Investment Policies
in the
Arab Countries

Investment Policies
in the
Arab Countries

**Edited by
Said El-Naggar**

**Papers presented at a Seminar held in
Kuwait, December 11 - 13, 1989**

International Monetary Fund ◆ 1990

Library of Congress Cataloging-in-Publication Data

Investment policies in the Arab countries / edited by Said El-Naggar.
    p. cm.
    "Papers presented at a seminar held in Kuwait, December 11–13,
1989."
"Sponsored by ... the Arab Monetary Fund ... [et al.]"—P.
    ISBN 1-55775-140-4
    1.   Investments—Government   policy—Arab   countries—
Congresses. 2. Investments, Foreign—Government policy—Arab
countries—Congresses.
    I. El-Naggar, Sa' id, 1920– II. International Monetary Fund. III.
Arab Monetary Fund.
HG5816.A3I58   1990
332.6'732'09174927—dc20   90-34408
                                                                                   CIP

Price: US$18.50

Address orders to:
International Monetary Fund, Publication Services
700 19th Street, N.W., Washington, D.C. 20431, U.S.A.
Telephone: (202) 623-7430
Telefax: (202) 623-7491
Cable: Interfund

Sponsoring Organizations

- The Arab Monetary Fund
- The Arab Fund for Economic and Social Development
- The International Monetary Fund
- The World Bank

Foreword

This is the third seminar volume to be published jointly by the IMF and the Arab Monetary Fund. As before, it focuses on an issue of particular significance to the Arab countries, namely, their investment policies. The increased level of institutional interest engendered by the debates on issues concerning the Arab world demonstrates the relevance and usefulness of the series.

The quality of expert participation speaks to the importance of the themes that have been selected for discussion in these seminars. We at the Fund are pleased to have helped launch the series and to have been again associated with the Arab Monetary Fund, and for the first time on this occasion, with the Arab Fund for Economic and Social Development, as well as the World Bank. The involvement of Professor Said El-Naggar as the moderator of this as well as the previous seminars has provided not only a useful continuity to the management of the discussions and their editing, but his own contributions have been of great value, given the clarity of his thinking and the lucidity of his expression in Arabic and in English.

The impact of macroeconomic and microeconomic policies on the investment climate in the Arab countries, the efficiency of public investment, and the role of foreign direct investment—the recurring themes of the seminar—are issues that are topical for all developing countries. I hope that the publication of this volume, like its predecessors in the series, will contribute to a broader understanding of these important economic issues, and not only in the Arab world.

MICHEL CAMDESSUS
Managing Director
International Monetary Fund

Acknowledgment

This is the third in a series of seminars dealing with economic issues of particular importance to the Arab countries. The preceding seminars dealt with adjustment policies and privatization. The topic this time has acquired special significance because of the efforts of the governments concerned to promote private domestic and foreign investment and to raise the efficiency of public investment. The papers presented to the seminar cover a broad area ranging from investment guarantees to macroeconomic policies that have a bearing on the investment climate in the Arab countries.

The seminar was sponsored by four organizations: The Arab Monetary Fund, the Arab Fund for Economic and Social Development, the International Monetary Fund, and the World Bank. The interest and support shown by these organizations bear witness to the importance of the issues covered by this seminar.

On behalf of the participants, I would like to express my thanks to all those whose active support made this event possible, in particular, Messrs. Osama Faquih, Director General and Chairman of the Board, and Rasheed Khalid of the Arab Monetary Fund, and Azizali Mohammmed and Ahmed Abushadi of the International Monetary Fund.

A special word of thanks is due to Mr. Abdlatif Y. Al-Hamad, Director General and Chairman of the Board, Arab Fund for Economic and Social Development, and his collaborators, Ismail El-Zabri and Mirvet Badawi, for the excellent organization of the seminar and for their hospitality during our stay in Kuwait. I would like also to thank Elin Knotter of the International Monetary Fund for editing this volume for publication.

Said El-Naggar
Moderator

Contents

The following symbols have been used throughout this book:

... to indicate that data are not available;

— to indicate that the figure is zero or less than half the final digit shown, or that the item does not exist;

– between years or months (e.g., 1987–88 or January–June) to indicate the years or months covered, including the beginning and ending years or months;

/ between years (e.g., 1987/88) to indicate a crop or fiscal (financial) year.

"Billion" means a thousand million.

Details may not add to totals shown because of rounding.

The term "country," as used in this book, does not in all cases refer to a territorial entity that is a state as understood by international law and practice; the term also covers some territorial entities that are not states, but for which statistical data are maintained and provided internationally on a separate and independent basis.

1

Investment Policies in the Arab Countries: The Basic Issues

Said El-Naggar[1]

Since the onset of the debt problem in the early eighties, developing countries have been in the grip of a deep and protracted economic crisis. For them the decade of the eighties has been aptly described as a lost decade as their standard of living suffered stagnation or even deterioration. Most of them have incurred unsustainable external deficits and experienced high rates of inflation, crushing debt-service burdens, and sluggish growth in gross domestic product (GDP). Part of their woes is undoubtedly ascribable to an unfavorable external environment, notably, mediocre growth in the industrial countries, a rising tide of protectionism, stagnation of financial flows, and worsening terms of trade. While these factors are important, they fail to offer a satisfactory explanation. A good part of the blame lies with domestic factors. In a large number of cases poor economic management is responsible for widespread macroeconomic and structural distortions and for failure to implement timely and effective programs of adjustment in the face of deteriorating external conditions.

The same can be said of the majority of Arab countries. For countries such as Algeria, Egypt, Morocco, the Syrian Arab Republic, Sudan, and Tunisia, the decade of the eighties was marked by poor economic performance as reflected in substantial external and internal imbalances. For the oil-rich Arab countries, as might be expected, it was somewhat different. With the sharp increase in oil revenue, they were able to make remarkable progress. However, the later debacle in the oil market gave rise to a wide range of economic problems. In this group of countries, as in the rest,

[1]The views expressed in this paper are the author's and do not necessarily represent those of the seminar.

1

adjustment to a changed economic environment has become imperative.

Against this background, the Arab Fund for Economic and Social Development and the Arab Monetary Fund, in cooperation with the International Monetary Fund and the World Bank, convened a seminar on "Investment Policies in the Arab Countries."

There are two ways in which the term "investment policies" can be interpreted. In a narrow sense, investment policies refer to those policies specifically designed to strengthen incentives and eliminate impediments that impinge on investment decisions. In this sense investment policies cover such topics as tax holidays, investment guarantees, and free zones. Broadly interpreted, however, investment policies refer to the investment climate, that is, the totality of policies and institutions that have a bearing, directly or indirectly, on investment decisions. In this sense there can be no meaningful discussion of investment policies without reference to the macroeconomic and microeconomic policies of the country concerned. Investment policies are intimately intertwined with monetary, fiscal, and trade policies in addition to questions related to banking institutions, legal and judicial systems, labor and tax laws, as well as regulatory arrangements.

At the seminar that took place in Kuwait on December 11–13, 1989, investment policies were tackled on the basis of both a narrow and a broad interpretation. Eight papers were discussed.

- A. Shakour Shaalan: "The Impact of Macroeconomic Policies on Investment"

- John W. Wall: "Efficiency of Public Investment: Lessons from World Bank Experience"

- Dale Weigel: "Foreign Direct Investment: The Role of Joint Ventures and Investment Authorities"

- Abdel Rahman Taha: "Investment Guarantees: The Role of the Inter-Arab Investment Guarantee Corporation"

- Heba Handoussa: "Egypt's Investment Strategy, Policies, and Performance Since the Infitah"

- Abdullah Al-Kuwaiz: "Investment Process in the Gulf Cooperation Council States"
- Abdel-Monem Seyed Ali: "Investment Policies in Iraq, 1950–87"
- Bachir Hamdouch: "Investment Policies in Morocco"

In addition, written comments on these papers were prepared by designated discussants, and general remarks by Ibrahim F.I. Shihata on the encouragement and promotion of foreign and Arab investment were circulated.

It is neither feasible nor useful to summarize the content of all papers, as they cover such a vast and complex area. An attempt will be made, however, to highlight some of the recurrent themes in the seminar.

The Macroeconomic Impact

One of the major themes in the seminar was the impact of macroeconomic policies on investment. As pointed out earlier, macroeconomic policies constitute one of the important determinants of the investment climate. Not infrequently, the invest ment climate in developing countries, including Arab countries, is vitiated by macroeconomic distortions. Substantial budget deficits, overvalued exchange rates, and negative real interest rates are typical of such distortions. Insofar as a budget deficit is financed through money creation, as often happens, it becomes a major source of inflation. Inflation militates against the investment climate. It undermines confidence in the national currency, weakens the incentive to save, encourages unproductive forms of investment such as holding foreign currency deposits and inventories, and causes capital flight. Part of the budget deficit is financed by borrowing from the local market. In countries like Algeria, Egypt, and the Syrian Arab Republic, for example, a good portion of domestic savings is under the control of pension funds, social security funds, and insurance companies. Since they are all public sector institutions, the government avails itself of their financial resources to cover part of the budget deficit. This form of financing may not be inflationary, but it can have a detrimental effect on the quality of investment by crowding out productive private sector projects in favor of less efficient public spending. Thus, a certain portion of productive investment is pre-empted by this type of financing of the budget deficit.

Overvalued exchange rates exercise a similar impact on investment. They inhibit the inflow of capital and induce the outflow of domestic savings. By cheapening imports artificially, overvaluation of national currency encourages investments with a high foreign exchange component. The same can be said of negative real interest rates, which go a long way toward explaining the phenomenon known as the "dollarization" of the national economy, reflected in the widespread recourse to foreign currency deposits by residents whenever it is legally permissible. Simultaneously with dollarization, negative real interest rates are behind a good deal of capital flight from developing countries. These distortions deprive developing countries of badly needed domestic savings. No less important is that negative real interest rates encourage the use of capital-intensive techniques of production in countries with an abundant supply of labor. Worse still is that they virtually eliminate the cost of capital as a means of rationing credit among competing users. Under conditions of negative real interest rates, the mere fact of securing credit becomes a source of windfall profit. As a consequence, demand for credit at prevailing interest rates tends to outstrip the supply of savings. Since interest rates are not allowed to rise in response to market forces, the only way of achieving equilibrium between supply and demand is through direct allocation of credit among potential investors. The amount of waste involved in this method of allocation can be substantial. There is no guarantee that credit goes to investments with the highest rate of return. Moreover, when the banking system is itself part of the public sector the method of direct allocation is sure to result in further crowding out of the private sector.

It is important to point out that macroeconomic distortions are interrelated. Budget deficits and excessive credit expansion lead to inflation, which underlies negative real interest rates and overvaluation of currency. By giving rise to the phenomenon of dollarization and by inducing capital flight, negative real interest rates intensify pressure on the national currency and can be a significant factor in the overvaluation of exchange rates. Thus, the economy slides into a vicious circle where each macroeconomic distortion feeds, and is fed by, the other. The combined effect of this vicious circle thoroughly distorts the investment climate.[2]

The preceding analysis applies to many Arab countries. It is particularly true with respect to macroeconomic policies in Egypt and Morocco.[3] The case of Iraq is somewhat different. For the major part of the post–Second World War period, investment was almost completely dependent upon oil revenue, which accounted for an overwhelming proportion of public revenue. Foreign borrowing, up to the outbreak of the war between Iraq and the Islamic Republic of Iran, was conspicuous by its absence. Tax revenue as well as private domestic savings played a minor role as a source of financing investment. While stability of the price level was always a matter of concern for the Government, neither exchange rates nor interest rates played an important role as instruments of investment policy.[4]

Microeconomic Distortions

The efficiency of investment is largely, but not exclusively, determined by microeconomic considerations.[5] In many countries a great deal of waste is accounted for by distortion of relative prices. Prices of a wide range of goods and services are typically subject to strict administration controls. Accordingly, they fail to respond to changes in market forces, and when they do, it is usually too little and too late. After a certain period of time during which market forces are ignored, prices cease to reflect the relative scarcity of resources, that is, they cease to be economic prices and become social or political prices. Three types of price distortions can be identified.

- Deviation of domestic prices from international prices. In some instances, domestic prices are well above international prices.

[2]A. Shakour Shaalan, "The Impact of Macroeconomic Policies on Investment," Chap. 2 below. See also comments by Mohamed El-Diri and Fareed Atabani.

[3]Heba Handoussa, "Egypt's Investment Strategy, Policies, and Performance Since the Infitah," Chap. 7 below. Bachir Hamdouch, "Investment Policies in Morocco," Chap. 10 below. See also comments by Ahmed El-Ghandour and Abdelrazaq El Mossadeq.

[4]Abdel-Monem Seyed Ali, "Investment Policies in Iraq, 1950–87," Chap. 9 below. See also the comments by Abdel Wahed Al-Makhzoumi.

[5]See comments by Fareed Atabani.

This is true of heavily protected industries where protection takes the form of exceedingly high tariffs together with quantitative restrictions and other nontariff barriers. This type of distortion injects a bias against export industries and in favor of import-competing industries. As a consequence, investment resources are artificially diverted from the more productive export industries to the less productive but more profitable import-competing industries. In other instances, domestic prices are well below world prices. This is the case for industries whose output enters as input in the import-competing industries (for example, energy) as well as those whose output is subject to a government monopsony making profit from the differential between domestic and international prices (for example, cotton in Egypt). Here again the allocation of investment resources on the basis of artificial prices falls short of the optimum pattern that would otherwise have prevailed.

- Divergences in price-cost relationships. This type of distortion arises because the incidence of government controls is uneven owing to administrative weaknesses and because different goods and services are not subject to the same rules and regulations. In the political scheme of things, some goods and services are more important than others. Consequently, some prices are fixed while others are left to find their own level following changes in market forces. In due course relative prices become divorced from relative costs with the result that certain investments become highly profitable compared with others, not because of the interaction between supply and demand but because of the uneven incidence of government policy. This consideration explains why in Egypt there is less than optimum investment in the production of cotton, which is subject to a system of compulsory delivery at artificially low prices, and more than optimum investment in the production of fruits, the prices of which are left free. It also explains why there is a scarcity of housing for rent, which is subject to strict controls, and an abundance of housing for sale, which is unrestricted.

- Multiplicity of prices for the same commodity or service. In many instances there is no single price for, say, sugar or wheat flour, but many prices for different categories of users. There is one price for sugar used by candy factories and other prices for different groups of consumers according to their presumed income levels. The same applies to wheat flour, where there is one price for making bread, another for making pastry, and there is also differentiation according to whether the buyer is a public or a private sector entity. This type of distortion is a common phenomenon and has the effect of destroying the price mechanism as a means of allocating investment resources.

Efficiency of Public Investment

In many Arab countries a high proportion of investment is accounted for by the public sector. This is true for Algeria, Egypt, Sudan, the Syrian Arab Republic, and the People's Democratic Republic of Yemen. In these countries public investments are as high as 70 percent or more of total investment. In other Arab countries the proportion of public investments is not as high but is still important.

In countries with a high proportion of public investment, public enterprises dominate a wide range of economic activities. Banking, insurance, foreign trade, the modern manufacturing sector, mining, construction, public utilities, transport, and many other activities are typically under the sway of public enterprises. The rationale for this state of affairs varies from one country to another. In some cases, the government of the day opted for a socialist orientation based on public ownership of the means of production or a drive to control the so-called commanding heights of the economy. In others, the explanation lies in pragmatic considerations such as the appropriation of surpluses or the absence of a private sector willing and able to undertake major projects.

Whether ideological or pragmatic, the dominance of the public sector was expected to make a positive contribution to development. The experience of the past twenty years or so seems to point in the opposite direction. The performance of the public sector in developing countries has been the subject of extensive studies. These studies are virtually unanimous in concluding that the results have been far from satisfactory. Performance was measured in terms of several indicators: overall deficits, impact on the government finances, rate of return on capital invested in public enterprises, impact on the balance of payments, and share of external indebtedness. It was found that, with a few exceptions, the public sector incurs substantial losses, contributes significantly to budget deficits, earns exceedingly low rates of return, has a negative impact on the balance of payments, and is responsible for a good part of external indebtedness.

The first step in reforming the public sector is to recognize the constraints set by the managerial capacities of the countries concerned. In many developing countries evidence shows that the public sector is overextended and that the proper role of the government needs to be redefined on the basis of a realistic assessment of development imperatives as well as of available financial and administrative resources. It is equally well recognized that under conditions of underdevelopment the state will continue to play an important economic role This situation is unavoidable given the limitations imposed by small domestic markets, lack of factor mobility, weakness of the private sector, and, above all, imperfections of the market. However, the present scope of the public sector typically goes far beyond what is justifiable in terms of these considerations. It is difficult to justify that in many Arab countries, the government continues to be involved in such activities as grocery and department stores, bakeries, flour mills, printing, bookshops, advertising, hotels, travel agencies, contracting, cattle and poultry farming, fisheries, and scores of other activities. These are normally the kinds of activities that are better and more effectively undertaken by the private sector.

At the other extreme there are activities that constitute the core of the public sector. They include the traditional role of government in health, education, defense, maintenance of law and order, as well as the macroeconomic management of the economy. To a large extent the public sector should also continue to be involved in the provision of basic physical infrastructure including roads, water supply, telecommunications, electricity, flood control, irrigation, and sanitation facilities.

Between these two extremes a vast gray area exists about which it is difficult to generalize.[6] The proper mix between the public and private sector is a matter that varies from one country to another depending on the stage of development as well as the availability of private capital and entrepreneurship. It is important,

---

[6]Abdullah Al-Kuwaiz, "Investment Process in the Gulf Cooperation Council States," Chap. 8 below. See also the comments by Mahsoun Galal.

however, to keep in mind that there are limits to what the public sector can do and that excessive involvement in the production process is certain to be at the expense of those services that only the government can provide. As John Wall puts it, "Spending too little on basic government services while spending too much in areas that the private sector could have served is perhaps the biggest and most costly loss of efficiency. . . ."[7]

Apart from the proper mix of the public and private sector, economic performance suffered greatly because governments tend to saddle public enterprises with mixed mandates, including social objectives that often conflict with considerations of efficiency. Public enterprises have been required to play a role in the implementation of government policy of guaranteed employment to university graduates. This policy meant that they were forced to appoint annually a certain number of candidates allocated by the government although there were no jobs for them to perform. The policy of guaranteed employment has had a profoundly adverse effect on the performance of public enterprises. Not only has it resulted in swelling the ranks of disguised unemployment, but more important, it has undermined the work ethic, created intolerable working conditions, and inflated the wage bill with nothing to show for it.

Public enterprises were also required to contribute to the anti-inflationary policy by holding down the prices of goods and services they produced. The policy is thought to protect the low-income groups by offering essential consumer goods at reasonable prices. The result is the opposite of what is intended. It was not possible to hold down prices without heavy subsidies from the government budget. In due course subsidies became a major factor in the budget deficit, which is itself the principal source of inflation. The adverse effect of inflation on income distribution is too well known to warrant elaboration. Nor has this policy succeeded in achieving the objective of helping the low-income groups. Most of the benefits of open-ended subsidization have in fact accrued to petty middlemen, corrupt officials, and higher-income groups with much better access to supplies than the targeted groups.[8]

[7]John W. Wall, "Efficiency of Public Investment: Lessons from World Bank Experience," Chap. 3 below. See also comments by Mohamed A. Diab.

[8]For a more detailed analysis, see *Privatization and Structural Adjustment in the Arab Countries*, ed. by Said El-Naggar (Washington: International Monetary Fund, 1989), p. 12.

The policy of mixed mandates has been costly in terms of efficiency. It has inevitably resulted in pervasive cost-price distortions and, consequently, considerable misallocation of resources. No less important, it has compelled the government to protect public enterprises from competition as a means of generating rents to pay for the social burdens. They were protected from foreign competition by extensive tariff and nontariff barriers. At the same time, domestic competition was frequently thwarted by a system of licensing designed to control new entry, especially of private firms.

In the light of these considerations it is incumbent that the policy of mixed mandates be discontinued. Evidently, unemployment cannot be dealt with through a policy of guaranteed employment in public enterprises. There is no substitute for a growing economy that could provide adequate opportunities for productive employment. Similarly, interference with the price system is an ineffective and inefficient tool to protect vulnerable consumers. If prices are to perform their principal function of resource allocation, they have to be responsive to market forces and reflective of relative scarcities. This is not to ignore considerations of social equity, which is better served through the taxation system.

This analysis points clearly to the nature of reform. Public enterprise should be allowed to operate on the same basis as the private sector. Efficiency and profitability in a competitive environment should be the sole criterion by which performance is assessed. It remains to be seen whether this expectation is realistic given the history of the public sector over the last twenty-five years.

Role of Foreign Investment

So far foreign direct investment has played a minor role in the economic development and the adjustment process of capital importing Arab countries. Like other developing countries during the seventies, the Arab countries resorted to foreign borrowing to meet their external financing requirements. For a variety of reasons, foreign borrowing rather than foreign direct investment was the preferred form of financing. Newly independent countries that had just emerged from a long period of colonial domination were anxious to maintain control over their own economic and political affairs. Foreign direct investment that was in the majority of cases closely associated with multinational companies was perceived to be incompatible with this goal. There was also a tendency to discount the presumed advantages of foreign direct investment compared with other forms of financing. Not infrequently multinational corporations were not interested in developing export-oriented industries but rather in supplying the home market behind a high protective wall. The impact on employment was seen as minimal in view of the capital-intensive techniques imported from the home country; the transfer of technology was seen as a mirage as multinational corporations were secretive about their methods of production, and training of local personnel was kept within the narrowest possible limits. Equally important was concern about the distribution of benefits between the host country and the investing corporations in terms of tax revenue, value added, and reinvested profits. The prevailing view in most developing countries was that through dubious methods and practices such as transfer pricing, multinational corporations arrogate to themselves the lion's share of the benefits from investment.

These were some of the considerations behind the relative decline in the role of foreign direct investment during the seventies. The trend was abetted by the fact that borrowed funds were readily available. After the sharp increase in oil prices, a large proportion of world savings shifted to the oil exporting countries. These countries were either unable or unwilling to undertake direct investment abroad on a significant scale. Most of their savings were kept in deposits with commercial banks in the industrial countries and became available for lending to developing countries that were only too happy to use this source of financing. For the first time commercial banks emerged as a major source of lending to developing countries. This development obviated to a large extent the need for foreign direct investment.

In contrast to the sixties and seventies, the decade of the eighties saw a revival of interest in foreign direct investment. On the part of multinational corporations an effort was made to establish standards for acceptable business conduct. They became more sensitive to the concerns of developing countries and more flexible in the particular forms of investment. This change included a greater willingness to accept innovative arrangements such as joint ventures, turnkey projects, build-own-transfer (BOT) arrangements, and licensing agreements rather than the traditional wholly owned subsidiary. Developing countries, on the other hand, became more experienced and confident in dealing with multinational corporations. Moreover, they can, if they so wish, receive assistance and advice in negotiations with multinational corporations from institutions established within the framework of the United Nations and its specialized agencies such as the UN Centre on Transnational Corporations and the Investment Promotion Service (IPS) of the United Nations Industrial Development Organization (UNIDO).

The most important factor, however, underlying the changed attitude toward foreign direct investment is the recent developments in the international financial system. The debt crisis of the early eighties has underscored the serious limitations of heavy dependence on foreign borrowing. A heavy debt-service burden combined with variable interest rates on a large proportion of their debt made the heavily indebted countries particularly vulnerable to external shocks. A prolonged recession in the industrial countries, in addition to the high cost of energy and the collapse of prices of principal export commodities, have conspired to undermine their payment capacity. The result was a debt crisis of unprecedented severity, which inflicted untold hardships on the indebted countries and threatened their growth prospects—not to mention the integrity of the international credit system. In contrast, remittances of dividends and profits on foreign direct investment are much more responsive to changes in business conditions. By their very nature they increase with prosperity and fall with recession. They are more in tune with changes in the payment capacity of the host country. More important, the debt crisis has had a profound impact on the international sources of finance available to developing countries. Commercial bank lending has all but dried up not only for balance of payments support but also for project financing. Most commercial bank lending is presently undertaken in the context of adjustment programs supported by the International Monetary Fund. Outside this type of concerted or "involuntary" lending, most is limited to collateralized or guaranteed loans. Other sources of finance are also subject to severe constraints. The tight budgetary situation in most industrial countries has been a serious obstacle to expanding bilateral sources of finance whether concessional or nonconcessional.

Moreover, recent developments in the socialist countries of Eastern Europe are certain to give rise to an enormous demand for external financing from the major industrial countries, which could easily impinge on the financial resources available to developing countries. This situation leaves the multilateral sources of finance, particularly the World Bank and the International Monetary Fund, as a possible alternative. But it is clear that even under the most optimistic assumptions on the growth of their capital base, these institutions cannot play the role of commercial banks in international financing.

Such dim prospects for other sources of external financing are likely to enhance the role of foreign direct investment and raise a number of issues about the most appropriate policies to attract and maximize the benefit from it.

Incentives, Restrictions, and Guarantees

The first issue relates to the relative importance of macroeconomic policies and special incentives as factors in attracting foreign investment. It was pointed out earlier that macroeconomic policies are highly relevant to investment decisions. This is particularly true with respect to foreign investment. Empirical investigation shows that a stable macroeconomic environment is perhaps the most important single factor in the calculations of the foreign investor. High rates of inflation, overvalued currency, sudden and sharp devaluation, administratively fixed interest rates, or a weak banking system are not the kind of conditions that attract foreign investment.[9] In this context it is important to note that some countries have succeeded in attracting a considerable volume of foreign investment on the basis of a stable macroeconomic environment although they have little by way of natural resources and only limited special incentives. To this category belong countries such as Hong Kong, Singapore, Taiwan Province of China, and the Republic of Korea. In some other countries, by contrast, generous incentives have failed to attract significant foreign investment because of macroeconomic distortions. Egypt is a case in point. Law No. 43 of 1974, recently replaced by Law No. 230 of

[9]Ibrahim F. I. Shihata, "Promotion of Arab and Foreign Investment: General Remarks," Chap. 6 below.

1989, offers advantages, exemptions, and guarantees that are virtually unequaled by other developing countries of comparable development potential. However, the impact on foreign investment has been extremely limited.[10]

It is also important to note the relationship that exists between macroeconomic distortions and incentives. To compensate for the disadvantages arising from macroeconomic distortions, host countries are likely to offer incentives in various forms. The deeper the distortions, the more extensive are the incentives. But incentives are not without cost to the host country. Often foreign investors are exempt from all forms of taxes, duties, and fees for periods that could extend for 10 and 20 years. Expansion of capacity is similarly exempt even if it takes place long after the expiry of the original period. The loss to the treasury could be considerable. At the same time, this method of attracting foreign investment weakens the fragile foundation of the taxation system, encourages tax evasion, and discriminates between different types of investment. In the light of experience it might be concluded that tax exemptions and similar incentives should be used selectively to compensate for externalities that interfere with the optimum flow of investment.

Debt-equity swaps provide another type of incentive for the promotion of foreign investment in the heavily indebted countries. They are dual-purpose instruments, as they serve both to reduce the size of outstanding foreign debt and to increase the volume of equity and direct investment. This policy is predicated on three basic assumptions.

- The existence of a foreign debt owed to commercial banks or private creditors with a secondary market in which debt instruments are traded at less than their face value.
- A potential investor—whether foreign or national—who is interested in making equity or direct investment in the indebted country and who buys a debt instrument at a discount in the secondary market.
- A government that is prepared to allow the holder of the debt instrument to sell it against local currency and to use the proceeds of the sale in equity or direct investment.

[10]Handoussa (cited in fn. 3).

If these assumptions are satisfied, each party to the debt-equity transaction will have an incentive to proceed with the deal. The creditor commercial bank has the incentive to sell the debt at less than face value to clear its books of nonperforming assets. The potential investor buys an instrument whose face value is more than it costs to acquire it. The government of the debtor country— or the central bank—has the incentive to reduce the stock of outstanding debt at no cost in foreign exchange while promoting foreign investment.

A number of indebted countries, particularly in Latin America, have undertaken debt-equity swaps, with varying degrees of success.[11] The heavily indebted Arab countries could benefit from similar programs if they are well designed. A question that arises in this context is the type of investment that would be allowed under the program. In some countries investments are limited to pre-designated priority sectors while others exclude such investment activities as the acquisition of stocks in existing companies, buyouts, and financial restructuring. Another question is the rate of exchange that is applicable to the conversion of the debt instrument into local currency. There are various approaches to this issue aimed at dividing the benefit of the discount between the government and the potential investor. Finally, there is the question of control over the pace of debt-equity swaps to avoid aggravating inflationary pressures from excessive growth in money supply. The Egyptian Investment Law No. 230 of 1989 contains provisions that permit debt-equity conversions (Article (3)b). Investments are limited to the priority sectors specified in Article 1. Proceeds can only be used to establish a new project or to expand the production capacity of an existing company. By implication, debt-equity swaps could not be used simply to finance buyouts or financial restructuring. However, the investor who qualifies under this program would benefit twice: once from the discount on the debt instrument, and a second time in being exempt from all types of taxes. Such a double benefit seems extravagant. Moreover, under the present provisions a host of questions are left unanswered. For a country like Egypt with a heavy debt burden and, at the same time, anxious to promote foreign investment,

[11]Joel Bergsman and Wayne Edisis, "Debt-Equity Swaps and Foreign Direct Investment in Latin America," IFC Discussion Paper No. 2 (Washington: World Bank, International Finance Corporation, 1988).

debt–equity swaps are sufficiently important to warrant treatment in separate legislation.

Finally, some countries, including a number of Arab countries, use the system of free zones to encourage foreign investment. However, the precise function of such a system varies greatly between countries. A distinction should be made between three types.

- Export processing free zones have existed for a long time in a number of countries—developed as well as developing. The purpose of this arrangement is to provide facilities for carrying out certain processing operations on imported goods without going into the customs formalities to which such goods are subject. Typical of processing operations are packaging, bottling, and labeling. Moreover, they serve as facilities for the transit trade.
- Export free zones involve more than simple processing. The purpose is to create a zone in which full-fledged manufacturing can be carried out, including the importation of raw materials, technology, and management. Foreign investments are attracted to these zones to take advantage of cheap labor, developed infrastructure, and exemptions from taxes and duties without going into the maze of bureaucratic procedures and regulations that apply to inland projects. Put differently, the purpose is to create an island of economic freedom in an ocean of statism. The underlying assumption is that free zones of this type are effective tools for the development of export-oriented industries.
- Export-import free zones perform the same functions as the preceding ones but, in addition, they operate as depots for the supply of imported goods to the mainland. Goods enter duty free to the zone but are dutiable when they cross the border into the mainland.

The first type of free zone poses no problem and is advantageous to the host country. The situation is different with respect to the export-import free zones. Experience shows that they soon cease to do much by way of export-oriented industries and concentrate instead on the easier and more lucrative business of supplying the domestic market with imported goods. Because import duties are frequently excessive, the temptation to smuggle highly taxed goods is well-nigh irresistible. The cost in terms of lost public revenue and unfair competition with home industries can be considerable.

As to the intermediate type, the export free zones, it is difficult to generalize, assuming that they are strictly confined to the development of export-oriented industries. On balance, however, the cost could well outweigh the benefit to the host country. The most serious drawback of such arrangements is that they tend to create a dangerous illusion, namely, that the host country can escape the negative consequences of stifling bureaucratic controls through creating isolated islands of economic freedom. They weaken the resolve for economic reform and divert attention from the need to eliminate distortions that damage the overall investment climate.

Restrictions and performance requirements go hand in hand with incentives. Here again the more important the incentives, the greater is the temptation to impose restrictions. The most common restrictions relate to local content requirements, export performance, and trade balancing and ownership requirements. Some of these restrictions have a distorting effect and give rise to misallocation of resources. This is obvious for local content requirements, which operate in much the same way as trade restrictions. But it is also true of export and trade balancing requirements. This consideration explains why some industrial countries insist on their inclusion as trade distorting investment measures in the Uruguay Round of trade negotiations currently under way in Geneva.[12]

It is also clear that restrictions and performance requirements act for the most part as disincentives to foreign investment. For this reason countries differ greatly on the extent of restrictions they impose on foreign investment. Joint ventures are a case in point. In many countries foreign investors are required to enter into partnership with domestic capital with or without a majority share. The deterring effect of this requirement has led some countries to adopt more liberal provisions. "We can conclude," says Dale Weigel, "that developing countries are re-examining the role of forced joint ventures between foreign and local investors. The

---

[12]Cynthia Day Wallace, *Foreign Direct Investment in the 1990's: A New Climate in the Third World* (Dordrecht; Boston: Martinus Nijhoff, 1990), especially Chap. 2.

trend is clear—to allow foreign and local firms increasingly to make their own arrangements."[13]

Investment guarantees have a different footing. They belong of course to the category of incentives, but they do not affect the taxation system and have a moderate cost to the foreign investor and the host country. Following the emergence of substantial investable surpluses in the oil exporting countries, the Inter-Arab Investment Guarantee Corporation (IAIGC) was established in mid-1975 with the purpose of providing the Arab investor with insurance coverage in the form of reasonable compensation for losses resulting from noncommercial risks as well as carrying out activities that are complementary to the Corporation's main purpose, in particular research related to the identification of investment opportunities and the conditions of investment in the Arab countries.[14] Noncommercial risks include nationalization and confiscation, war or political unrest, and inability to transfer earnings or invested capital outside the host country in a convertible currency. As noted by Nour El-Din Farrag, the issue of guarantees for foreign investments made in the industrial countries does not arise as the rights of foreign investors are protected by a strong legal and judiciary system. The goal of the Arab countries should be to reach a stage where the foreign investor does not feel the need for a special arrangement to protect against noncommercial risks—in other words, to dispense with the system of investment guarantees altogether. In the meantime the system currently in force, together with provisions in national legislation as well as the Multilateral Investment Guarantee Agency (MIGA), plays a role in promoting inter-Arab and foreign investment. It bears repeating, however, that "the role played by guarantees in attracting investments is an ancillary or complementary one, and an improved investment climate, in all its various political, economic, and institutional aspects, is really the key factor in attracting direct foreign investments to the Arab world."[15]

[13]Dale Weigel, "Foreign Direct Investment: The Role of Joint Ventures and Investment Authorities," Chap. 4 below. See also comments by Abdulaziz M. Al-Dukheil and Ezzedin M. Shamsedin.

[14]Abdel Rahman Taha, "Investment Guarantees: The Role of the Inter-Arab Investment Guarantee Corporation," Chap. 5 below. See also comments by Nour El-Din Farrag.

[15]Abdel Rahman Taha (cited in fn. 14).

2

The Impact of Macroeconomic Policies on Investment

A. Shakour Shaalan

This paper looks at investment in developing countries, its relationship to growth and development, and the macroeconomic conditions and policies through which investment and growth can flourish. It draws heavily on recent empirical studies by the International Monetary Fund in this area and brings out some of the issues surrounding the efforts by the Fund to support policies conducive to higher savings, investment, and growth in the context of adjustment programs.

Investment and Growth

While experience has varied from one region to another, and even more markedly between different countries, real output growth in the developing world has slowed from an annual average rate of 5½ percent in the 1970s to about 3 percent in the 1980s. With relatively high rates of population growth and much weaker terms of trade, this slowdown translated into a marked decline in per capita income in many countries.

Though there are many factors responsible for the deceleration of growth, the one that stands out is the contemporaneous decline in capital formation—a vital ingredient and precondition for growth. Again, for the entire group of developing countries, domestic investment declined from 27½ percent of national income during the period 1976–81, to 23½ percent in the five years following the outbreak of the debt crisis (1983–87).[1] Underlying the decline

---

[1]Data weaknesses require that these estimates (and those for savings cited below) be treated with some caution. Both investment and savings are "gross" (they include depreciation) and include reinvestment by individual entities (and

in investment was a sharp reduction in financial resources not only in the form of foreign capital but also—and more importantly, as I will show—from national savings (which fell from 27 percent of national income to 22½ percent over the same period).

The restoration of a satisfactory rate of growth in the developing world is a matter of urgent concern and one of high priority in the Fund's work. Referring specifically to those countries with debt-servicing difficulties, the recent communiqué of the Interim Committee notes: "These countries should intensify efforts to raise national saving and investment, promote efficiency through structural reforms, curb inflationary pressures, encourage the return of flight capital, and promote foreign direct investment. . . ."[2]

Much of what I have to say involves an elaboration of these policy prescriptions. The consensus is that the achievement of satisfactory growth requires steady increases both in the domestic capital stock and in the efficiency with which it is utilized. To be sustainable, however, higher investment must be achieved in consonance with a viable external payments position (including a manageable external debt situation)—a constraint that underlines the need for greater emphasis on mobilization of domestic savings. I shall consider these issues in turn.

The Level of Investment

An ample body of evidence is available inside and outside the Fund that supports the relationship between investment and growth in developing countries. Indeed, the contribution of investment to growth is generally found to be larger in developing countries than in the industrial world, although there are large differences between different subgroups of developing countries.

This relationship between investment and growth was examined in a recent Fund study covering 125 capital importing developing

---

thereby exceed savings and investment as intermediated by the financial system). Gross domestic investment includes investment in plant and equipment, residential construction, and changes in stocks. National saving is derived by adding (subtracting) the external current account deficit (surplus) to (from) gross domestic investment. Savings and investment ratios are based on national income, defined as gross national product plus net foreign transfers.

[2]*IMF Survey* (Washington: International Monetary Fund, October 16, 1989), p. 310.

countries.[3] The study found the relationship to hold for all country groups, with a 10 percentage point increase in the ratio of investment to gross domestic product (GDP) raising the growth rate of output by 1½ percentage points on average. (This result is broadly confirmed by other studies.)

Efficiency of Investment

Studies such as these, though they point to a positive and relatively strong relationship between the absolute level of investment and the rate of growth, ignore such elements as the efficiency of resource use, as reflected, for example, in the allocation of resources and the quality of capital. Partly for this reason we find a large residual in such analyses, implying that only part of the growth process can be explained in terms of the absolute capital stock. However, we can be confident, a priori, that a shift in the allocation of resources toward more productive projects (for example, in favor of viable export-oriented ventures rather than protected import-substituting ones) and investment in human capital (health, education, and training) will bring about gains in output through increased efficiency.

Clearly, data weaknesses and problems in devising appropriate techniques for measuring the quality of investment limit empirical work in this area. Nevertheless, some studies have attempted to allow for quality variation in inputs, and they do indeed reveal larger relative contributions by capital and labor to output compared with the results obtained when productivity or the quality of factors of production are not taken into account. Of interest in this context are the results of another Fund study,[4] which attempted to evaluate the relative contributions of factor inputs (capital and labor) and total factor productivity in the growth of output of groups of developing countries classified by region. (The contribution of a factor input is defined as the average share of that factor in output times its growth rate, while total factor productivity measures all other influences on growth.)

This study reveals a wide variation between the various regional groupings not only in the relative contribution of factor inputs to

---

[3]*World Economic Outlook: A Survey by the Staff of the International Monetary Fund* (Washington: International Monetary Fund, April 1988).

[4]Also published in *World Economic Outlook* (cited in fn. 3).

growth but also in the contribution of factor productivity (the proxy for efficiency). For example, over the period 1974–81, total factor inputs accounted for about 70 percent of the growth of output in the non-oil Middle Eastern countries, leaving the remainder (accounting for about 1¼ percentage points of GDP growth annually) to be explained by improvements in factor productivity (or efficiency). Improvements in efficiency also contributed to growth in developing countries in Asia and Europe. In Africa and the Western Hemisphere, on the other hand, declining factor productivity (suggesting resource misallocation) offset the contribution to growth of total factor inputs by about one half of a percentage point annually.

During 1982–87, indications are that factor productivity declined for all regional groupings of developing countries—with the exception of Asia. The Middle Eastern countries, for their part, succeeded in maintaining positive productivity gains (contributing about three fourths of a percentage point to GDP growth annually) as against zero or negative contributions in the remaining regional groupings (Africa, Europe, and the Western Hemisphere).

In sum, this study confirms that while capital accumulation per se has made a significant contribution to growth in developing countries, improvements in the quality of resources and the efficiency with which they are used are also very important.

The External Constraint

The gap between domestic investment and national saving is reflected in a country's external current account position. Thus, when investment exceeds the financing available through national savings, recourse to foreign financing is required. The existence of a current external deficit is not necessarily a cause for concern, but a number of caveats deserve emphasis.

First, external financing can only be a supplement to, not a substitute for, national savings. This is evident from the relative magnitudes involved. Thus, national savings have financed by far the greater share of investment in developing countries—about 90 percent on average. With the focus of attention being on the supply (or lack) of foreign financing in the wake of the debt crisis, this fact is sometimes overlooked: what it means, of course, is that higher investment ultimately hinges on greater mobilization of *domestic* resources through policies aimed at strengthening financial savings and keeping them within the country.

Second, while foreign financing can be an important supplement to national savings, its *form* is also important. In light of recent experience, commercial borrowing is likely to continue to play a much less important role in balance of payments financing in the developing world in the years ahead compared with the pre-debt crisis period. Meanwhile, the relative importance of official financing and direct investment has increased, and both sources of finance are more closely linked to domestic policies. Increasingly, bilateral donors are paying attention to domestic macro- and structural policies, while foreign direct investment, by its very nature, is aimed at a commercially acceptable rate of return. The latter, in turn, depends not only on the economic environment but on the political atmosphere as well—notably confidence on the part of potential investors that their assets and earnings are not subject to arbitrary action on the part of the host country.

Improved domestic policies and a greater receptiveness to foreign investment—which is often accompanied by technology and managerial expertise—should help improve the productivity of domestic as well as foreign-financed investment. Strengthened domestic policies are also a key to addressing the problems of capital flight—an irony in borrowing countries—which is essentially the consequence of perverse incentives and a general lack of confidence in economic management.

Finally, reliance on external borrowing must be kept within manageable bounds. This point has been amply demonstrated by the experience in recent years of many developing countries that relied too heavily on external borrowing—frequently on commercial terms—as a source of capital. As debt service obligations rose, these countries became vulnerable to exogenous shocks— arising from the global recession, higher interest rates, terms of trade losses, and so on—that characterized the early 1980s and culminated in the debt crisis.

The general principle is that orderly repayments will be ensured if debt is incurred up to (but not beyond) the point where the marginal productivity of capital is equal to the real interest cost of the borrowed funds. In such a framework, debt-servicing difficulties can be viewed as having arisen either because the marginal productivity of capital was overstated, or because exogenous shocks lowered the return on capital relative to the cost of borrowing. Our empirical work in the Fund in recent years has brought out the overwhelming importance of the former explanation. Although external shocks have had adverse implications for the economies in many countries, the pre-eminence of domestic economic policies is clearly established as the governing influence on economic performance.

Lessons from Recent Experience

This point can, I believe, best be illustrated by examining in more detail the recent experience of two distinct groups of developing countries: those that experienced debt crises and those that did not. This is a useful dichotomy for analytical purposes because a great deal of data on the respective economic policies and performance of the two groups has been assembled by the Fund in connection with our continuing studies for the *World Economic Outlook*. In addition, the contrasting experience of the two groups provides a graphic illustration of the consequences of two markedly different economic strategies on saving and investment, on the one hand, and growth on the other, and hence offers valuable lessons for policy.

At the most general level—real GDP growth—we find that the two groups of countries had identical growth rates during the 1970s (5.2 percent annually). Investment ratios (relative to national income) were also comparable for the two groups (in the range of 27–28 percent). What differed, however, were the financing sources for investment, with the countries that were to avoid debt problems relying much more heavily on national savings. National savings in these countries accounted for 26 percent of national income during the late 1970s, compared with only 23 percent in the countries that were later to experience debt problems. This discrepancy was reflected in the differing external positions of the two groups, with the countries with future debt problems relying much more heavily on foreign savings, as indicated by their much larger external current account deficits (which represented 4 percent of national income annually during the late 1970s, compared with less than 2 percent for the other group).

The onset of the debt crisis in the early 1980s had severe consequences for the countries that had been relying heavily on foreign

savings during the previous decade. The virtual cessation of external commercial financing (which was in part cause, in part
effect, of the debt crisis), combined with the continuing large
outward transfers from these countries needed to service their
massive external debt, resulted in a very large contraction of the
net external financial resources available to them. This forced on
these countries a rapid external adjustment. Their current account
deficit fell from over 4 percent of national income in the years
leading up to the debt crisis to about 1 percent in the following
five years. Moreover, national saving in these countries fell to
about 18 percent of national income after 1982 from about 23
percent in 1976–81.

How was this sharp fall in both domestic and foreign resources
reflected in domestic absorption (that is, consumption plus investment)? The answer explains why many of these countries have
failed to restore growth: Not only did investment bear the full
brunt of the reduction in resources, but domestic consumption
was allowed to *rise*, thereby further constricting investment. In
the event, investment ratios fell sharply, from 27 percent of national income in 1976–81 to about 19 percent after 1983. As a
consequence, real GDP actually declined by 3 percent during 1981–
83. And while adjustment efforts in many of these countries helped
to restore the average growth rate for the group in the second half
of the decade, it remained relatively low (3 percent) and uneven.

The countries that avoided debt-servicing problems and, thereby,
did not lose access to foreign financing, also maintained their national savings rates at about 26 percent of national income (6 or 7
percentage points higher than in the countries experiencing a debt
crisis). Thus, they were able to *maintain* domestic investment during the 1980s—at about 27 percent of national income—and succeeded in *increasing* their real GDP growth in the 1980s compared
with the late 1970s (6 percent versus 5.2 percent).

Behind these contrasting performances were a number of policy
differences between the two groups that are worth recounting.
Compared with the countries that avoided debt problems and
achieved sound investment and growth performance, the crisis-
prone countries

- had large budget deficits
- had loose monetary policies (artificially low interest rates,
  high rates of monetary creation)

A. Shakour Shaalan

- recorded relatively high rates of inflation
- did not make active use of the exchange rate
- failed to achieve strong export growth
- cut investment rather than consumption in their approach to adjustment.

Macroeconomic Policies and Investment

The final topic of my remarks is the crucial role for macroeconomic policies in establishing a climate conducive to saving and investment, in ensuring that capital is efficiently utilized, and in keeping reliance on external resources within manageable bounds.

Fiscal Policy

High and rising fiscal deficits have been a central cause of excess demand pressures—as indicated by inflation and large external payments deficits—in many countries. These conditions, which were symptomatic of the countries that experienced debt crises, hurt domestic investment in a variety of ways. For example, large public sector financing requirements pre-empt resources that might otherwise be used in the private sector, frequently more efficiently.[5] Also, public sector borrowing often takes the form of loans from the central bank, which is highly inflationary.

Because of rigidities in some prices, inflation has distorting effects that produce misleading signals and interfere with the efficient allocation of resources. Rigidities of exchange rates and interest rates are a particularly common problem, leading to a weakening external position as incentives are shifted away from exports in favor of imports, and in favor of spending and capital flight rather than financial saving. It is not surprising to find, therefore, that countries with high inflation have saved and invested significantly less in recent years than countries with low inflation rates.[6] In

---

[5]Mohsin Khan and Carmen M. Reinhart, "Private Investment and Economic Growth in Developing Countries," IMF Working Paper, No. 89/60 (Washington: International Monetary Fund, July 1989).

[6]During 1982–88, developing countries with high inflation rates recorded savings rates equivalent to about 18 percent of national income and investment rates of about 20 percent. Low-inflation countries saved and invested on average 28 percent of national income.

addition, as I pointed out in a paper some twenty-five years ago,[7] inflation tends to alter the composition of investment, toward less efficient ventures (for example, inventories) offering short-term gains, and away from productive projects involving larger gestation.

Because of the prevalence of large fiscal deficits, and their role in contributing to excess demand, fiscal restraint is typically a key component of adjustment programs supported by the Fund. While the impact of fiscal restraint on domestic saving and investment will vary according to the structure of the economy and the particular circumstances, a few generalizations are possible. A reduction in *public consumption* (current expenditures), for example, is unlikely to have a significant effect on private consumption in developing countries and would normally lead to an increase in national savings. The rise in national savings, in turn, could stimulate private investment if it were to lead to lower domestic real interest rates, or if it were to result in the expectation of a lower burden of taxation in the future.

If, on the other hand, the fiscal adjustment takes the form of *increased revenues*, private saving is likely to fall, particularly if the tax increase reduces the after-tax rate of return on saving (which would tilt the pattern of expenditure toward consumption). Similarly, if the incidence of the tax falls on profits, private investment may suffer. If increased investment is not forthcoming, the rise in national saving will simply replace foreign saving; that is, it will result in an improvement in the external current account position.

Cuts in *public investment* could affect private investment in a number of ways. If, for example, the public investment projects that are curtailed compete directly with the private sector, private investment may receive a net stimulus. On the other hand, a reduction in public investment projects that are complementary to the private capital stock could lead to an improvement in the current account position but to a lower rate of economic growth.

Credit Policy

The restraint of aggregate demand through limits on the expansion of domestic credit—another central element of adjustment

[7]A.S. Shaalan, "The Impact of Inflation on the Composition of Private Domestic Investment," *Staff Papers*, International Monetary Fund (Washington), Vol. 9 (July 1962).

programs—also influences saving and investment. Much depends upon whether interest rates are relatively free to respond to market forces or are administered (fixed). If interest rates have some flexibility, a more restrictive credit policy would tend to raise interest rates and stimulate private financial saving. With credit restricted, higher saving will serve to strengthen the external position. Meanwhile, however, if the credit restraint is an element of a broader program of adjustment, confidence may rise to the extent that individuals seeking to increase investment seek alternative (non-inflationary) financing—through reduced consumption, for example.

With rigid interest rates, a tightening of credit will be less effective in strengthening the balance of payments (since there is likely to be little effect on domestic financial savings), while the necessary tightening of credit rationing may further undermine allocative efficiency. In these circumstances, the direct effects of credit restraint on private investment will be unfavorable. However, stabilization programs usually attempt to mitigate such adverse effects on private investment by applying subceilings on credit to the public sector, which seek to shift the composition of credit toward the private sector within the overall ceiling. Further negative effects on investment could prove to be short term if the restrictive credit policy succeeds in bringing inflation under control. As the domestic macroeconomic situation improves, the medium-term outlook for investment would become more favorable.

Interest Rate Policy

While there is disagreement over the influence of interest rates on the volume of *total* savings, interest rates have been shown to be important in determining the *form* in which savings are held. Thus, while an increase in interest rates may stimulate total savings by making future consumption less expensive relative to current consumption (substitution effect), it may also tend to reduce saving by lowering the amount of present saving necessary to buy a given amount of future consumption (income effect). Empirical evidence on the relative importance of these two effects is mixed, but there is evidence that the interest rate has a significant effect on the volume of *financial* savings.

In countries experiencing prolonged bouts of financial repression (for example, negative real interest rates), a large proportion of savings are held as inflation hedges such as real estate, consumer durables, precious metals and gems, and foreign currency. Where such countries have significantly increased interest rates, a large positive effect on financial savings has been observed. In addition, where the interest rate increase has been accompanied by appropriate macropolicies leading to greater confidence in the exchange rate, capital flight has been curbed or even reversed, thus augmenting the supply of resources for domestic investment.

Developing countries often keep interest rates artificially low in an effort both to keep down the cost of government borrowing and to stimulate private investment. In practice, however, such a strategy has many disadvantages. Insofar as low real interest rates depress financial savings and encourage capital outflow, the supply of resources for investment will be reduced. At the same time, artificial suppression of real interest rates tends to lower the productivity of investment as scarce financial resources have to be rationed by administrative means (rather than through the market). The success of allocation of credit by administrative means depends on the ability of policymakers to identify correctly the most productive sectors and to control the end use of funds allocated to them. Neither of these tasks is easy. Moreover, the low cost of funds reduces the necessity for careful evaluation of projects by enterprises. Finally, low interest rates together with downward rigidity of real wages distort relative factor prices in a manner that encourages a bias in investment toward capital-intensive techniques with detrimental effects on employment.

In a recent study covering 33 developing countries over the period 1965–85, the relationship between real interest rates and growth was examined. The study showed that increases in interest rates, toward modestly positive levels, are associated with increased saving and investment and with increased financial depth (monetization). And financial depth, in turn, is strongly associated with more productive investment, thus improving prospects for growth.

Financial Sector Development

There is abundant evidence that policies aimed at assisting the development of the financial sector can improve the climate for private sector investment. (Indeed, this subject forms the basis for the 1989 *World Development Report* of the World Bank.) Informal finance, as it exists in many developing countries, involves unequal opportunities for potential lenders and borrowers and, since it is by definition unregulated, is exposed to greater risk of fraud and instability. As economies grow, informal financing arrangements need to be replaced by the more sophisticated and comprehensive services that organized institutions like commercial banks, investment houses, and organized capital markets can supply. These institutions are capable of mobilizing financial savings on a large scale and of transforming their maturity structure by intermediating between the many small depositors, usually with a preference for liquid assets, and fewer large borrowers who typically need long-term finance for investment. Government policy can help foster and develop financial systems in a context of broad macroeconomic stability by building better legal, accounting, and regulatory frameworks.

Exchange Rate Policy

Exchange rates are a key administered price in almost all developing countries, and one which is frequently subject to considerable rigidity. Because of the pervasive influence of the exchange rate on domestic prices (via its direct effect on the domestic currency price of imported goods and exportables), governments are often reluctant to depreciate their currencies lest such action should aggravate domestic inflationary pressures. Failure to depreciate in conditions of inflation (when domestic prices are rising faster than in trading partners) has been a widespread problem. The resulting price distortions divert investment into importing and import-dependent industries at the expense of exportables, and, as the balance of payments weakens, confidence in the currency declines, leading to a drain on domestic savings in the form of capital flight.

Overvalued exchange rates often give rise to other price distortions as well. Governments often respond to capital flight, for example, not by allowing interest rates to find a market level, but by seeking to control capital flight directly—an endeavor that has rarely been fully successful. The deterioration in the balance of payments is often addressed not by fundamental measures of adjustment but by the intensification of trade and payments restrictions or by recourse to foreign borrowing. Restrictions directly undermine efficiency by compounding price distortions and hence the allocation of investment, and by breeding corruption—a dubious prescription for growth. I have already discussed the perils of undue recourse to foreign borrowing as a means of augmenting domestic savings.

While depreciation is best not postponed in the circumstances I have been describing, it is not a panacea. Adjustment to a realistic exchange rate needs to be backed by a comprehensive macroeconomic program aimed at reining in aggregate demand and restoring a viable external position. Without such a program, the changes in relative prices induced by the depreciation would be quickly eroded by domestic inflation, and the earlier distortions would quickly reappear, again undermining savings, investment, and growth.

Uncertainty and Policy Credibility

A final consideration relates to the credibility of policies. A number of recent studies have emphasized the irreversible nature of investment expenditures because capital, once installed, is company- or industry-specific and cannot be put to use elsewhere without considerable cost. In view of the irreversible nature of investment, uncertainty plays an important role in investment decision making. In this context, the perceived stability and predictability of the incentive structure and the macroeconomic policy environment are probably as important as the policies and incentives themselves. Various studies have analyzed the different forms of uncertainty relevant for investment decisions. For example, uncertainty regarding future demand or future real exchange rates or interest rates may cause companies to refrain from investment even if existing conditions made entry profitable. Equally, uncertainty deters potential foreign investors, thus depriving the country of access both to foreign equity capital and to the management and technology that frequently accompany it.

A corollary of this issue is the credibility of policy *reform*. This could be related to investors' perceptions about both the internal consistency of a reform package as well as the government's willingness and ability to carry out the reform in the face of short-run social costs. Credibility in this sense could become an important factor in investor response. This factor would be especially significant in economies that have attempted, but failed, to carry reforms to their successful conclusion in the past. It is difficult to suggest how credibility could be improved by government actions in the short run, but the adoption of sound macroeconomic policies that support domestic and external balance is a start in the right direction. The issue is also related to the choice between gradual and abrupt reforms, which in the end would largely depend on the specific conditions prevailing in a particular country.

Concluding Remarks

I would like to conclude with some additional comments regarding savings, investment, and growth in the Middle East—a region which has been the subject of rather limited empirical work. I shall speak first of the oil exporting countries and then of the non-oil developing countries of the region.[8]

Oil Exporting Countries

Trends in the capital-surplus major oil exporters have moved in line with the changing fortunes of the world oil market. National savings (to which fiscal surpluses contributed importantly in past years) declined from as much as 43 percent of national income in the second half of the 1970s (when budget surpluses were typically very large) to about 30 percent in the first half of the 1980s. The debacle in the world oil market in 1986 led to a further contraction in national savings, which fell to about 17 percent of national income in 1988.

Domestic investment in these countries showed greater resilience. Indeed, in the first half of the 1980s, investment (at about 29 percent of national income) was somewhat higher than in the second half of the 1970s (27 percent of national income), though it fell sharply after 1986 to about 20 percent on average. The eventual decline in investment reflected a desire in most countries to conserve foreign assets and was facilitated by the completion by most countries of much of their infrastructure development programs.

These diverging trends in saving and investment were accompanied by a substantial increase in the share of consumption in national income—a process that has continued without interruption during the 1980s. This, in turn, has contributed to the emer-

[8]The country coverage corresponds to that of the Fund's Middle Eastern Department (with the exception of a few countries that have been excluded on account of data limitations). The oil exporting countries comprise the Islamic Republic of Iran, Kuwait, Libya, Oman, Qatar, Saudi Arabia, and the United Arab Emirates. The non-oil economies are Bahrain, Egypt, Jordan, Pakistan, the Syrian Arab Republic, and the Yemen Arab Republic.

gence of a current external deficit for the group as a whole in the range of 2–3 percent of national income. Although the external reserve position of the majority remains comfortable, affording considerable scope for policymakers, the more constrained external position combined with the continuing uncertainty surrounding the prospects for the world oil market calls for caution and prudence in domestic policies. More compelling reasons exist now, for example, for these countries to subject domestic investment to more rigorous scrutiny to ensure that new ventures are remunerative and productive. In more restrictive budgetary circumstances, most countries also are seeking to improve the efficiency of government expenditures by curbing subsidies and raising charges and fees for government services. These policies promise to strengthen budgetary positions (augmenting national savings) and to minimize the distortions in domestic price structures that can give misleading signals for investment.

As budgets have shifted from surplus into deficit in recent years, new financing mechanisms are being introduced, including bonds and other government securities. Such investments offer new vehicles for domestic savings and are leading to more flexible interest rate policies in some countries. Such a step can be helpful not only in raising government finance but also in integrating domestic capital and money markets and in enabling governments to influence external capital flows more effectively—an important consideration in countries with unrestricted exchange and payments systems.

Non-Oil Developing Countries of the Middle East

The direction of change in savings and investment in the non-oil countries of the Middle East is similar to that of the oil exporters, though the magnitudes differ significantly. In brief, national savings fell from 18½ percent of national income during 1976–81 to about 14 percent in the early 1980s and have since declined to about 12 percent. Investment ratios now stand at about 16 percent of national income—six points lower than in the late 1970s. Meanwhile, in these countries too, consumption ratios have been on the rise.

These trends are a reflection in part of adverse external (exogenous) factors and in part of weaknesses in domestic policy. The contraction of the export earnings of the oil exporting countries in the 1980s, coupled with the weakening of domestic demand

and activity in their non-oil sectors, had profound implications for the non-oil countries of the region that depend upon the oil exporters—to a greater or lesser degree—for financial support, for outlets for their surplus labor (and associated remittances), and for export markets. More generally, the external economic environment during the 1980s for the Middle Eastern non-oil group has been mixed, with relatively high interest rates and weak commodity prices over most of the decade being partly offset by moderately strong (if uneven) world trade growth.

On the whole, these economies have been susceptible to adverse external influences on account of shortcomings in domestic policies and delays in adjustment (compounded in some cases by hostilities and civil strife) that are reflected in large external imbalances and external financing difficulties (current account deficits are in the range of 4–5 percent of national income on average).

At the root of these imbalances are large, and, in some cases still rising, public sector deficits as expenditures have risen in the face of poor revenue performance. The liquidity expansion associated with the financing of these deficits, together with rigidities in domestic prices and interest rates, has been fueling excess demand pressures as reflected in high or rising rates of inflation and deteriorating external positions. Despite these pressures, some countries continue to maintain overvalued exchange rates and complex exchange and trade systems in an effort to moderate price increases. However, this has put downward pressure on exchange rates in parallel markets and, together with negative real interest rates, has contributed to capital flight in some countries.

The policy requirements are clear for many countries in this group, and determined action is necessary. It is encouraging to note that two countries in this group have recently embarked on comprehensive adjustment programs in collaboration with the Fund, and discussions are under way in one or two others.

Thus, the issues I have discussed in broader terms in the earlier sections of this paper have a clear relevance for the Middle Eastern countries, particularly in current circumstances. I would hope that this seminar will be able to address in more specific, policy-related terms the challenges countries of this region are facing today in mobilizing savings and ensuring both that capital is profitably utilized and that the recovery that has been emerging can be sustained through sound policy choices.

Comment

Mohamed El-Diri

Without going into every detail of Mr. A. Shakour Shaalan's important paper on the relationship between investment and growth in the context of the macroeconomic policies adopted by developing countries and supported by the International Monetary Fund, it seems to me that three fundamental points warrant emphasis here. The first revolves around a general retrospective analysis of the relationship between investment, external financing, and growth; the second relates to macroeconomic policies aimed at improving investment ratios; while the third emphasizes the present chronic problem of foreign debt and its impact on investment—and therefore growth—within developing countries.

Investment, External Resources, and Growth

Most developing countries have been relying on foreign resources to raise their level of income. The nature, importance, and institutional framework of those resources have changed radically over the years. Nevertheless, external resources have almost become an autonomous factor of production, whose consequences are considered two of the main factors that subsequently contributed to the debt problem.

The underlying concept behind the promotion of foreign resources in the developing economies was based on the assumption that, since those resources were not associated with direct performance, they helped somewhat to reduce the need for certain factors, such as savings or foreign exchange, so as to achieve fast growth and correct imbalances. However, the achievement of those objectives depends on the fulfillment of certain prerequisites for sustainable growth and for the gradual elimination of dependence on foreign resources.

One of the prerequisites for achieving the objectives is the ability of developing countries to adjust their productive structures to cope with the changes taking place in domestic and foreign demand. This condition may have particular importance in a fast-

growing economy, thus requiring a significant increase in the supply of inputs for production, raw materials, and manufactured
goods. Since developing countries in general import those materials, any limitation on their import would reflect negatively on
the level of growth. Consequently, controls would be tightened,
thus impeding investment. Moreover, the increasing shortage of
imported materials caused by a lack of foreign resources results in
the use of potential savings to finance domestic consumption demand at the expense of productive investment, which leads to
weak aggregate demand. It has been proved, however, that while
foreign capital has a positive impact it poses certain dangers:

- This capital might lead governments to postpone the implementation of necessary reforms;
- Foreign capital could lead the government to borrow excessively.

With this in mind, let us review the developing countries' experience from the early seventies to the early eighties.

Although the practical experience of the developing countries
varies from region to region, and from country to country, as Mr.
Shaalan has pointed out, growth in the developing countries in
general witnessed a considerable slowdown throughout the eighties
compared with the seventies. It is also evident that this slowdown
was due to several factors, such as population growth, weakening
terms of trade, instabilities in currency exchange markets, and the
resurgence of protectionism. But the most important cause of
decelerating growth during the eighties was without doubt the
decline in capital formation that immediately followed the outbreak of the debt crisis, which was attributed in turn to scarce
financial resources, both domestic and foreign.

During the seventies and up to the eighties, external capital
flows, especially private flows, to developing countries increased
in momentum, as manifested in greater borrowing from commercial banks, whose share in recent total capital flows to developing countries rose from 15 percent in 1970 to 36 percent in
1983. As a result, these countries became more vulnerable to external debt-servicing difficulties, for three reasons:

- The volume of loans greatly exceeded the volume of direct
  investments, leading to an imbalance between capital and debt.
  New investments in developing countries thus fell from an

annual average of $14 billion in 1975–79 to $7.8 billion in 1983.

- Floating interest on loans increased markedly, placing the burden of debt squarely on the borrower whenever the interest rate grew.
- Repayment time was significantly reduced, especially following the decline in the share of public capital and public debt in total external contributions. It should be recalled that foreign investments declined before bank loans became scarce, which also explains the reduction in the ratio of direct investments to total external contributions in favor of developing countries from 48 percent to 12.5 percent in 1983.

Thus, most developing countries, especially from 1978 to 1983, began to encounter serious difficulties that became so chronic that many of these countries turned to commercial borrowing payable on terms different from and at odds with the phased planning of investment financing or the time spans in which these investments become remunerative. Abetting this action was the abundant liquidity at the disposal of commercial banks during that time, which made it easier for developing countries to obtain these loans, made without sufficient concern for the areas and terms of assignment.

On the other hand, one must acknowledge that many of these countries did not undertake sufficient restructuring of their economies when these external debts began to mount, while external funds were frequently improperly assigned. Indeed, the presence of foreign capital does not necessarily preclude raising the level of domestic saving, whether private or public, since such capital can only supplement and does not replace domestic saving. The principle applied in this regard requires taking into consideration the same measures for determining domestic saving and investment levels as are applied in estimating acceptable levels of external borrowing. One can infer from this principle that managing and adjusting external capital flows is an essential bridgehead to managing the macroeconomy.

Macroeconomic Policies and Investment

The diverse situations in which developing countries found themselves enable certain lessons to be derived about the impact of government intervention in the various economic sectors. First, most developing countries failed to display sufficient flexibility before the uncertainties surrounding international economic conditions arose. Second, foreign capital, as well as domestic resources, was not utilized or channeled effectively, because, as a rule, investment yields should exceed official resource costs if sufficient surpluses are to be generated to cover interest, award shareholders, and secure profits.

Without repeating the figures quantifying the experience of developing countries in this regard, which Mr. Shaalan has already provided, I should like to summarize some of the salient features of this experience for economic policy. Three areas of activity may be delineated, each involving certain distortions and constraints that developing countries have been unable to resolve adequately:

- The greatest value corresponds to the opportunity cost, for through it productive structures can achieve sufficient flexibility and the activities in which the country has a comparative advantage can be encouraged. If price subsidies are introduced, it should be done with care. On the other hand, because the price structure, including interest rates, influences investment decisions, this area of activity should not be ignored.
- The rate of exchange and commercial policy also play an important role. During the seventies and until the early eighties, many developing countries sometimes allowed their currencies to become overvalued and their commercial policies to suffer distortions, thereby encouraging imports and discouraging exports. As a result, macroeconomic equilibria in many developing countries were upset.
- Domestic demand must be limited to a level compatible with domestic production and external realities. The absence of such compatibility will lead to problems in performance and the depletion of exchange reserves.

These three areas of activity actually suggest a macroeconomic policy for restoring growth and ensuring its progress through improved savings and ways in which these savings may be employed in productive investments. Long-term growth is effectively linked to a combination of structural economic variables, such as domestic savings ratios, human capital formation, growth in exportables, real interest rates on external debt, and population growth.

For the first three variables, one anticipates that they would have a positive impact on development; the other two are more likely to hamper development.

One recent study that endorsed this line of thought attempted to incorporate it in an evaluation of the experience of 55 selected countries, starting from 1970.[1] Among the results obtained was that exports were the principal determinant of growth for over 95 percent of these countries for 1970–85, with growth increasing by 2.6 percentage points on average. It was also shown that domestic savings ratios have a positive effect on economic growth, possibly to the same extent as exports. The study contends that a unit increase in domestic savings yields a tenfold percentage increase, raising per capita GNP by 1–2 percentage points a year. Investments in human capital during this period increased by 4 percent a year; this type of investment, according to the study, had a tangibly positive impact. As for population growth and real interest on external debt, both had a negative effect on per capita GNP (with the former effecting a slight decline of about 2 percentage points), which was to be expected.

However, upon interpolating these results, one notes that the variables that were regarded as the greatest determinants of growth (exports and savings) had themselves been subject to external limitations since the early seventies. Consequently, the results of the adjustment programs endorsed by the developing countries during this period fell short of expectations. The programs revolved around the revival of exports in particular, strengthening market mechanisms, deregulating prices, reducing expenditures, and so on.

The adverse consequences of an unstable global environment characterized by the prevalence of protectionist policies in the industrial countries cannot benefit exports from developing countries. On the other hand, if one contends that prices should be determined exclusively by the market, one may point to the example of the farming sector in the industrial countries, which benefits greatly from financial aid to countries, and which therefore confirms the asymmetrical nature of adjustment efforts.

By the same token, the contraction of expenditures required for

[1]See Ichiro Otani and Delano Villanueva, "Theoretical Aspects of Growth in Developing Countries: External Debt Dynamics and the Role of Human Capital," IMF Working Paper, No. 88/54 (Washington: International Monetary Fund, 1988).

adjustment programs was most glaring in productive investments
and in the education and health sectors, where a clear drop occurred
in both physical and human capital formation.

Similarly, the growing external debt, on the one hand, and the
dramatic drop in external flows, on the other, have led to a reverse
transfer of resources. These transfers will most likely diminish the
amount of savings earmarked for investment.

All these pressures, in addition to the negative social consequences entailed, led to the failure of the various adjustment programs pursued by the developing countries. One can conclude
therefore that the success of any adjustment program must involve
an adequate amount of external financing. Without it the programs
will have contrary results at intolerable economic and social costs.

External Debt, Investment, and Growth

We cannot in all honesty decry the credit policies pursued by
developing countries still in the early stages of growth. The procurement of intermediate goods and equipment through loans is
a necessary gamble in the first stages of growth—a process that,
the economists agree, is a long time maturing. But when debt
becomes a cumulative phenomenon, the question of the externalities of that debt, as well as domestic utilization, automatically
arises.

With regard to utilization, we can assume that the country facing
accumulating debt has not been able to direct the loans obtained
productively, enabling a normal repayment of the debt and an
expansion of the base for economic growth.

What needs to be emphasized here are the many forms that this
debt takes in developing countries, reflecting at the same time the
diversity in domestic use of credit, the structural development of
the economies concerned, and the state of the international economy. But it is evident that the kinds of loans extended to developing countries were not their choice but were imposed on them.
The fall in the share of public loans in total external flows to
developing countries, their replacement by commercial bank loans,
the setting of multivalued interest rates, and the instability of exchange markets—all combined to leave developing countries no
room for choice. At the same time, interest rates grew at a be-

wildering rate during the seventies, and maturities grew shorter and shorter.[2]

This situation of a burgeoning foreign debt that exceeds the capacity of developing countries to cope is what impelled these countries to prod for a rescheduling of their debts, the initiation of adjustment programs, and the restructuring of their economies.

One of the consequences of this state of affairs is that new loans are being used to cover interest on old loans and to renew the principal. In 1979, the amount of interest owed by non-oil developing countries exceeded the level of new loans, with only a year's duration separating them. As the balance of trade of these countries is registering a very large deficit in the wake of the second oil shock, to achieve equilibrium in their balance of payments they are resorting to short-term loans at a time when these loans are tied to extremely high costs.

Although these countries have scored some success in this effort during the past few years, the record shows that they remain unable to achieve the goals to which they aspire.

As a result, the debt question continues to be the subject of heated debate, as the rescheduling of conventional debts is a very costly endeavor. Meanwhile, no tangible progress is apparent on additional flows to developing countries while fluctuations in international economic conditions continue.

The recovery of investment and growth to a sound footing under prevailing conditions is therefore inextricably tied to the resolution of the debt crisis. The question of private and public debt and their costs and the achievement of thoughtful solutions that accord with the conditions and aspirations of developing countries must therefore be addressed.

Resolving the debt crisis, curtailing protectionism, stabilizing exchange markets, and reviving domestic investment—so that the developing countries may become genuine contributors to international production and trade—are the problems that, if solved, would provide a sound and viable basis for restoring investment and for progress in development in developing countries.

[2]According to the Organization for Economic Cooperation and Development, the interest rate ranged from a fixed rate of 4.5 percent in 1972 to a variable rate reaching 17.4 percent in 1981.

Fareed Atabani

I read with great interest Mr. Shaalan's refreshingly clear exposition both of the theoretical relationships between investment and growth and of the growing empirical evidence resulting from work inside and outside the Fund to buttress this relationship. Let me say at the outset that I have no quarrel with Mr. Shaalan's contribution and find myself in complete agreement with the eminently sensible things he had to say. In my comments I will therefore attempt to clarify and elaborate some of the major policy issues that seem to me to be behind much of Mr. Shaalan's paper.

To do this one should pose a number of questions: Why, given the theoretical framework and the evidence on investment and growth, are the economies of most developing countries experiencing low rates of growth and substantial dislocations? What if anything is the role of macroeconomic policy in the context of growth and what is the role of government in the process of economic development? Answers to these and similar questions would, I believe, clarify the necessary conditions—already implicit in the paper—for maintaining high and sustained levels of investment and economic growth.

The source of present-day trouble in most developing countries, I think, lies in the rejection by many economists (and the acceptance of this rejection by policymakers) of some of the basic tenets of economic theory based on the assumption that economic theory is irrelevant for present-day developing countries. In its simplest and most prevalent form, it is argued that microeconomic relationships, particularly relative prices, cannot be applicable to developing countries in which markets, among other things, are neither perfect nor competitive in the textbook sense. Separated from its microeconomic foundations, concern with macroeconomics then shifted to identifying and then manipulating major (undifferentiated) aggregates like investment, consumption, and savings in an attempt to obtain more output from the economy. The emphasis of macroeconomic policy is therefore shifted to demand management based on the view that higher levels of investment are beneficial, with little or no concern for how these are to be achieved or what type of investment it is. By contrast, microeconomics, concerned with relative prices as the signal for resource allocation, focuses on the supply side, that is, on efficiency and the proper allocation of resources and not merely on the *increase* of the *rate* at which they are used.

The macroeconomic concern with aggregates implies that all supply relationships are fixed. This gives rise to all sorts of concepts that are surprisingly still fashionable in current thinking about economic development—concepts that have ossified into dogma. Perhaps the most prevalent is the denial of the possibility that workers will respond positively to changes in incentives, or the possibility of substituting one good for another in response to changes in prices, or the idea that export earnings or import requirements of most developing countries are fixed for any given scale of production. The most important implication of fixed supply relationships is that prices can, without harm, be stripped of their proper function of allocating scarce resources to their most efficient uses. Prices then are viewed merely as a passive instrument for government manipulation, for example, to curb inflation through price controls or perhaps to be tampered with to increase government revenues.

This view of economic relationships leads direct to the concept that to bring about economic development in most underdeveloped economies their governments will need only to *control* and *direct* the major economic activities with no reference to relative prices. I believe that therein lies the major problem in formulating economic policy in most developing countries in the postwar era. Government policy then attempts to achieve what relative prices are meant to, that is, allocate resources. But bureaucracies in most countries are not able to cope with the stringent requirements needed to stay on top of the system, thereby causing irreparable damage to the efficiency of the economy.

Mr. Shaalan in his paper refers to the markedly different effects of the debt crisis on two sets of countries: those that relied "heavily on foreign savings during the previous decade"—certainly the majority—and those "countries that avoided debt problems and achieved sound investment and growth performance"—a minority. He then goes on to enumerate a number of policy differences between the two groups, such as large budget deficits, loose monetary policies, high rates of inflation, and overvalued exchange rates. To my mind these are the symptoms of a much deeper malaise. The first group consists of those countries that have tampered with the price system and refused to allow relative prices to do their job, while the second group consists of those countries that left their domestic price systems largely intact and, by and large, allowed relative prices to perform their function.

In the first group, what started off as attempts to foster economic growth through government intervention (since prices cannot be relied on because markets are not perfect) ended up by causing macroeconomic mismanagement resulting in monumental distortions that eventually hampered economic growth. The trouble with this approach is that advocates of intervention, in their haste to reject the market mechanism, have failed to pose the really important question. Since it is generally admitted that markets in most developing countries are imperfect, the proper question to pose is whether to rely on imperfect markets or imperfect governments. The history of economic development over the past forty years indicates quite clearly that, in most developing countries, imperfect markets work better than imperfect governments. Experience shows that governments use their powers not only arbitrarily but also incompetently. In most developing countries the administrative capacity to intervene intelligently and in a non-distorting manner is lacking.

If this is true, the question remains, what is the appropriate role of economic policy in fostering investment and hence economic development? First, it is necessary that the price system be allowed to function with minimum interference by the government so that relative prices can allocate scarce resources to their most beneficial uses. Only then can the quality of investment be improved and investment reflect resource endowments and comparative advantage. At the macro-level, it is obvious that economic stability is a prerequisite for economic growth. Policies that ensure such stability are a noninflationary monetary policy and a tight control of public finances. The aim of macroeconomic policy is to ensure that the rate of inflation in the economy is both low and stable. With low and stable inflation, investors can, at the very least, be confident that major shocks, such as sudden currency depreciations or emergency measures that could choke businesses, will not be needed. Experience shows that when this deceptively modest goal is achieved, development will proceed in a more or less satisfactory fashion. It also shows that when macroeconomic policy attempts to achieve something bolder, the results are usually disappointing.

What, then, beyond the delivery of a stable macroeconomic environment that fosters both the level and the efficiency of investment, is the role of government in the process of economic development? Obviously, governments have an important supporting role where their own scarce resources can be of maximum benefit. Perhaps the most crucial role is the creation of an effective and impartial legal system. By this I do not mean only the adoption of clear rules that define property rights, contracts, limited liability, etc. but also, and perhaps more important, the means of enforcing these rules impartially. In addition, spending on improved infrastructure, the provision of education and training, and the delivery of adequate health services are prime areas for government activity, since investment in these areas tends to foster and improve the quality of private investment in the creation of goods and services. In addition, in most developing countries, if the government does not provide these public welfare services, the need is likely to remain unmet and to grow, with detrimental effects on the quality of investment and economic growth.

3

Efficiency of Public Investment: Lessons from World Bank Experience

John W. Wall

The efficiency of public investment is quite a relevant and timely subject in Arab countries, because the public sector invests heavily, and because all resources for development are becoming increasingly scarce. In these countries, public investment is high both as a proportion of total investment and as a percentage of gross domestic product (GDP). This means that in the long run the growth of output, the standard of living, and welfare crucially depend on the efficiency of public investment. As Arab countries have adjusted to the reduced inflows of foreign resources that started in the early 1980s, the tendency has been to reduce public investment, meaning that maintaining any semblance of past growth rates depends on increasing the efficiency of the investment that remains.

The appendix contains graphs that allow comparisons of public investment as a percentage of GDP in selected Arab countries and a group of 30 comparator countries (Pfeffermann and Madarassy, 1989). A glance at these graphs indicates that many Arab countries have higher levels of public investment than most other countries, and that most countries, Arab and non-Arab alike, have experienced a declining trend in public investment in the 1980s. Growth rates of GDP and total investment have also fallen over the same period, in some cases to less than the rate of population growth, implying that living standards are falling. This is an unsatisfactory state of affairs. Reversing these trends in the face of scarce resources for development will require substantial improvements in the efficiency with which available resources are used.

The relevant issue is not whether to undertake public investment, but under what circumstances is public investment efficient. While there is some literature that directly compares the efficiency of public and private investment (Balassa, 1988), in modern economies some level of public investment is inevitable to create the environment and infrastructure necessary to make economic activities of all kinds possible and more efficient. This paper addresses two related issues: what is the appropriate mix of public and private investment; and what criteria can be used to ensure that the public investment is efficient.

The World Bank undoubtedly has had more experience in reviewing public investment plans and their implementation than any other organization in existence (Kavalsky, 1986). Over the past four decades, World Bank staff regularly have reviewed the public investment plans of its borrowing countries, and now conduct perhaps 10–15 such reviews a year. There have been such reviews in many Arab countries— during the 1980s at least once each in Egypt, Jordan, the Yemen Arab Republic, the People's Democratic Republic of Yemen, Bahrain, Morocco, Tunisia, and Algeria. In conjunction with its project lending, often directly to governments for public investment, the Bank closely scrutinizes individual investment projects, works closely with implementing agencies, and follows the progress of projects it helps fund with regular field visits. The research departments of the World Bank have undertaken cross-country macroeconomic and sector studies of the experience with various forms of public investment to draw lessons learned in one context for assistance in finding solutions to development problems in another. The experience built up through this effort has led to an appreciation of how diverse individual country situations are, but also to some firm conclusions as to what leads to efficiency in public investment.

Establishing Priorities for Public Investment

Basic Governmental Responsibilities

The most important step in ensuring the efficiency of public investment is choosing the appropriate mix of public and private investment in the first place. (The World Bank's 1988 *World Development Report* discusses this general area in some detail.) Efficiency depends as much if not more on what the public sector

chooses to do as on how well it does it. There is a wide spectrum
of experience among countries with respect to public ownership,
organization, and control of economic activities; some countries
have minimal involvement in the direct provision of goods and
services while the involvement of others is pervasive. As in most
other aspects of life, there are trade-offs that are reconciled differently in different situations. Most would agree that public ownership and control involve a dilution of incentives to husband
resources with care, resulting in welfare losses. Most also would
agree that some economic activities, those that display inherent
externalities, natural monopolies, or other types of market failures,
cannot be left to the unfettered operation of market forces. The
very existence of governments is a recognition that some activities
are best handled as public undertakings. The challenge is to identify
those activities and organize them in the most efficient way possible, fulfilling governmental responsibilities to create a favorable
environment in which human welfare can flourish.

The public organization of various activities can be seen as a continuum, ranging from the least controversial type, which almost
all would accept as governmental responsibilities, to the other
extreme, which most would agree is better left to private initiative.
At the beginning of the continuum would be basic defense services,
maintenance of law and order, supply of justice, control of money,
establishment of standards, funding of basic research, and collection and dissemination of basic statistics and information. A little
further on, but still at the noncontroversial end, would be the
governmental provision of social services—education, health, and
poverty alleviation—often in conjunction with private organization of the same or similar services in the private sector. Basic
physical infrastructure—roads, water supply, telecommunications, electricity, flood control, irrigation, and sanitation facilities—is almost everywhere subject at least to pervasive public
control and often public ownership and investment.

These public responsibilities are perhaps the most basic undertaken by most developing countries. They should constitute the
priorities for public investment. Where there are constraints to
resource mobilization for public investment, these should become
the core of investments to be protected in times of resource scarcity. Spending too little on basic government services while spending too much in areas that the private sector could have served is

perhaps the biggest and most costly loss of efficiency in public investment.

World Bank staff have conducted research into the question of whether public investment is complementary or competitive to private sector investment (Chhibber and van Wijnbergen, 1988). On the macroeconomic level, public and private investment clearly compete for the same resources. Higher public investment requires either increased foreign borrowing or higher private sector net saving, requiring higher domestic interest rates. Either of these means of financing in a world of scarce resources means lower private sector investment. The question returns to which sector makes better use of the resources. Chhibber and van Wijnbergen show with quantitative analysis that in the case of Turkey public investment in infrastructural activities (broadly defined to include expenditures on health and education) is largely complementary with private investment; and public investment in noninfrastructural activities crowds out private investment and reduces overall rates of return to investment. Public investment of the right kind reduces the costs of private activities and creates the conditions for higher private sector profitability.

Public Sector Enterprises

Many developing countries have gone further along the public-private continuum to set up public sector enterprises (PSEs) to undertake a plethora of activities. Some Arab countries—Egypt, Algeria, and the People's Democratic Republic of Yemen—developed public sectors that were dominant in most areas. In the more recent past, as a result of disappointing performance by PSEs, these three countries have started to move back from the extreme public sector end of the continuum by encouraging the private sector to take on more responsibilities, although a very large part of economic activity still remains under public control.

Ironically, many PSEs originally were set up to make governmental activities *more* efficient. That is, activities that were at first handled by government departments that were separable functions (for example, electricity or oil production, railways, hospitals) were spun off from the government itself to create a more businesslike environment. The idea was to protect these entities from political interference by separate budgets, cost accounting, cost recovery through pricing, rational employment policies, and management autonomy and accountability. The present-day problems of many of these PSEs attest to the difficulty of actually protecting these entities from political interference, despite the original intentions of doing so.

Often, countries expanded public ownership and control beyond those activities with strong externalities or natural monopolies to others that are elsewhere left to the private sector. Examples of these are production of steel, cement, and fertilizer, road transport, agricultural marketing, housing, health care, and commercial banking. The rationale used was some mixture of the following: appropriation of surplus, the size of the minimum investment required, the large impact of the produced items on consumers' budgets, and the lack of private initiative. Comprehensive and ambitious development planning often led to the establishment of such PSEs, as it soon became obvious to planners that, left to its own resources, the (often incipient) private sector was not forthcoming in fulfilling the investment plans as formulated.

Experience with Public Sector Enterprises

The experience in developing countries with large-scale public investment in productive enterprises has not been an altogether happy one. While there are examples of efficient, financially viable, and flourishing PSEs, there are also many examples of the opposite. World Bank staff have often been requested to review the experience of public sector enterprises by the governments involved, such as a major study done recently on Egypt. World Bank research staff have distilled lessons from many such studies in papers that indicate a pattern of similar problems (*World Development Report, 1988* and Shirley, 1989a).

Despite the desire to provide a businesslike environment for their operation, governments tend to saddle PSEs with mixed mandates, including not only financial targets but also social objectives that often conflict with the efficient operation of these entities. Governments find many reasons to control the output prices of PSEs—to protect vulnerable consumers, fight inflation, and maintain low input prices for other PSEs. Governments also seek to influence employment policies for social objectives such as general employment generation, placement of unemployed university graduates, establishment of minimum wages for the low-skilled, enforcement of maximum wages for managers and professionals for equity reasons, and appointment of senior managers on the basis of political patronage.

Because of these burdens of mixed mandates, governments often protect PSEs from competition as a way of creating rents from which the costs of the social burdens can be paid. PSEs are often protected from import competition through quota restrictions and high tariffs on outputs; and from domestic competition through restrictive licensing of domestic capacity (investment control), preferential access to (subsidized) inputs, and other rules rigged to benefit PSEs over the private sector. This protection holds two negative consequences for efficiency: the protection further weakens the economic efficiency of PSEs themselves beyond that introduced by the social burdens; it also introduces distortions into the entire domestic structure of production, weakening private firms as well.

Perhaps the ultimate protection from competition offered is the unwillingness of governments to allow PSEs to go out of business. Irrespective of ownership or motivation, some good ideas turn out badly in practice, and some originally viable undertakings become nonviable when circumstances change. Problems created when an investment turns sour disappear when the capital and labor are redeployed in other activities. These problems continue and escalate when governments refuse to allow the redeployment, either by continuing the operation of PSEs, or, sometimes, by converting failing private firms to public ones. The motivation is often the protection of employment of labor in these entities or the continued provision of goods and services for which no other private sector alternatives exist. More fundamentally, it protects labor and capital from the stress of adjustment to new employment at the cost of tying up these economic resources in inefficient firms. This unwillingness forces governments to protect sick PSEs further from competition, introducing further distortions, or direct subsidies in one way or another from the government budget.

Mixed mandates and protection from competition not only lead to economic inefficiency but also to financial distress, both for the PSEs and for the government. This financial distress shows up in the rising contribution of PSEs to overall public sector deficits, growing foreign indebtedness, interagency arrears in payments due, and increasing borrowing from the domestic banking system. When the scale of PSEs in the total economy is large, as it is in several Arab countries (Egypt, Algeria, and the People's Democratic Republic of Yemen), financial distress in PSEs can lead to large macroeconomic imbalances in the economy as a whole—uncontrollable budget deficits, balance of payments deficits, and excessive growth of domestic credit. These imbalances tend to persist and grow as long as governments are unable to correct the root causes—inefficiencies in PSEs.

Reform of Public Sector Enterprises

The solution to this problem is inherent in the diagnosis: the best cure is prevention. Public investment should concentrate on those activities that are the core of governmental responsibilities, and scarce financial and administrative resources should be deployed to make these activities as efficient as possible. Those activities that can be should be left to the market to provide.

Where there is a legacy of a large public sector with inefficient and financially troublesome parts, restructuring of those parts is called for. The basic tools of public sector restructuring are divestiture, financial strengthening, and introduction of more market competition (Shirley, 1989b).

A growing number of countries with problematic PSEs have decided to divest public ownership or control, using a variety of mechanisms, none of them easy to implement. One is the straightforward option of selling selected PSEs by negotiation or auction, often with some restructuring before or after the sale. Countries that have embarked on such a policy have found it no simple matter, as it is difficult to let go of the healthy ones and to sell the sick ones. Such a program requires careful preparation and determination. Another option is sale to employees. While this option has the advantages of divestiture and employee protection, it requires creative solutions to difficult financial and managerial problems. A third option that is not quite divestiture is to arrange private management contracts with suitable incentives for performance.

Countries that have initiated PSE divestiture programs have found that a change of ownership (or management) is not a complete solution. Where legacies of the burdens of mixed mandates remain and/or the economic environment is distorted by noncompetitive policies, changing ownership or management is only a partial solution. In some cases, the terms of sale of a PSE even worsen the situation, when governments agree to protect the PSE even further from competition as an incentive to complete the sale. In the long run, there is no escape from addressing the financial and competitive problems that caused the deterioration of the health of the PSE in the first place. The World Bank policy staff have embarked on a major research project to study the results of various divestiture programs in several countries.

When financial problems of PSEs are large and pervasive enough to create macroeconomic imbalances, the solutions involve changing the fundamental cost/price relations and instilling financial discipline. There is no creative financial engineering, such as conversion of debt to equity that will solve the problem for long, although such financial engineering is often needed as part of the rehabilitation of the PSEs that have fallen into a financial mess. It is even less useful simply to impose more stringent financial targets for PSEs by fiat without changing the rules under which they operate. The need is to rationalize pricing policies, limit subsidies, control borrowing, improve investment decisions, eliminate interagency arrears, improve financial reporting, and increase the financial accountability of managers.

The path to efficiency requires more than financial restructuring. With enough control over markets, governments could rig financial profitability in a highly distorted environment. This would send signals to managers to improve financial performance while wasting resources and reducing welfare. To increase economic productivity it is necessary to change the environment in ways that send economically correct signals. There is a growing consensus that the most important way to change the environment in pursuit of increased efficiency is to introduce more market competition, both at home and from abroad. Many governments with large public sectors surround PSEs with protection from domestic competition in the form of capacity licensing and cost-plus pricing rules, and from foreign competition by quota restrictions or prohibitive tariffs. These effectively remove all competition from the environment of PSEs and engender complacency in cost control, technical innovation, product quality, and the attitudes of both labor and management.

Changing this environment requires the removal of this cocoon of protection. A first step is to allow firms in the same industry

to compete with each other on the basis of costs—by having each
PSE face the same ex-factory price rather than calculating this
price based on the cost of production of each PSE. A next step is
to allow these firms to compete on the basis of price—allowing
firms to set their own prices, which is tantamount to allowing the
market to fix the price. Introducing competition from the domestic
private sector means setting PSEs and private firms on the same
basis with respect to both the freedom to invest and access to
inputs, including credit and foreign exchange. A further step is to
introduce competition from abroad by removing quota restrictions
and reducing high tariff protection.

Removing the cocoon of protection is often painful, as it exposes
some PSEs that have become inefficient and noncompetitive un-
derneath the protection. Removal of cost-plus pricing rules and
their replacement with unified output pricing often exposes PSEs
with outdated, high-cost technology to competition with other
PSEs in the same industry with newer, lower-cost plants. Setting
prices at a level that covers the costs of the highest-cost producer
means high prices, and setting them to cover the costs of the low-
cost producer means other firms in the industry make financial
losses. Exposing PSEs to domestic private sector firms often reveals the higher costs of PSEs owing to overmanning or lax management. Removing import protection exposes PSEs to the
lowest-cost producers in the world. For these reasons, the removal
of protection must be done gradually, along with carefully designed restructuring plans to avoid large-scale disruptions.

Efficiency Criteria for Public Investment

In addition to choosing the appropriate fields for public investment, economic efficiency depends on how the public investment
chosen is carried out. The timing of the investment, its consistency
with the macroeconomic environment, the economic evaluation
of investments, and the adequacy of their financing all impinge
on the returns the economy receives. When setting up and carrying
out investment criteria, it is important not to lose sight of the
basic development objectives that public investment is designed
to serve. Among other things this means realizing that some noncapital development expenditures are as important as those clas-

sified as investment, and that sources of funding should not distort national development objectives or strategy.

Timing

The timing of public investment is a crucial determinant of its efficiency. Investing too early or too late sharply reduces economic returns. Two independent studies by World Bank staff have found that economic returns to public investment depend heavily on its timing (Shah, 1988, and Chhibber and van Wijnbergen, 1988). The basic issue turns on whether the economy is pressing up against capacity constraints in areas of public responsibility. When excess capacity exists in basic infrastructure—often when a slow-down of economic activity occurs for macroeconomic reasons— then additional public investment yields low or negative returns. Also, when short-term resource imbalances cause an unusually high opportunity cost to public resources, limiting public invest-ment only to those projects whose returns exceed the higher op-portunity costs means a cut in the overall investment program. In fact, it is often public investment that gets cut when governments find themselves in a financial bind.

Cutting public investment when macroeconomic imbalances are large sometimes results in public investment that is too little too late from the point of view of the future growth of the economy. Some of the most important governmental responsibilities—basic infrastructure—require investments with long gestation periods. If these are cut when resources are out of balance, then, in a few years, after the economy resumes growth, it runs into infrastruc-tural constraints (energy or transport) that could only have been avoided by earlier investment. This is a basic dilemma of devel-opment planning that can be reconciled only by setting and fol-lowing clear priorities for public investment to ensure adequate funding for the most important activities.

Macroeconomic Consistency

World Bank staff, when they review public investment plans, often encounter overblown investment programs that have too many projects with too little funding for timely implementation. This results from a legacy of project proliferation owing to an inability by central ministries to prevent line ministries from initiating projects despite inadequate funding. Line ministries have learned that once started, no matter how small the initial funding, approved projects continue to be funded and eventually are completed. This situation leaves the public investment program overprogrammed and underfunded, with much of its scarce resources tied up in slow-moving projects with much delayed benefits. The same level of resources, concentrated so as to complete priority projects expeditiously, results in earlier benefits and raises the efficiency of the total investment program. When priorities are formulated, governments should be mindful of the future infrastructural needs of continued growth. Given the situation they often face when reviewing public investment plans—a large list of ongoing projects, scarce (and often overestimated) resources, and the need to protect investments in basic infrastructure—the World Bank often recommends creating a "core" public investment program whose funding should be protected for timely implementation, with other projects to be funded only if additional resources become available. This solution is clearly second best. The best would be to scale the whole investment program back to a level that can be implemented in a timely way with priority projects necessary to fulfill the most important public responsibilities.

Economic Evaluation of Project

Development literature places great emphasis on economic evaluation of individual projects as a primary means of ensuring economic efficiency of public investment plans. The World Bank also places great emphasis on project evaluation and has been instrumental in developing and spreading techniques to undertake such evaluations (Kavalsky, 1986, and Squire and van der Tak, 1975).

Economic evaluation of individual projects is actually the last step, in a long and complex process, whose usefulness is largely in confirming that an already formulated program of public investment meets minimum efficiency criteria. No country formulates its public investment plans by calculating economic rates of return for every conceivable project, ranking them high to low, and then approving from the top of the list as far down as resources allow. Even if tried, the information costs of such an approach would be impossibly high. In any case, governments do not try (Leff, 1985). The process of formulating a public investment program is subtle and involves both economic and noneconomic criteria.

Formulating an efficient public investment program requires several key components. First, someone needs to supply a vision of a development strategy. This is a highly intellectual element but indispensable if the actual program elements will be mutually supportive, a necessary requirement for efficiency. The strategy must be developed within a macroeconomic framework that relates investment, growth, and resources consistently and realistically, resulting in a resource envelope that defines the scale of the feasible investment program. Individual projects that exhaust the available resources must be prepared in the context of sectoral strategies and development programs designed to fulfill these strategies. Such strategies and programs are necessary to define which projects are worth preparing to the stage they can be rigorously evaluated. A rigorous evaluation, then, is the last stage. It is nevertheless quite an important stage. Quantitative project evaluation of its technical, financial, and economic characteristics is a check on the realism of all the assumptions that have gone into the project formulation.

Foreign Financing

Maintaining a close correspondence between the individual projects approved and the development strategy is an important element of efficiency. One threat to the coherency of a public investment program is the influence foreign financiers sometimes have on the individual investment decisions. While foreign sources usually want to help finance the high priority investments, they sometimes have agendas of their own that are not fully coordinated with the investment strategy of the government. Where foreign financing is small in relation to the total size of the public investment program, it usually is not difficult to find projects that mutually meet the priority development strategy of the government and the agenda of the lender, whereas where it is large, finding an identity of views is more difficult. Governments should take care that all projects, irrespective of their financing source, are fully integrated with the planning and budgeting of the public investment program and reflect the country's development strategy. Any hidden costs of foreign financing, such as tied procurement, should be considered when deciding how to finance a project. Foreign-financed projects should avoid becoming enclaves with special treatment vis-à-vis the rest of the government.

Capital Versus Noncapital Expenditures

Although the topic of this paper was the efficiency of public investment, it should be noted that noncapital development expenditures are as important as capital ones. At least two issues with respect to noncapital development expenditures are important. One is the operation and maintenance costs associated with investment projects. The other is that in some sectors noncapital expenditures are considerably more important in development programs than capital expenditures.

Operation and maintenance requirements of investment projects create future burdens on the government budget and must be considered when formulating the investment program. For this reason, among others, ministries of finance should be involved in the planning and approval of public investment. By the same token, future operation and maintenance costs must be provided to ensure the realization of future benefits.

In sectors such as health, education, and agriculture, the most important development programs often require only modest capital expenditures, compared with their recurrent expenditure requirements. Government involvement in these sectors usually takes the form of provision of services, which is more staff intensive than capital intensive. For this reason, the World Bank has increasingly emphasized in its work the review of public *expenditure* programs rather than just public *investment* programs.

Illustrative Application of Criteria

It would be revealing to see how these criteria would be applied to an actual case. As an illustration, a few examples can be drawn from Egypt's second Five-Year Plan, 1987–92, which the World Bank reviewed at the Government's request in March 1987 (unpublished official document). A full citation of the Bank's analysis and recommendations would far exceed the patience of this paper's audience, but it is possible to relate the issues identified to the criteria for efficiency developed here.

Macroeconomic Consistency

Egypt's second Five-Year Plan modestly estimated the resources available for public investment during the period (LE 27.4 billion in 1986/87 prices), despite a highly ambitious GDP growth target (6 percent per annum). Bank staff supported the macroeconomic investment target but estimated that the cost of the investments proposed exceeded this target, owing to various elements of undercosting. The Bank recommended that the total program be scaled back somewhat while protecting the "core" investments needed to enable growth in the future. It pointed to projects in some sectors (for example, transport and land reclamation) where the economic returns looked low and the implementation capacity was constrained.

Timing

There were many timing issues in Egypt's second plan. An important one concerned the rate of investment in electric power generation. The original power generation investment plan was based on an extrapolation of past trends that were unlikely to continue in the future because of slower GDP growth and the demand-dampening effects of the Government's pricing policy. This meant that the original plan called for investment in capacity before it would have been needed. Once the plan included a consensus demand projection and a revised generation investment program, it was important to fund this program fully to ensure that the capacity needed to supply the projected demand would be available. Another timing issue concerned the development of natural gas. As natural gas should be developed as rapidly as possible in Egypt, the issue was simply to ensure that the natural gas development program was fully funded for maximum development. A third timing issue was in the transport sector, where the need for new roads was relatively modest compared with the pressing need to maintain roads and bridges.

Economic Evaluation of Projects

The economic evaluation of projects influenced the plan and the Bank's recommendations in many instances. In an important sense, some view of the economic rate of return permeates the whole

planning process and the Bank's views of the plan. The view that
the land reclamation program was too large was based on a view
that some of the projects included in the program earned low or
negative returns. On the other hand, the drainage program is
expected to earn high returns and fully deserves its prominent
place in the investment program. Similarly, the high returns from
gas development motivate the recommendation to proceed quickly
with its development. The industrial sector's public investment
plan contained many potential projects whose economic return
was questioned, leading the Ministry of Planning to exclude them
from the plan.

Foreign Financing

The Government of Egypt has established a Ministry of International Cooperation to coordinate the foreign aid financing of
development projects. This ministry works closely with the Ministry of Planning to ensure that projects financed by such aid fit
into the Government's priorities. The Ministry of Planning has
an established mechanism to deal in an orderly way with the additional aid that becomes available in the period after investment
plans are made.

Capital Versus Noncapital Expenditures

Egypt's second Five-Year Plan included many examples of development programs where the noncapital expenditures were more
important than the capital ones. Many agricultural programs essential for the growth of productivity (such as research and extension) require salaries and facilities of a largely noncapital type.
Most of the education and health expenditures are similarly noncapital in nature. Even in some typically capital-intensive sectors
such as transport, the main need during the plan is for rehabilitation
and periodic maintenance rather than new investment.

Bibliography

Anderson, Dennis, "Economic Growth and the Returns to Investment," World
    Bank Discussion Papers, No. 12 (Washington: World Bank, 1987).
Balassa, Bela, "Public Finance and Economic Development," Policy Planning
    and Research Working Papers, WPS 31 (Washington: World Bank, August
    1988).

Binswanger, Hans, "The Impact of Infrastructure and Financial Institutions on Agriculture Output and Investment in India," unpublished, World Bank, 1988.

Blejer, M. I., and Mohsin S. Khan, "Government Policy and Private Investment in Developing Countries," Staff Papers, International Monetary Fund (Washington), Vol. 31 (June 1984), pp. 379–403.

Chhibber, Ajay, and Sweder van Wijnbergen, "Public Policy and Private Investment in Turkey," Policy Planning and Research Working Papers, WPS 120 (Washington: World Bank, October 1988).

Handoussa, Heba, and Mieko Nishimizu, "Productivity Change in Egyptian Public Sector Industries After 'The Opening,' 1973–1979," Journal of Development Economics, Vol. 20 (January–February 1986), pp. 53–73.

Heady, Christopher, "Public Sector Pricing in a Fiscal Context," Policy Planning and Research Working Papers, WPS 179 (Washington: World Bank, April 1989).

Jorgensen, D. W., "Econometric Studies of Investment Behavior: A Survey," Journal of Econometric Literature, Vol. 9 (December 1971), pp. 1111–147.

Kahnert, Friedrich, "A Longer-Term Strategy for Public Expenditure Analysis in EMENA," World Bank Working Paper, Report No. EMN3 (November 1988).

Kavalsky, Basil, "Reviewing Public Investment Programs," Finance and Development, Vol. 23 (March 1986), pp. 37–40.

Landau, Daniel, "Government Expenditure and Economic Growth: A Cross-Country Study," Southern Economic Journal, Vol. 49 (January 1983), pp. 783–92.

Leff, Nathaniel H., "Optimal Investment Choice for Developing Countries: Rational Theory and Rational Decision-Making," Journal of Development Economics, Vol 18 (August 1985), pp. 335–60.

Little, I.M.D., and J.A. Mirrlees, Project Appraisal and Planning for Developing Countries (New York: Basic Books, 1974).

Mishan, E.J., Cost-Benefit Analysis: An Introduction (New York: Praeger, 1971).

Nellis, John, "Public Enterprise Reform in Adjustment Lending," Policy Planning and Research Working Papers, WPS 233 (Washington: World Bank, August 1989).

Paul, Samuel, "Emerging Issues of Privatization and the Public Sector," Policy Planning and Research Working Papers, WPS 80 (Washington: World Bank, September 1988).

Pfeffermann, Guy, and Andrea Madarassy, "Trends in Private Investment in Thirty Developing Countries," International Finance Corporation, Discussion Paper No. 6 (Washington: World Bank, September 1989).

Ram, Rati, "Government Size and Economic Growth: A New Framework and Some Evidence from Cross-Section and Time-Series Data," American Economic Review, Vol. 76 (March 1986), pp. 191–203.

Shah, Anwar, "The Public Infrastructure and Private Sector Profitability and Productivity in Mexico," Policy Planning and Research Working Papers, WPS 100 (Washington: World Bank, September 1988).

Shirley, Mary M. (1989a), "Evaluating the Performance of Public Enterprises in Pakistan," Policy Planning and Research Working Papers, WPS 160 (Washington: World Bank, March 1989).

————(1989b), "The Reform of State-Owned Enterprises: Lessons from World Bank Lending," Policy and Research Series, No. 4 (Washington: World Bank, June 1989).

Squire, Lynn, and H.G. van der Tak, *Economic Analysis of Projects*, (Baltimore; London: Johns Hopkins University Press, 1975).

Sundararajan, V., and Subhas Thakur, "Public Investment, Crowding Out, Growth: A Dynamic Model Applied to India and Korea," *Staff Papers*, International Monetary Fund (Washington), Vol. 27 (December 1980), pp. 814–58.

World Bank, *World Development Report, 1988* (New York: Oxford University Press, 1988).

Appendix

Public Investment as Percentage of GDP
(weighted averages)

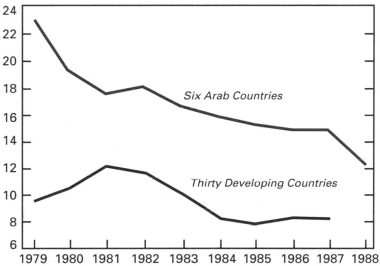

Public Investment in Arab Countries
(as a percentage of GDP)

Comment

Mohamed A. Diab

Mr. Wall's paper addressed two related issues:

(a) What is the appropriate mix of public and private investment; and

(b) What criteria can be used to ensure that public investment is efficient.

He also attempted to bring to bear on these issues the strategy of the World Bank in assisting Middle Eastern countries in their efforts to formulate policies concerning public investments and related public expenditures.

I wish to indicate that I find myself in agreement with the general tone of his paper, its underlying philosophy, and the explicit as well as the implicit conclusions and recommendations it contains. Moreover, I would like to express some views that support his position.

The controversy on the role of the state in the economic life of a nation is as old as political economy itself. The increasingly rapid technological, social, economic, and political developments in western societies have sharpened professional debates on the subject ever since Adam Smith articulated his theory of the judicious invisible hand in solving the problem of resource allocation and income distribution. The major political and social upheavals that have occurred in European societies in the past two centuries are nothing but a manifestation of the tug of war between antagonistic parties about the role of the state in the organization of productive resources and in the distribution of the goods and services produced. Governments have fallen and new regimes have risen in the name of achieving more economic efficiency and more social justice. The controversy continues, albeit less violently and more maturely than hitherto.

In the Arab Middle East, and since the Second World War, the role of the state in the economic life of the community and the size of the public sector have evolved in stages, each with its own set of motivations and causes. The first was the post-independence stage in the Levant countries and in Iraq, where existing public utilities such as electricity generation and distribution, city transportation, and railways that were owned by foreign concessionary companies were nationalized. This was followed many years later in Egypt by the nationalization of the Suez Canal, a culmination of the surging desire of the Arab nation to eradicate all politico-economic vestiges of foreign dominance. During that period increasing financial resources were put at the disposal of national governments not only to provide for an expanding army but also to fund activities that it was felt should better be carried out by the state—such as building roads, airports, seaports, dams, schools, hospitals, and public buildings, laying railways, and installing electricity generation and distribution networks. These infrastructural activities were carried out by governments and regimes that believed in the "sanctity" of private property and individual enterprise, but felt that, because of the relative immensity of these projects, the state was in a far better position to undertake them with speed and efficiency. Along with the expansion of the public sector and the military, an expanding public bureaucracy developed: more self-confident and more assured of its ability to organize resources and to manage centers of production. The observation that I wish to make here is that the expansion of the public sector was very much encouraged and supported by decision makers in the private sector. The expansion of the public sector was looked upon as complementary to and not as competing with the private sector. The economy was expanding fast enough to accommodate the need for resources in both sectors.

As to the efficiency of the public sector in managing the resources put at its disposal, it should be noted that most of the commodities produced have no competitive alternatives, and therefore their production costs and prices cannot easily be checked for economic efficiency by the market mechanism. However, it is safe to say that, on the whole, the work conduct of public sector managers at that time was guided by nationalistic fervor and high ethical standards that ensured, to a large degree, that resources were managed and put to use as efficiently as possible.

The second phase in the evolution of the role of the state in the economy in these countries is marked by the laws of agrarian reform, but more important, by the nationalization acts in the early sixties. Here the expansion of the public sector was brought about with a vengeance. Socialism was declared the new economic order, and the boundaries of the public sector were expanded to include any sizable industrial firm in sight, regardless of its industrial classification! Socialist ideology dictated that all modern means of production should be owned, and consequently managed, by the state. The question of the appropriate mix between the public and the private sectors was, by a stroke of the pen, summarily answered.

A different scenario evolved in the Arab oil producing countries. The gush of wealth took its nationals and governing bodies by surprise. In the sixties, there was hardly any public sector to speak of. Nation states had to be built up practically from scratch. The task was thrown into the lap of burgeoning public institutions because hardly any other actor or vehicle was in sight. Public institutions, and a modern infrastructure, were built up with a scope, resources, pace, and lavishness that is unprecedented in the annals of economic development. The cost in terms of resources and social values may have been great, but financial resources were so abundant, the task and the desire to build rapidly were so great, and the general mood was so euphoric that hardly anybody seriously bothered to note whether resources were properly allocated, whether income distribution was becoming dangerously skewed, or whether public institutions and enterprises were efficiently run. The methodical search for an appropriately demarcated public sector was overtaken by the ability of the state to undertake any enterprise whatsoever.

The role of the state in the economies of the Arab countries has during the past quarter of a century gained an importance beyond the wildest dreams of Arab students of economics of the sixties. When we look now at the map of the public sector in these economies, we find that public enterprises occupy practically all the high ground. Aside from the very heavy investment in infrastructure, the state owns all extractive industries and their ancillary transportation networks, all armament industries, practically all significant manufacturing industries, major food processing industries, and high-quality tourist facilities.

The conclusion to be drawn from this brief description of the expansion of the public sector in selected Arab countries is that its motivations and causes have been quite diverse, and that its size and composition have been brought about more by politics, ideology, and the sudden surge of wealth in some countries than by a gradual and willful evolution of a national concept of a particular pattern of resource allocation between the public and the private sectors. This point is important because it is related to the question of involvement, commitment, and accountability on how resources are allocated and how enterprises are run.

In the Arab countries, the role of the state in the organization, allocation, and management of resources—whether through the public sector or through the maze of rules and regulations, incentives and penalties, coercion or persuasion, encouragement and discouragement—has recently come under increasing scrutiny, sometimes in the open, but more often through the grapevine! The questions that are being asked about the role of the state in the politico-economic systems that have emerged are simple:

- Have resources put at the disposal of the state been wisely allocated?
- Has the role manifested a strategy of development that enabled a "big push" to break through the structural barriers to economic expansion?
- Has it allowed the mobilization of resources that the community could muster locally and abroad?
- Has it tempted decision makers to indulge in the establishment of "white elephant" projects?
- Has it led to distortions in the price structure, to inflation, and to significant depreciation of local currency?
- Has it led to rapid economic development?
- Has its performance been compatible with expectations?
- Has it brought about increasing involvement by the community in the decision making on resource allocation?
- Has the system led to concentration of political and economic power in the hands of a few?
- Has it been instrumental in the development of dedicated social work ethics that hold the community welfare as an objective?
- Has it been amenable to more corruption and abuse of economic power?
- Has it been germane to practices that have benefited a few privileged officials at the expense of the community?

- Does the system inherently give immunity from account-ability both politically and economically?
- Does the system inhibit creativity and innovation in the man-agement of public enterprises?
- Does the system provide an attractive climate for the deploy-ment of dynamic resources locally and from abroad?
- Is the system capable of meeting the challenges of the new technological revolution with all that it entails, and of opening up to creative, innovative, and risk-taking senior and mid-career managers and technicians?
- Are public enterprises better poised to "engage" foreign cen-ters of production for the transfer of technology and joint efforts to produce goods and resources?
- Is a democratic political system a necessary prerequisite for an efficient and a nonexploiting public sector?

Answers to questions of this nature fundamentally shape the preferences of individuals, and consequently the community, about the appropriate or desirable mix of the public and the private sector.

The market economy, despite its many shortcomings in areas of monopolistic practices and of social equity, provides a reason-able mechanism for allocating resources where they are needed through daily monetary voting on the part of consumers and inves-tors alike. Decision makers in an economy with a large public sector need to be fed constantly with information about what the community wants in terms of the size, the composition, and the management of the public sector. Entrepreneurs in a market econ-omy would find themselves out of business if they did not display adequate foresight in anticipating consumers' wishes, and/or if they did not provide efficient management of their enterprises. This is not necessarily the fate of decision makers in an economy characterized by a large public sector. Here the economic and the political decision-making process is so intertwined that the trans-mission of the communal preference for resource allocation and its efficient organization and management can only be accom-plished through the political system. To the extent that the political process allows the free articulation and expression of the com-munal preference and makes political and economic agents ac-countable for its implementation, one can say that the question of "what is the appropriate mix of the public and the private sector" is answered.

Ailments in any economic system are recurring diseases requiring continuous recognition, diagnosis, and medication. A community needs lots of *glasnost* if it is to undertake *perestroika*. Utopia is, however, a mirage—but a mirage that could serve as a beacon directing and guiding human endeavors toward higher plateaus of communal happiness and welfare.

4

Foreign Direct Investment: The Role of Joint Ventures and Investment Authorities

Dale Weigel

This paper will discuss the policies that require foreign investors to enter into joint ventures with local firms, and the institutions used by host countries to promote, screen, and service foreign direct investment. These are related topics because the kinds of institutions that host countries need to put in place to deal with foreign investors will depend on the policies they are trying to implement. If the host country does not intend to screen foreign investors, or require them to enter into joint ventures with local investors, there may be no need to establish a procedure or an institution to deal with foreign investment. Brazil, for example, has had a very open attitude toward foreign direct investment, and therefore has not established a specific institution to regulate an investment approval process.

Joint venture policies and investment authorities are specific aspects of the panoply of policies and institutions that regulate foreign direct investment in most developing countries. These investment policies and the institutions that administer them should be consistent with the objectives the host country hopes to achieve through the use of foreign direct investment. For example, if direct investment is expected to increase the country's exports, then policies at all levels must make exports attractive. If a country wants foreign investors to participate in a broad range of activities, then macroeconomic policies, as well as specific policies affecting foreign investors, must be directed toward this end. Policies inconsistent with the objectives and inherent characteristics of a country result in frustration both for the country and for the foreign inves-

**Table 1.   The Stock of Foreign Private Investment
in Relation to GDP**
(Data for 1979)

	(percent)
Singapore	19
Malaysia	15
Kenya	9
Costa Rica	8
Chile	7
Brazil	7
Ghana	6
Côte d'Ivoire	6
Philippines	6
Argentina	5
Colombia	5
Mexico	5
Pakistan	4
Korea, Republic of	3
Morocco	2
India	2
Thailand	2
Nigeria	1
Egypt	1
Algeria	1
Turkey	1
Yugoslavia	1

Sources: Organization for Economic Cooperation and Development, *Development Cooperation Review*; World Bank, *World Bank Atlas*, 1981.

tor. Likewise, the objectives of policies may be frustrated by institutions that are not consistent with those policies.

That governments of developing countries have had a wide
range of objectives, policies, and institutions governing foreign
direct investment is suggested by Table 1.[1] The wide variation in
the stock of foreign direct investment in relation to GDP among
the 22 developing countries shown in the table reflects not only
differences in investment opportunities but also differences in their
objectives, and their success in translating objectives into effective
policies and institutions. Some countries have not wanted much
foreign direct investment (for example, India). Others have wanted

[1]Table 1 is taken from Dale Weigel, "Investment in LDCs, the Debate Continues," *Columbia Journal of World Business*, Vol. 23, No. 1 (Spring 1988), pp. 5–
9.

it (for example, Yugoslavia), but have not been successful in formulating policies, or establishing institutions to get the amount or type of investment desired. Still others (for example, the Republic of Korea) have envisioned a limited role for foreign direct investment, but have been reasonably successful in putting appropriate policies and institutions in place to achieve these objectives.

The remainder of this paper discusses a particular set of policies—those to require joint ventures between foreign and local investors—and alternative institutional arrangements to administer investment policies. In the course of this discussion, it will be helpful to bear in mind that these policies and institutions should be evaluated in the broader context of the opportunities for foreign investment as well as the objectives of the host country in relation to such investment.

Policies Requiring Joint Ventures

Among developing country governments, and the international development community, it is almost taken as an axiom that joint ventures between foreign and local firms are more beneficial to the host country than are wholly owned foreign ventures. International development institutions act on this belief and actively encourage joint ventures. The International Finance Corporation (IFC), for example, has a policy of helping to finance projects involving foreign investors only when a substantial local partner is involved in the project as well.

Many developing countries introduced measures to require joint ventures and other ownership restrictions during the late 1960s and 1970s. Some countries also introduced provisions that required foreign firms to divest shares to local owners over a specific period of time. The phase-out provisions of Decision 24 of the Andean Common Market were the most famous divestment requirements, but similar measures were introduced in other countries such as Indonesia and Malaysia.

These restrictive provisions were aided and abetted by the increasing availability of foreign loans to developing countries in the 1970s. With the increasing availability of loans, there was both increased desire, and the ability to "unbundle" the package of capital, technology, and management that is direct investment.

With capital being available at low, and sometimes negative, interest rates, developing countries tried to get foreign firms to provide the complementary technology and management skills in "new forms" of investment with reduced ownership and reduced control of the resulting ventures.

Host Country Views of Joint Ventures

There are a number of reasons why developing countries have favored joint ventures when foreign direct investment is allowed at all. One is simply a desire to protect sovereignty: to ensure that foreign firms will not control key decisions in the economy. This desire is particularly strong in countries that have recently gained their political independence.

In addition, it is thought that joint ventures are a good way to encourage the transfer of technology and to train local business people in the operation of a modern firm. By being a part of a joint venture with foreign partners, it is expected that local engineers and managers will learn from their foreign counterparts. (It is curious in this context that many countries that require joint ventures also restrict the numbers of foreign managers and technical people who can be employed.)

Another rationale for forcing joint ventures is more complex— they are viewed as a way in which the local economy can participate in what are thought to be monopoly profits of multinational firms operating in the host country. It is recognized in this context that most firms making international investments are large and operate in oligopolistic industries. These firms have certain skills and technologies that are the basis of their size and profits. Developing countries think that by forcing these firms to enter into joint ventures, they will be able to capture some of these "monopoly" profits for the country, either for the government or for local investors who are in the joint venture.

Most, if not all, developing countries prohibit foreign investment in some sectors and require joint ventures in others. For example, the appendix shows the ownership restrictions of the countries of the Association of South East Asian Nations, a group that is generally regarded as following liberal policies toward foreign investors.

The ownership restrictions imposed by Arab countries vary widely. A recent study ranked the degree of restrictiveness of these

Dale Weigel

Table 2. Foreign Ownership Restrictions—Rankings
of Arab Countries[a]

Algeria	2	Kuwait	3	Sudan	5
Egypt	4	Libya	2	Syrian Arab Rep.	2
Iraq	1	Morocco	5	Tunisia	5
Jordan	2	Saudi Arabia	3		

[a]1 = very restrictive; 5 = very liberal.

measures, as shown in Table 2.[2] A value of 1 denotes very stringent restrictions on ownership (for example, Iraq), while 5 indicates very liberal ownership policies (for example, Morocco). While it is possible to take issue with these rankings, they reflect how an outside observer views ownership policies of Arab countries in relation to those of other developing countries at the time the study was completed.

Foreign Investors' Views of Joint Ventures

Multinational enterprises also see benefits in joint ventures and voluntarily enter into them in some circumstances. This is a trend in developed countries, where even the largest firms are seeking alliances to develop technology, enter markets, and improve production techniques. In developing countries, some firms enter into joint ventures voluntarily with local firms to incorporate their knowledge of managing the local labor force, the market, and to help in interactions with the government.

Involuntary joint ventures, however, are viewed by foreign investors as a major disincentive to investment. A recent survey of 300 of the largest U.S. multinational corporations showed that 65 percent of these firms view ownership restrictions as being a critical negative factor in assessing the viability of an investment.[3] Econometric evidence also shows the negative impact of ownership restrictions on investment decisions.[4] That developing coun-

[2]Frost and Sullivan Inc., "Measurement of the Investment Climate for International Business," a study conducted for the U.S. Agency for International Development, 1988.

[3]Cynthia Day Wallace, *Foreign Direct Investments in the Third World: U.S. Corporations and Government Policy* (Washington: Center for Strategic and International Studies, 1989).

[4]Ben Gomes-Casseres, "MNC Ownership Preferences and Host Government Restrictions," in *An Integrated Approach* (Harvard Business School, August 1988).

tries appreciate the disincentive effect of ownership restrictions is shown by their actions—almost without exception, when they decide that they want to encourage more foreign investment, one of the first things they do is to liberalize their ownership restrictions.

Liberalizing Ownership Restrictions

Developing countries in ever greater numbers have been liberalizing ownership restrictions in the 1980s. Since 1982 the Andean Pact countries have taken back the power to conduct their own negotiations with foreign investors, and in many of these countries the ownership phase-out requirements of Decision 24 have been modified or dropped. In Indonesia, initial foreign ownership percentages have been increased, phase-out periods have been extended, and in some industries they have been eliminated. Malaysia has relaxed its laws requiring a progressive increase in ownership by ethnic Malays. Many African countries have opened up a larger number of sectors to foreign investors, as has the Republic of Korea.[5] Most striking, a number of socialist countries that had previously excluded foreign direct investment altogether, now encourage it. In fact, recent laws passed in Hungary, Poland, and Yugoslavia are among the most liberal in the developing world, allowing wholly owned foreign ventures in a wide range of circumstances. China has taken the unusual step of setting a minimum share that the foreign investor has to provide.

In May 1989, Mexico was the most recent country to announce a liberalization of its ownership policies. These policies previously had required foreign investors to enter joint ventures and take a minority position in ventures with Mexican firms. The liberalized Mexican policies, like those in many other countries, allow foreign investors to have a majority in export-oriented ventures, in those bringing advanced technology, and in those investing outside the more developed regions.[6]

---

[5]See Sheila Page, "Developing Country Attitudes Towards Foreign Investment," in *Developing with Foreign Investment*, ed. by Vincent Cable and B. Persaud (London; New York: Croom Helm, 1987), pp. 28–43.

[6]This is just the latest turn in Mexican policies, which were relatively liberal in the 1950s and 1960s. In 1973, perhaps reflecting the increasing availability of resources from other sources, a new foreign investment law made ownership restrictions more stringent. That law remains in force but its administration has been liberalized.

There are several reasons for this historic change in the policies
of so many developing countries. One is their need to encourage
foreign capital inflows of all types after the worldwide recession
of 1980–82 and the world debt crisis both increased the need for,
and reduced the supply of, foreign resources. The trend toward
liberalization, however, began before the debt crisis and may also
reflect a disenchantment with the supposed benefits of joint ventures. There is evidence, for example, that forced joint ventures
are less efficient than majority or wholly owned firms in the same
industry.[7] Moreover, if forced joint ventures allow greater local
participation in monopoly profits of foreign firms, it is usually
only a few privileged individuals who participate, not the society
as a whole. Finally, the usefulness of joint ventures as a vehicle
for technology and managerial transfer depends on the capabilities
of the local partners. The more capable they are, the more transfer
will occur. On the other hand, the more capable the local partner,
the less need there will be to force a joint venture—it will be
undertaken voluntarily.

We can conclude that developing countries are re-examining the
role of forced joint ventures between foreign and local investors.
The trend is clear—to allow foreign and local firms increasingly
to make their own arrangements.

This is a trend that should be encouraged. Many of the reasons
for ownership restrictions have been lost in history while the costs
of ownership restrictions in terms of loss in investment have become clearer. If sovereignty is an issue, it can be dealt with by the
use of government power to regulate, tax, exclude undesirable
investment, and prosecute abuse. Virtually all countries of the
Organization for Economic Cooperation and Development (OECD)
follow this approach. More developing countries are doing so as
they realize that requiring joint ventures does not bring the control
they hoped for, and as they gain increasing confidence in their
ability to exercise normal government power in relation to foreign
investors.

---

[7]A study of the efficiency of Mexican firms by the World Bank shows that
firms with minority foreign shares in most industries were less efficient than
wholly owned Mexican firms and majority-owned foreign firms. Majority-owned
foreign firms, in turn, were more efficient than wholly owned domestic firms
in most of the industries where both types operated.

The Role of Investment Authorities

The trend toward liberalizing ownership restrictions is only one aspect of a more general trend of liberalizing foreign investment regulation in developing countries. Moreover, developing countries are increasingly focusing on the need actively to promote foreign direct investment to increase the flow of foreign capital, technology, management, and access to foreign markets that they deem essential for their development.

It is in the context of these changing policies that developing countries are reconsidering the nature and functions of the institutions that deal with foreign investors. These institutions have typically had a number of functions, including screening and monitoring on the one hand, and promoting and providing services to investors on the other. Developing (and developed) countries have tried a wide range of institutional arrangements to carry out these functions, sometimes combining all of the functions in one institution, and at other times dispersing them to several organizations. Individual activities, such as screening, have also been handled in different ways, in some cases being centralized in a single organization, and in others being decentralized in various ways to existing government departments and ministries. This section describes some of the alternative approaches to the screening of foreign investment, and then considers whether it is desirable to combine the screening and promotion functions.

Organization of Screening

Developing countries screen and monitor foreign investment to try to assure that it both conforms to established policies, such as those on ownership discussed above, and contributes to the achievement of development objectives. Screening is thus meant to keep out those investments that would not benefit the host country, including inefficient firms that benefit from high levels of protection.

Governments use a wide range of organizational approaches to carry out the screening function. Some countries have not coordinated their policies and insist that investors deal with a whole network of government agencies. Others have sought to coordinate government policies by establishing some kind of a central authority to screen and evaluate foreign direct investment, to negotiate transactions with foreign investors on behalf of the government, and to monitor their activities.[8] In some cases, this centralization applies only to projects in certain zones, such as export-processing zones, or in specific sectors. Other countries have entrusted this regulatory function to an already existing government ministry.[9]

Absence of a Comprehensive Institutional Structure

Some countries have no comprehensive institutions for screening and monitoring foreign direct investment. Foreign investors are generally free to invest, with some exceptions that may be adopted from time to time reflecting the country's development priorities. The basic attitudes of these countries can be described by three characteristics: an essentially favorable disposition toward foreign direct investment; a system where treatment of foreign direct investment has been clear and fairly constant over time, but also flexibly and informally applied; and a set of sectoral priorities for foreign direct investment.

Brazil is the example of a major host country without comprehensive foreign investment legislation and institutional infrastructure for screening foreign investment proposals. No government approval is needed for foreign direct investment unless a foreign investor wants to take advantage of investment incentives (industrial or regional), and no government body evaluates foreign direct investment.[10] A foreign investment must be registered by the Cen-

[8]Whatever approaches countries may take toward screening foreign direct investment in general, they tend to make special arrangements for investment in a sector of the economy that is of special importance to the country's development plans and objectives (for example, the petroleum industry).

[9]Some central investment authorities are responsible for dealings with foreign investors (and domestic alike) only when such investors wish to avail themselves of investment incentives (such as the Board of Investment of Thailand), or when, regardless of incentives, foreign investment exceeds prescribed limits (such as the Board of Investments in the Philippines).

[10]Foreign direct investment is excluded from several sectors (for example, petroleum exploration, exploitation, and refining, communications media, and most domestic transport). Furthermore, a significant part of the computer and associated industries have recently been reserved for domestic companies. It is also true that Brazil influences the decisions of investors through the use of incentives and uses government regulations to preclude decisions, such as the establishment of major new investments in congested urban areas.

tral Bank, which satisfies itself that the basic laws are complied with and that the value of the requested investment is accurately stated.[11] Among the benefits of this approach is the greater predictability of the outcome of the approval process for both government and investor compared with the inevitably more ambiguous outcome associated with selective policies. Consequently, the potential costs for an investor considering entry are likely to be low. On the other hand, in the presence of large price distortions resulting from tariffs, subsidies, and limited competition, an "open door" policy, such as that followed by Brazil, may result in the entry of those investments that may not necessarily be economically desirable for the host country.

Decentralized Mechanism

Some countries adopt a decentralized screening process that is dispersed across several government ministries and agencies whose interests could be affected by an investment. Usually, the agencies participating in the screening include ministries of finance, industry, or trade, the central bank, as well as other functional government bodies. This direct involvement of many government bodies and entities can have the advantage of bringing to bear the technical expertise necessary for evaluating proposals for a specific industry. On the other hand, many of the agencies and ministries involved in screening may have little technical knowledge or limited experience with a particular industry. Diffuse units operating autonomously may also have little ability to evaluate overall net benefits of foreign direct investment in light of larger policy objectives. Moreover, each agency involved in screening may be pursuing its own narrow objectives, and these may be inconsistent with each other, and with broader policy objectives.

As a result of these considerations, a decentralized approach is likely to be costly to the foreign investor because the period of negotiation is likely to be longer and the results unpredictable at the outset. The potential investor with only marginal interest may possibly go elsewhere, while other investors, responding to the conflicting demands of approval agencies, may reshape investments in ways that are inconsistent with broad national objectives.

[11]Investments in mining, insurance, rural land, and financial activities are treated separately. In these areas, prior government authorization is required before a foreign investment can be made.

Interministerial Mechanism

In recognition of the potential costs that a diffused decision-making process can impose on foreign direct investors, some host countries have developed interministerial mechanisms to coordinate the foreign investment approval process. Such coordination entails the creation of decision-making structures whose operations cut across the existing functional divisions of government and whose membership comprises representatives of affected government agencies.

Many of the disadvantages associated with diffusion of the decision-making process may be overcome by coordinating bodies. Such entities provide a single focal point for foreign investors in all their dealings relating to a particular venture and avoid, to some extent at least, investors tramping from department to department to secure the necessary approvals. Coordinating mechanisms also can recognize the necessary link through planning, promotion, screening, approval, and monitoring of ventures— they can ensure that what is being planned, for example, is reflected in the screening criteria, and what is being monitored reflects the key considerations that have arisen during the screening and approval process. Finally, coordinating mechanisms can allow a streamlining of decision making by avoiding the need to involve government agencies that are only peripherally concerned with a particular investment decision.

Gaining these advantages may entail serious internal political costs, however, since a participating ministry may feel its influence is diminished if it cooperates fully with a coordinating body. To preserve influence, politically powerful ministries may be tempted to send only low-level people to meetings and later impose their power over the investor administratively.

As a result of such political considerations, the power of a coordinating agency in relation to individual board members can vary greatly from country to country. In some countries, coordinating bodies serve only as a clearinghouse for information, while the real power rests with individual ministries. In other countries, a board may have final decision-making authority and truly serve as a one-stop agency, at least for the major negotiating issues. Coordinating boards may be dominated by one or a few members, or power may be diffused among all members. Whatever the specific span of control and authority of a coordinating agency, its existence in a country indicates that the government is attempting to emphasize foreign investment issues, whether the government's interest lies in attracting or in controlling foreign investors.

Interministerial bodies may either be permanent or ad hoc in nature. The National Commission on Foreign Investment in Mexico, the Board of Investment in Thailand, and the Malaysian Industrial Development Authority are examples of permanent, interministerial bodies.[12]

Centralized Authority

To overcome some of the costs associated with the operation of coordinating bodies, several countries have centralized the foreign investment decision process in a single government ministry or department or, in a case of a particular sector, have given screening authority to a state enterprise. In Korea, for example, approvals are handled by the Ministry of Finance, in Colombia by the National Planning Department, and in Yugoslavia by the Ministry of Foreign Economic Relations.

Some countries, to take advantage of available technical expertise in a single industry and to optimize organizational learning with regard to that industry, have delegated the screening of foreign investment proposals in that industry to specialized government agencies or state-owned enterprises. In Indonesia, for example, foreign petroleum firms have dealt primarily with PERTAMINA, the national oil company. By contrast, in the Philippines, such negotiations are the province of the Ministry of Energy. In this way, the costs of negotiating and of interministerial conflict are likely to be reduced, while organizational learning is enhanced. However, while obtaining these benefits, certain costs are incurred. By delegating authority to state-owned enterprises and other agencies that possess knowledge of the industry, many of the same shortcomings of diffuse decision making may be experienced; larger policy issues such as the net national benefit of

[12]The government bodies represented on the Board of Investment in Thailand are Industry, Finance, Agriculture and Cooperatives, Commerce, Defense, Interior, Foreign Affairs, Judicial Council, the Bank of Thailand, and the Industrial Finance Corporation of Thailand.

investment and the spillover of negotiations on other investors will likely be ignored.

Delegation of Centralized Decision Making

The entry control function, regardless of the form it takes (diffused ministerial approach, single authority, interministerial bodies), is carried out in almost all cases by the central government authorities only. However, some exceptions to this general practice hold for fully export-oriented projects. Export-oriented firms can locate their plants in any of a number of countries that offer cheap production resources. In most cases, they need only inexpensive labor, sufficient infrastructure, and good transportation and communication facilities. Given this common perception, the competition for these "footloose" investors is usually quite intense. Fearful of losing the battle for such investors, a number of countries have delegated powers to approve investments in export projects to authorities separate from the central investment agency. The goal is to create an organization that can act quickly and decisively, thereby increasing the attractiveness of the country to such investors.

Accordingly, in some countries potential investors for export plants have had the option of investing in export-processing zones. Not only do these zones offer infrastructure, but they generally are run by an organization that is fully vested with authority to reach agreements quickly with foreign investors. In the Philippines, for example, a firm producing wholly for export may choose to negotiate with either the Board of Investment or the Export Processing Zone Authority, or both, depending upon where it seeks to locate and what incentives it seeks to enjoy. In Sri Lanka, the Greater Colombo Economic Commission Authority is the sole agency for approving any investment in the export-processing zones. Indonesia is currently considering the establishment of four export-processing zones and the creation of an Export Processing Zone Authority that will be relatively autonomous from the Capital Investment Coordinating Board of Indonesia.

Sometimes, the authority for specific functional issues, such as taxation and investment incentives, may be delegated to regional governments. In Brazil, for example, investment located in one of the less developed regions (North-East and the Amazon) can apply to regional agencies for specific regional ventures.

Selecting the Form of Investment Organization

The preceding discussion illustrates the wide range of alternative institutional forms a host government can employ to screen foreign investment, and provides a basis for determining the most appropriate form in particular circumstances. It is in this context that centralized investment authorities, popularly known as "one-stop shops," can be evaluated. It is also possible to evaluate the desirability of combining the screening function with investment promotion and investment service activities.

The Role of Centralized Investment Authorities

The main issue in selecting the most appropriate organizational form for investment screening is the extent to which decision making within the government can and should be centralized. The most important point to remember in this context is that there is no need to centralize investment decision making if there are liberal and automatic investment policies—there is no need for a central authority if, in fact, there are few decisions to be made. The example of Brazil discussed above is a case in point, as is the practice in almost all OECD countries.

Centralized investment authorities are useful to cut through a myriad of regulations. If there are relatively few regulations, or if decisions are based on transparent criteria, the role of an investment authority is much less apparent. Moreover, it needs to be remembered that central investment authorities can serve to block foreign investments just as easily as they can facilitate them. Some of the countries that have been the most active in restricting foreign investment have done so through the mechanism of an intransigent central investment authority. Such authorities, therefore, are not inherently facilitators of investment and, if that is the intent, their activities will have to be carefully monitored by the political authorities.

A second point to be borne in mind when evaluating the feasibility of establishing a true centralized investment decision-making authority is that the various parts of government that normally participate in these decisions will yield authority to a central body only reluctantly. It is for this reason that true one-stop shops are quite rare. They are found almost exclusively in small countries. Most countries that claim to have a central investment authority in fact have a coordinating agency with limited decision-making power. These bodies sometimes have difficulty in cutting through the investment regulations that were the reason for their establishment in the first place.

Rather than establishing a compromise investment authority, it may be more productive to work on the investment policies, making them more transparent and less restrictive. In that way, the need for a central agency can be reduced, and a more decentralized mechanism might suffice.

Organizing for Investment Promotion

The main task of a centralized investment authority may be investment promotion rather than investment screening. Investment promotion is an activity that demands a central focus to present the country to the foreign investment community. It is not an activity that can be easily decentralized either bureaucratically or geographically.

Investment promotion consists of three main activities:

- country image building;
- investment generation; and
- service to investors.

A complete investment promotion program will contain all three elements, but the main focus will be given to one of them at different stages in the life of the program. At an early stage, priority may be given to servicing existing foreign investors so that they will be happy and can serve as ambassadors for the country. As the program develops, greater attention will be given to country image building, assuming that the reality is consistent with the image that is being projected. Finally, the focus should shift to targeted investment generating activities.

The organization that carries out the investment promotion program can be in the government, in the private sector (although supported by the government), or in between the two as a quasi-government organization. The most successful promotion organizations have been of the latter type, with links to government, but with freedom particularly in hiring and setting salaries to attract the kinds of aggressive marketing people who are usually found in the private sector.

Combining Promotion and Screening

It is difficult to combine a vigorous screening organization with an aggressive promotion function. One or the other of these functions will dominate. If it is screening, the promotion function will most likely be neglected. On the other hand, if promotion dominates, the screening function is unlikely to be independent—promoters are unlikely to be willing to see the fruits of their efforts rejected by the screening process.

Screening and promotion have been successfully combined in a single central investment authority when liberal investment rules are in effect. In that case, foreign firms are relatively free to establish, and screening is carried out mainly to determine eligibility for investment incentives. Targets for investment promotion, however, are in a sense pre-screened, being selected for the contribution they can make to the development of the country. The promotion function dominates the investment organization, but screening criteria are taken into account in selecting targets for promotion.

Countries approaching investment promotion in this way generally are considered to have investment authorities that are one-stop shops. They provide a wide range of services to investors and grant incentives, as well as carrying out investment promotion. Good examples of such institutions are the Industrial Development Authority of Ireland and the Economic Development Board of Singapore. These organizations flourish in countries with liberal policies toward foreign investment. They would be difficult to conceive in more restrictive environments.

Conclusion

This paper has suggested several conclusions that can be the subject of further discussion. The first is that the role of an investment authority is linked to the policy framework the authority is expected to administer. In many developing countries these policies are being changed to open more sectors to foreign investment and to allow greater involvement of foreign investors in individual enterprises. An increasing number of developing countries are abandoning requirements that foreign investors participate in joint ventures with local investors.

These changes are taking place as developing countries have come to doubt the benefits of joint ventures and have seen their costs. As they redefine their economic goals, and as they gain confidence in their ability to control the activities of foreign investors regardless of their share in the ownership of individual enterprises, developing countries see less value in earlier policies to require joint ventures.

In these circumstances, investment authorities are becoming more concerned with promotion and allocation of incentives, and less with screening and control. It is difficult to contemplate the coexistence of rigorous screening and promotion functions in the same organization. These functions require different types of people, and a different mentality.

The evolution of the single investment authority is thus predicated on liberalization of investment policies that makes it possible to de-emphasize the screening function and give greater attention to promotion. This is now the trend in many developing countries. The challenge faced by these countries, of course, is to put in place a general policy framework that encourages beneficial foreign investments, and to identify specific investments as targets for the promotion effort.

Appendix

Foreign Equity Ownership

	1981	1988
Brunei		No restriction.
Indonesia	Maximum of 80 percent but must be diluted to 49 percent within 10 years.	If project exports 100 percent and is located in a bonded zone, 95 percent foreign ownership is allowed. Otherwise must increase local ownership to 51 percent within 15 or 20 years.
Malaysia	Export-oriented industries based substantially on imported components are allowed to have majority foreign ownership.	1. For applications received before December 31, 1990, 100 percent foreign ownership is allowed if project exports 50 percent of its production or employs 350 full-time workers and does not compete with domestic manufacturers. 2. For applications received after 1990, must export 80 percent to qualify for 100 percent ownership; 51–79 percent if between 51 percent and 79 percent of production is exported; 30–51 percent if between 20 percent and 50 percent is exported; maximum of 30 percent if less than 20 percent is exported; (other factors, e.g., size of investment, location, value added, and technology will also be taken into account).

Foreign Equity Ownership (*continued*)

	1981	1988
Philippines	1. Foreign ownership of 100 percent if 100 percent is exported; in pioneer area; if registered with the Export Processing Zone.	1. Foreign ownership of 100 percent if 70 percent of its production is exported or in pioneer area specified in IPP; in areas not exploited by Filipinos and requiring no incentives.
	2. If exporting less than 100 percent, the enterprise must divest 60 percent of shares to Filipinos.	2. Up to 40 percent in any other activities not reserved for nationals only.
Singapore	No restriction.	No restriction.
Thailand	Foreign control is possible for promoted companies engaged in priority activities as approved by the Board of Investment.	1. Foreign ownership of 100 percent if 100 percent of production is exported.
		2. Majority foreign ownership if 50 percent of output is exported.
		3. Up to 49 percent for nonexport manufacturing. (The criteria may be waived depending on size of investment, technology, location, and employment.)

Comment

Abdulaziz M. Al-Dukheil

Before commenting on Mr. Weigel's paper, I would like to present a condensed summary of the main points in his paper. The reason for this is to make sure that I have read it carefully and to take the reader through the basic structure of Mr. Weigel's paper before going through my own comments.

Summary

Policies and institutions required to manage foreign direct investment (FDI) in the context of developing countries is the subject of Mr. Weigel's paper. In most developing countries, policies mean objectives of joint ventures, and institutions mean investment authorities. The form of institution is influenced by the policies pursued.

Both policies and institutions should be consistent with the goals to be achieved from FDI. For example, if export promotion is the main economic objective, then FDI policies should be directed to achieving this goal. Likewise, institutions and objectives ought to be consistent.

Joint Venture Policies

Mr. Weigel has rightly mentioned that there is no uniformity among developing countries regarding their need for FDI. Some countries need it (for example, Yugoslavia), some do not (for example, India), and some need it in a limited amount (for example, the Republic of Korea).

The author then deals with policies required to promote joint venture relationships between foreign investors on the one hand and local investors and institutions on the other. On the policy side, it is almost taken as a rule by developing countries that a joint venture is the most beneficial policy for them. Sovereignty is one of the reasons for restricting ownership by foreign investors. Transfer of technology, profit sharing, and keeping some sectors out of the hands of foreign investors are the other reasons. Table 2 lists the foreign ownership restrictions of some Arab countries. Morocco is ranked very liberal and Iraq very restrictive.

Foreign investors favor unrestricted (voluntary) over restricted foreign investment. Many developing countries are taking a more liberal attitude toward joint ventures and, thus, are either minimizing the restriction or dropping it completely. The trend now seems to favor a position where it is left to foreign and local parties to decide on the issue of joint ventures. This is a trend that Mr. Weigel suggests should be encouraged.

Institutions: The Investment Authority

Screening and promotion of foreign investments are the two important functions of the investment authorities.

Screening

Screening keeps out the investments that would not benefit the host country. The organization that deals with this policy usually takes one of the following forms:

- No comprehensive institutional structure is needed if the government is taking a flexible and liberal attitude toward foreign investment.
- A decentralized form of organization is adopted if many agencies are involved.
- An interministerial commission is established when it becomes too complicated to coordinate among these agencies.
- A centralized form is used when the problems associated with coordination among the government agencies become complicated.

Regardless of the form screening takes, the control function is usually handled by a single authority. A centralized investment authority is needed if investors have to deal with many regulations. Otherwise, there is no need for any organization, the paper suggests. The other point in evaluating the need for a centralized investment authority is that government agencies do not actually delegate real power.

Investment Promotion

Investment promotion is best served by a centralized organization of a semigovernmental nature. It is difficult to combine the tasks of screening and promotion under a regime of restricted foreign investment policy. Only under a liberal policy can a combination of both activities under one umbrella work.

In his conclusion, Mr. Weigel says that " . . . developing countries see less value in earlier policies to require joint ventures" and therefore "investment authorities are becoming more concerned with promotion and allocation of incentives and less with screening and control . . . ."

Comments

I offer the following comments on Mr. Weigel's paper.

Mr. Weigel has rightly emphasized the point that developing countries should first determine clearly whether they need FDI or not and, if they do, then what purposes are these investments going to serve (that is, objectives). Clear objectives will determine appropriate policies and institutions. Among the major contributions of FDI to the economies of developing countries are foreign exchange earnings, foreign market outlets, and transfer of technology and employment. Developing countries with their different levels of development and resources do associate one or more of these objectives with their FDI policy. Thus, we can say that FDI is needed in one way or another unless a country takes a stand against FDI from an ideological point of view.

In the long-term interests of the host country, a foreign investor should be obliged to structure a joint venture vehicle in which he and a local partner or partners share and run the business. In this regard, I differ with Mr. Weigel, who does not see a strong need for imposing a joint venture policy on foreign investors, if my reading of his conclusions is correct. The percentage of foreign shares in the joint venture may differ from sector to sector, but the various aspects of the joint venture, such as management, the financial structure, and operations, should be left to the shareholders concerned.

The requirement of having a joint venture between foreign and local investors should not be left to the discretion of the foreign investor. Government policy should lend support to local firms in this regard, since local firms are in most cases in a weaker position compared with their foreign counterparts. The latter, in many cases, have the foreign exchange, the know-how, the managerial skills, and foreign market outlets. Therefore, from a practical point of view, a foreign partner may not find himself in need of a local partner. In such an environment, a government policy to enforce joint ventures as a mode of operation for FDI may be necessary. Such a policy will balance the bargaining power in favor of local firms and create a stronger long-term foundation for business activities.

For joint ventures between local and foreign firms to be beneficial to the economy, it is essential that the local partner have a minimum structure of business corporations operating in the same field as his foreign counterpart. Often, foreign companies not interested in transferring technology or managerial skills look for power centers in the host countries with which to form their joint ventures. These power centers act as agents and are not usually interested in developing local institutions to work hand in hand with foreign firms and learn the skills of running a business successfully. This attitude may find large acceptance among the foreign investors who do not have a long-term perspective. The host country agent with his short-term interest and lack of institutional setup is unable to provide genuine and professional services to the foreign firms. Thus, his position in the partnership will depend on his role as a manipulator of the public system and as a user and initiator of corrupt practices as a means of achieving unlawful personal ends.

Local professional firms, especially medium-sized and small ones, are not in a strong position to attract large international corporations. Therefore, government incentives to attract foreign direct investment should be linked to the promotion and development of joint ventures between professionally established local firms and foreign investors.

Many developing countries suffer from the lack of balance between their foreign exchange earnings and foreign exchange expenditures. At the heart of the matter lies the excess of consumption over production. In many cases, the government share in total consumption is the largest and the least efficient. Excessive government spending steered by the forces of corruption and financed through deficit financing contributes much to the shortage of foreign exchange in many developing countries. A successful FDI policy is not only a matter of whether a joint venture is required but, more important, whether a healthy business environment exists that would maximize the economic return from FDI for the benefit of the host economy. Red tape, bureaucracy, corruption, administrative problems, import licenses, and employment of skilled foreign labor could easily handicap the business and minimize its return. What FDI needs is not to be freed from joint venture obligations with a local partner but rather to be freed from:

- political uncertainty;
- uncertainty embodied in the lack of clear and sustained application of the law in general and commercial law in particular; and
- major shocks in fiscal and monetary policy.

Institutions needed to deal with foreign direct investment are mainly affected by the inefficiency of the government management system. In a system where corruption and an absence of accountability are dominant, any organizational structure will not work efficiently. Whether a centralized or decentralized form is adopted, the forces of corruption will be able to twist any system to their own ends. Thus, if the institutional structure to deal with FDI policy is to succeed, a minimum level of efficiency and account ability in the government management system must be accomplished.

In countries of the Gulf Cooperation Council (GCC), or those countries whose foreign exchange earnings and/or employment requirements are not compelling needs in the short run, joint ventures whereby the local firm enjoys a high level of sharing and participation are especially important. What these countries need most are efficient business institutions (corporations) able to absorb foreign skill and the technological capability necessary to create and run a business in a profitable and economically productive manner. This environment is one in which entrepreneurial skills and ability are born, and this is what an economy with a liberal economic strategy needs most.

In summary, Mr. Weigel has concluded his excellent presentation of the various aspects of the two thorny problems of foreign direct investment—joint ventures and the investment authority—

by recommending less emphasis on the policy of joint ventures by the host countries and an investment authority whose main concern is promotion of foreign direct investment rather than screening and control.

The liberalization of policies and procedures for foreign investment is accepted almost as a general rule by the majority of developing and developed countries. The winds of liberalism have swept over more areas on the economic and political map than has foreign direct investment, which is undoubtedly a move in the right direction. Nevertheless, liberalizing foreign direct investment should not, in my opinion, mean leaving the issue of the linkages between the foreign and local business institutions to the sole discretion of foreign investors or even to both parties. This would be the norm in the more advanced economies where there is some degree of compatibility and comparability between the two parties—the foreign and local investors—or where the host country is well advanced in the institutional, technological, and managerial aspects of investment, and all that is needed is the flow of financial assets to promote local production for local consumption or export. Developing countries, in many cases, have overlooked the importance of the long-term institutional, technological, and managerial benefits in the host country's long-term development and have concentrated on the short-term returns embodied in increasing production or employment directly. These objectives in a short-run framework would be achieved naturally by the foreign investors having a free hand in the mode of operation. Domesticating and institutionalizing the forces that lead to higher levels of production and employment in the long term is a much different and more difficult task. Liberalizing foreign direct investment in developing countries should be encouraged and directed so as to enhance the long-term benefits to the host country and the foreign investors.

A clear and well-defined government objective coupled with a liberal and market-oriented policy toward foreign direct investment through joint ventures between well-established institutions of the host country's private sector and those of the foreign investor is, in my opinion, the optimum policy. Though Mr. Weigel and I may differ on the need for joint ventures as a matter of policy we are not far apart on many other issues.

On the institutional side, I do think that a centralized approach in the form of an investment authority entrusted with all the powers to apply the strategy and to issue policies and procedures is a more efficient vehicle than any other. To ensure the success of the investment authority, it should be given all the ingredients in terms of either organization or by-laws that allow it to operate along the lines of the private market institutions. In this way, the authority can understand the problems facing private investors and can offer logical and efficient solutions.

Moreover, the general levels of discipline, accountability, and morality in the public system, as well as in the whole society, have a good deal of bearing on the working of whatever institutional structure is chosen to manage foreign direct investment. Thus, a means of improving the performance of FDI could be found in some areas that may seem at the outset to have no relationship to the issue.

Ezzedin M. Shamsedin[1]

Mr. Weigel's paper touches on an important and timely topic in view of the need of developing countries to increase the flow of nondebt resources and technology to compensate for the decline in other forms of capital flows. He is right in stating that policies and institutional approaches to encourage foreign direct investment (FDI) must be consistent with the objectives of host countries and what they hope to achieve through such investments. He is also right in suggesting that foreign investment policies should take into account specific country circumstances and must be evaluated on a case-by-case basis. There can be no general panacea or simple rules that are applicable to all countries across the board.

It is true that mistakes were made by a number of developing countries in the 1960s and 70s when they opted for a more dirigiste or overregulated approach to foreign investment, for a myriad of reasons: whether to protect sovereignty, encourage development of domestically controlled enterprises and technology, or to reg-

[1] I am grateful to Rumman Faruqi of the World Bank for his very helpful comments on an earlier draft of this paper.

ulate and control restrictive business practices by multinational corporations in an oligopolistic market setting. Some of the reasons for such a dirigiste approach can be easily explained and may have adversely affected the volume and pattern of foreign investment flows. But I would posit that a majority of developing countries did not fall between the two extremes of very restrictive and very liberal policy regimes, but somewhere in between. I am also not sure that the existence of a very liberal investment regime necessarily guarantees success in attracting FDI.

Mr. Weigel tries to draw a correlation between the stock of foreign investment and the country's policy stance with respect to FDI and concludes that countries with a hospitable business environment have in general been more successful in increasing the ratio of foreign investment to GDP. I found it difficult, however, to detect such a positive correlation from looking at Tables 1 and 2 of his paper. For example, Morocco and Tunisia are classified in Table 2 as having very liberal foreign ownership requirements, and yet neither of them has been successful in attracting the desired volume of foreign investment. Indeed, the share of FDI in Morocco's GDP at 2 percent is similar to that of India, which is one of the more restrictive economies with respect to FDI. I believe that in trying to present his evidence, Mr. Weigel has put more weight on the impact of national policies in determining the volume of FDI and too little emphasis on supply-side considerations as manifested by investment decisions of multinational corporations, which are frequently driven by their global strategy. Evidence suggests that irrespective of national policies, multinational corporations prefer to invest in countries that have a large and expanding market, or exploitable natural resources, or a trained labor force that could be used for offshore processing and exports. What all this suggests is that the direction and volume of FDI flows are hard to predict and are frequently determined by a complex of factors on the supply as well as on the demand sides with uncertain effects.

Regarding the influence of ownership policies of host countries and the decisions of foreign firms to invest, it is again difficult to draw firm conclusions. In some cases foreign investors may explicitly seek joint ventures with local partners. In others they may prefer wholly owned subsidiaries. The only empirical evidence of "involuntary" or "forced" joint ventures that Mr. Weigel presents is provided when he draws attention to a recent survey of 300 of the largest U.S. multinational corporations in which 65 percent of the firms interviewed thought that ownership restrictions were a critical negative factor in assessing the viability of an investment. My problem with the interview approach is that it is based on ex ante judgments. How a firm actually behaves when faced with an investment decision may be very different from the way it says it would. For this reason, I would apply a large discount factor to the interview approach and would prefer an ex post assessment when considering investment decisions. Also, some empirical evidence shows that concern with ownership questions may be very much a problem of U.S. corporations while Japanese and middle-sized European firms have generally favored joint ventures over wholly owned arrangements.

Even if ownership restrictions on FDI were a concern in the past, foreign investors may take comfort from Mr. Weigel's paper, which clearly indicates that in recent years an increasing number of developing countries have liberalized their FDI regimes by easing restrictions on ownership requirements and by opening up a large number of sectors to foreign investors. Many of them have also made major adjustments to reform their economies and allow the private sector as well as price signals to play an increasing role. The ball is now very much in the court of foreign investors and the industrial countries that have urged developing countries to have open FDI regimes. Unfortunately, Mr. Weigel does not discuss the policies of industrial countries or their impact on investment flows, nor does he discuss their need to adjust fiscal and tariff regimes and lower restrictions that inhibit FDI flows to developing countries.

In addition, I believe that Mr. Weigel could have used this opportunity to discuss in greater depth the role of political risks in influencing FDI flows and the possibilities of hedging against such risks. This is not an unimportant issue. We now have an institution, in the form of the Multilateral Investment Guarantee Agency (MIGA), as part of the World Bank Group, which is specifically designed to cover investors against such risks. As a member of the MIGA staff and head of its Foreign Investment Advisory Service, he could have thrown at least some light on the role of MIGA in promoting foreign investment and providing political risk cover as well as advice to countries in attracting and screening FDI.

Finally, let me say a few words about the role of national policies and investment authorities in monitoring, screening, and promoting FDI, which is the other question addressed in Mr. Weigel's paper. I agree that the form and scope of a national authority have to be tailored to fit country circumstances, and that in some cases a centralized arrangement may be more appropriate and in others a decentralized one. I also believe that simplifying approval procedures and avoiding delays in decision making would help attract foreign investment. Equally important would be to ensure that rules for regulating foreign investment are transparent and clearly set out so that there is no uncertainty about where the government stands with respect to FDI and its sectoral priorities for such investments. I would also add that in moving toward liberalization, the sequencing, speed, and depth of this process must be given due attention.

I need not belabor the point that a key challenge to policymakers in developing countries is how to provide sufficient incentives to foreign investors while ensuring that benefits are maximized and are consistent with long-term growth and development objectives. I believe that the World Bank Group can play a valuable catalytic role in this process by assisting countries to strengthen national capabilities for negotiating, absorbing, and prudently regulating foreign investment and technology flows so that they can obtain the best terms and conditions available in the international market.

Let me close by thanking the sponsors for organizing this timely seminar that should contribute to identifying issues and policies of critical importance to development, especially as we prepare to face the challenges of the 1990s.

5

Investment Guarantees: The Role of the Inter-Arab Investment Guarantee Corporation

Abdel Rahman Taha

The objective of this study is to highlight the salient features of the regional scheme of investment guarantees managed by the Inter-Arab Investment Guarantee Corporation (IAIGC)—an institutional offshoot of joint Arab economic effort—and to review the experience acquired by the Corporation since it commenced operations in 1975. Before proceeding with this, however, we should consider the concept of investment guarantees against non-commercial risks and briefly discuss international guarantee schemes, which provide a useful point of entry into the subject of inter-Arab investment guarantees.

Role of Guarantees in Promoting Foreign Direct Investment Flows

Three basic elements govern the decision-making process over direct investments in a country other than the investor's country. First is the existence of favorable investment opportunities in the country under consideration, namely, satisfying the investor's expectation of greater returns than could otherwise be obtained in another country or from international financial markets; this requires proof of project feasibility in every respect—technical, financial, managerial, and marketing.

Second is the need for a favorable investment climate; "investment climate" means the totality of political, economic, institutional, and legal conditions that may affect the success of an investment project in a given country. Here the political factor is paramount; it includes the extent of political stability enjoyed by

99

the country, the philosophy governing its economic imperatives, its efficiency in managing the national economy, and the policies pursued in regulating private domestic and foreign investments, foreign exchange, and credit. Also included are the degree of development of international financial markets, the stability of international relations, the various legislations for promoting or regulating or monitoring foreign investments, and the efficiency of the instruments on which they are based, in addition to the degree of development of infrastructure and its efficient performance.[1]

The third basic element governing direct investments is an evaluation of the noncommercial risks at work in the host country. These risks are essentially political, and in general they arise from those state-adopted measures that have a bearing on the political, economic, or security situation. These measures are invariably beyond the control of the investor, who normally cannot influence them or evade their consequences and repercussions on his investment project. The principal risks are the threat of nationalization and confiscation, war or political unrest in general, and the fear of being unable to transfer the invested capital or earnings accrued outside the host country into a convertible currency.[2]

If a good investment opportunity is found and the climate proves conducive for investment, the investor's evaluation of the noncommercial risks at work for the duration of the investment, whether real or imagined, becomes a decisive factor in his decision to invest. He cannot possibly proceed if his evaluation shows that the potential risks are greater than he can handle. By and large, the investor will use every legal (and perhaps illegal) means available to mollify the effects of the noncommercial risks. He may, for example, select investments that would accrue the greatest profit in the shortest time; these are unlikely to have a positive effect on the development of the host country. As a result, it comes as no surprise to find some investors' actions creating an opposite effect on the government of the host country, prompting it to impose precisely those restrictions that the investor seeks to avoid.

[1]For a detailed examination of the concept of "investment climate," see "The Elements of the National Investment Climate," Training Seminar on Financial Markets and Sources of Finance, Khartoum, Sudan, March 7–12, 1987 (Kuwait: Inter-Arab Investment Guarantee Corporation).

[2]See Charles Kennedy, Jr., *Political Risk Management: International Lending and Investing Under Environmental Uncertainty* (New York: Quorum Books, 1987).

It follows that a certain degree of legal protection, or insurance against political risks, would improve the investor's outlook and evaluation of the noncommercial risks surrounding a given project. This protection would tend to reduce the rate of investment return applied in the measurement of the *net present value*—which is the measure of the financial feasibility of a project—and thus increase the chances of the investor taking a positive decision toward entering into the project, without resorting to other, unwholesome, and possibly illegal, practices to curb the risks. Providing protection against noncommercial risks may therefore be the decisive factor in deciding to invest within foreign countries.

Evolution of the Concept of Investment Guarantees

There are, arguably, two principal methods of guaranteeing foreign investments. One is legal guarantees. These come in many forms, such as bilateral agreements between capital exporting and importing countries and national legislation designed to promote or regulate the inflow of foreign investments, provide protection, and safeguard such investments against all forms of political risk. There are also special agreements on specific investments, referred to as concession agreements; these agreements are between the host country and the investor, whereby the former grants the latter the right to invest in a specific area and awards certain privileges, incentives, and guarantees established by the state, which may be undertaken within the framework of prevailing investment laws or outside it.[3]

Most Arab countries (15 of them) have enacted laws to encourage or regulate investment.[4] Much of the legislation stipulates guarantees on foreign capital investments against nationalization, confiscation, seizure, or expropriation, except when, for reasons of public interest, it is so decided by specific legislation or by court order. Normally, such legislation requires that the state provide fair compensation and permit transfer of the value of that com-

[3]A detailed discussion of legal protection for foreign investments may be found in Chapter 2 of Zouhair A. Kronfol, *Protection of Foreign Investment: A Study in International Law* (Leiden: A.W. Sijthoff, 1972).

[4]See Arab League and IAIGC, *Investment Legislation in the Arab Countries*, a series on the laws governing investment in 15 Arab countries (Kuwait, 2nd ed., 1987).

pensation abroad if the same sum is found to have been previously transferred from abroad to the recipient country, in conformity with the prevailing currency laws. Moreover, it often stipulates that the state guarantee the transfer of net earnings accrued from the invested capital as well as the re-export of capital in the event of project liquidation, and in the same currency with which imports were obtained.[5]

Despite the importance of such state legislation and special concession agreements in encouraging and reassuring the foreign investor, their effect is undermined by the fact that the authorities of the host country are both the litigant and the judge where such guarantees are concerned. Furthermore, such legislation does not usually provide the foreign investor with a guarantee against political risks arising from the vulnerability of his investment's material assets to losses sustained during war or revolution or civil strife in general.

This leads to the second method of guaranteeing foreign investments, whereby institutions from the exporting countries or regional institutions or, more recently, multilateral institutions undertake to insure foreign investments against the noncommercial risks engendered.

Briefly, the concept of "investment guarantee" is the insurance against noncommercial risks provided for an investment outside the investor's own country as compensation for losses sustained by his investment, against pre-designated guarantee premiums. Though investment guarantees that are normally provided by public institutions are similar to business insurance in certain respects, there is a fundamental difference between the two. The latter applies the principle of the "law of large numbers"; through this law the insurer can calculate the probability of the risk to be insured against and thus the projected profit or loss when adopting a specific insurance plan. Naturally, this principle does not apply to investment ventures, as the number of projects here is relatively small, making it difficult to predict the incidence of noncommercial risks. Consequently guarantor institutions have relied on administrative and legal methods to diminish the effect of the risks

---

[5]For a typical case, see "Law No. 18 for 1975 Regarding Promotion and Regulation of Investment in the Yemen Arab Republic," in Chapter 2, "State Guarantees for Investment Projects," Articles (3) and (7), *Investment Legislation in the Arab Countries* (Kuwait: Arab League and IAIGC, 1987), pp. 9–10.

to their financial status and to strengthen their capacity to redeem financial compensation. One should add that these institutions do not normally pursue profits as a basic objective. Rather, they provide a general service, which is the provision of protection for an investment outside the investor's country. Thus, the institutions' vulnerability to loss—which is frequent—does not necessarily lead to their liquidation or phasing out, for they receive continuous government support from the public treasury on grounds of protecting the national interest that these guarantor institutions were in fact established to promote. The same can perhaps be said for multilateral guarantor institutions. Ultimately, they seek to help realize general development objectives, and the states that own them will certainly spare no effort to support and protect them whenever necessary.

Guarantee Schemes Outside the Arab World

National Guarantee Schemes[6]

There are 15 industrialized states that possess investment guarantee schemes.[7] Some are managed by the existing institutions themselves. This is the case in the United States, where the Overseas Private Investment Corporation (OPIC) provides insurance services in addition to funding. Other schemes evolved from within public agencies or ministries and were charged initially with managing export credit insurance plans; examples are the Export Credits Guarantee Department of the United Kingdom and Japan's Ministry of International Trade and Industry.

All such schemes are designed basically to guarantee their citizens' foreign investments against noncommercial risks; by and large, they revolve around three sets of risks: nationalization and confiscation, wars and civil strife, and the inconvertibility of the currency of the host country into a free currency. The programs differ in varying degrees as to underwriting policies, conditions

[6]Alan C. Brennglass, "Investment Guarantee and Political Risk Programs," Chapter 17, in *Political Risks in International Business: New Directions for Research, Management, and Public Policy*, ed. by Thomas L. Brewer (New York: Praeger, 1985).

[7]The United States, Japan, the Federal Republic of Germany, France, Canada, Australia, the United Kingdom, Austria, Belgium, the Netherlands, Finland, Norway, Italy, Sweden, and Switzerland.

of eligibility, the investment's gestation period and amount of coverage, guarantee premiums, and types of projects and investments eligible for guarantee or for precedence. Some of these schemes provide guarantees only in those countries with which they have agreements protecting investments, such as in the case of the United States.

Multilateral Schemes: The Multilateral Investment Guarantee Agency (MIGA)[8]

The idea of an international scheme for investment guarantees is nothing new and can be traced back to 1948. However, it did not materialize until quite recently, when the Multilateral Investment Guarantee Agency (MIGA) was formed in April 1988 as an institutional offshoot of the World Bank Group, and began its operations in mid-1989.

This Agency aims essentially at promoting the flow of investment funds (slanted toward development objectives) to the developing countries by insuring long-range investments against political risks, more specifically the risks surrounding currency convertibility, the threat of nationalization, confiscation, war, revolution or civil strife, and the failure of the state to honor its legal commitments. Promotion is achieved through the provision of ancillary consultancy services. The Agency's guarantees cover pioneer investments only and are restricted to its member countries. Pioneer investments include fresh financial infusions for project expansion, renewal, or financial restructuring, as well as for purchase of public institutions through privatization and the reinvestment of earnings open to transfer abroad.

The Agency insures a specific percentage of the investment; it may reach as much as 90 percent of the par value or about $50 million per project. Premiums on guarantees are determined on a per project basis, following the Agency's appraisal of several elements, including the nature of the risks to be covered and the project itself. The Agency also provides, in cooperation with the International Finance Corporation (IFC), consultancy services and technical assistance to member countries to help improve the in-

---

[8]Ibrahim F.I. Shihata, *MIGA and Foreign Investment: Origins, Operations, Policies and Basic Documents of the Multilateral Investment Guarantee Agency*, Part II (Dordrecht, Netherlands: Martinus Nijhoff Publishers, 1988).

vestment climate in these countries and develop their capacity to attract direct foreign investments. However, the Agency has not been able to conclude any investment contracts up to the date of issuance of its 1989 annual report although it has been providing consultancy and technical services.[9]

Arab Investment Guarantees

Objectives of the IAIGC

The Inter-Arab Investment Guarantee Corporation is an autonomous regional organization whose membership comprises all the Arab countries. Its main office is in the State of Kuwait and it commenced its activities in mid-1975.

The Corporation aims at promoting the flow of investments between the Arab countries by (a) providing the Arab investor with insurance coverage in the form of reasonable compensation for losses resulting from noncommercial risks; (b) carrying out activities that are ancillary and complementary to the Corporation's main purpose, in particular, research related to the identification of investment opportunities and the conditions of investment in the Arab countries.[10]

The Corporation's objectives crystallized from specific activities and programs, and it has developed an inter-Arab scheme for investment guarantees against noncommercial risks. The Corporation has also pursued intensive research to identify the investment climate and opportunities of the Arab countries and has provided services to promote these opportunities within Arab investment circles. It has also extended technical support services to member countries, in an effort to develop the legal and institutional facets of the investment climate therein and to upgrade the manpower of the institutions concerned with financing and promoting investment.

The Corporation has succeeded, over the past 15 years, in inculcating an indigenous technique for investment guarantee. The

---

[9]MIGA, *Annual Report, 1989* (Washington).

[10]Article (2) of the Convention Establishing the Inter-Arab Investment Guarantee Corporation. The Convention was subsequently modified to incorporate commercial risk associated with export–import credit facilities between the member countries (Corporation Council Decision No. 9 for 1987). The Corporation has developed a scheme for guaranteeing exports, which went into effect in 1986.

technique is new to the Arab world and developing countries in general, as it used to be confined exclusively to the industrial countries. By preparing and developing various model guarantee contracts, as well as contractual and coverage procedures, the Corporation was able to lay the groundwork for the first regional, multilateral scheme for Arab investment guarantees. We shall now highlight the main features of this scheme and the most salient features of its application.

Which Investor Is Eligible for Coverage?

To obtain IAIGC coverage, the Corporation's Convention requires the investor to be a national of a member state other than the host country, if he is a natural person (individual); if a juridical person, his stocks or shares must be *substantially* owned by nationals of member states, and his seat of control must be situated in one of these states.

Substantial ownership does not necessarily imply ownership of most of the capital; it is sufficient if a part of the capital of the juridical person enables its owners to influence the operation and management of the juridical person. In this case no condition is laid as to proof of nationality of the juridical person in the member state in the legal sense; it is sufficient if the company's headquarters is located within that state.

In addition to Arab individuals and companies that own substantial shares and are located in the Arab states, the Corporation's Convention permits the extension of its guarantees to firms outside its member states, provided that no less than half the capital of these firms is Arab owned. The rationale behind this stipulation stems from the conviction that Arab interests in such companies are large enough to warrant their falling under the aegis of Arab sovereignty, and so they are afforded the same treatment as private Arab companies. Extending coverage to such companies creates an opportunity to benefit from the technical capability needed in development and constitutes an incentive to reinstate to the Arab world Arab investments employed in international markets.

Investments Eligible for Guarantee

The IAIGC requires that, before providing guarantees for an investment project, two conditions be met:

(a) The project must be a pioneer enterprise, and investments employed prior to application for coverage are regarded as old and do not qualify for guarantee. The rationale behind this requirement is to render the guarantee an incentive for investors to explore new avenues of investment, as well as its being a contributing factor in the making of investment decisions. On the other hand, the reinvestment of earnings accrued from a previous investment are eligible for guarantee, as is the purchase of existing assets and projects so long as they involve foreign currency transfers to the host country.

(b) Prior approval must be obtained from the government of the host country for both implementation of the investment and its guarantee by the IAIGC.

There are no other conditions of eligibility for the IAIGC investment guarantee. All investments, whatever their type, are eligible for guarantee. This eligibility applies equally to direct and indirect investments (that is, full or part ownership of enterprises and their branches or agencies, ownership of shares, stocks, and bonds), and even to loans directed to financing a development project—provided the project's duration exceeds three years. The Corporation does not distinguish between private and public investments so long as the latter are managed according to business principles.

The IAIGC gives special priority—"subject to all operations being conducted on a sound basis and with the object of serving the interests of its investors"—to the following investments:

- Investments that promote economic cooperation between the Arab countries, in particular joint Arab projects and projects that promote Arab economic integration.
- Investments proved to the Corporation to be effective in the development of the productive capacities of the host country's economy.
- Investments in which the guarantee of the Corporation is considered to be an essential consideration in the decision to make them.

Types of Guarantee Contracts

The IAIGC provides guarantees through various contracts, each of which is designated for a specific type of investment.

Direct investment guarantee contracts cover investments consisting of total or partial ownership of the capital of a project, the overall and unlimited liability of which falls upon the guaranteed party, whether the party is a juridical person or not.

Equity participation guarantee contracts cover investments consisting of total or partial acquisition of shares or bonds of a company not subject to the control of the guaranteed party, who is thus not accountable for its obligations except within the limits of his participation. The rationale behind separating this type of contract from the previous one lies in the nature of the relationship between the applicant for the guarantee (investor) and the investment project, which differs in scope and nature in each case.

Loan guarantee contracts cover loans for financing investment and development projects, with the condition that their maturity should exceed three years and the loan be obtained from an Arab bank; the bank may be a joint Arab-foreign bank located outside the Arab world, in which case Arab participation must be at least 50 percent.

Contractors' equipment guarantee contracts were designed (in view of the importance of the contracting sector for the implementation of investment projects) to cover contractors' equipment used in the host country by the guaranteed party to implement a project, provided that this equipment is imported or purchased within the host country with foreign currency transferred from abroad for that purpose.[11]

The Risks Eligible for Insurance

The Convention of the Corporation (Article 18) drew up the general framework of the risks eligible for insurance by stipulating three generally agreed upon categories of noncommercial risks (expropriation and nationalization, inconvertibility, and wars and civil disturbance), thus rendering the IAIGC comparable with other guarantor institutions.

The guarantee contracts include detailed descriptions of these risks. The direct investment guarantee contract (as well as the equity participation guarantee contract) describes certain aspects

---

[11]The Corporation plans to issue a new guarantee contract for services; it would include a guarantee for contracting in addition to transportation and consultancy services.

of the measures taken by the public authorities in the host country to restrict substantially the ability of the guaranteed party from exercising his fundamental rights with respect to his investment; it also clarifies confiscatory measures, nationalization, sequestration, expropriation, and seizure of the investment.

As for the loan guarantee contract, its definition of risk concentrates on those risks that infringe upon the rights of the investor as a creditor. Its coverage is against any action taken by the public authorities of the host country that results in preventing the investor from exercising his fundamental rights as a creditor, such as preventing him from receiving his rights or disposing of his rights, or imposing a rescheduling of the loan, delaying repayment of principal and interest, or introducing any measure to the project that results in a failure to repatriate the creditor his due as stipulated in the loan contract.

As for the risk of inconvertibility, guarantee contracts define it as those measures introduced by the public authorities of the host country that prevent the investor from repatriating the principal of his investment or the remission of his earnings therefrom or the investment amortization installments. It includes delay of approval of the transfer and the imposition at the time of transfer of a clearly discriminatory exchange rate falling below 99 percent of the prevailing exchange rate.

The risk of war includes any armed foreign intervention, or armed violence or civil disturbance from within the host country, such as revolutions, coups d'état, insurrections, and other acts of violence that have a detrimental effect on the material assets of the investment project if it is a direct investment, on the equipment covered by the guarantee if it is a contractors' equipment guarantee, or on the creditor's material assets if it leads to inability to repatriate a loan, as in a loan guarantee contract.

Guarantee Premiums

The Corporation charges, against its commitment to guarantee, a standard guarantee premium applied in all Arab countries. However, the rate of the premium varies according to type of contract. For direct investment and equity participation guarantee contracts, it amounts to 0.6 percent (6 per thousand) of the current amount of the guarantee for each risk covered by the contract. For loan and contractors' equipment guarantee contracts, the premium is

0.45 percent (4.5 per thousand) of the amount of the guarantee.
The Corporation also charges a "commitment fee" of 0.45 percent
of the total amount of the guarantee for investment, equity, and
equipment contracts, 0.25 percent for loan contracts, against the
Corporation's commitment to guarantee the maximum amount
throughout the contract period.

The Corporation refunds the guaranteed party 25 percent of the
total guarantee premium paid at the end of the contract if no claim
(compensation) takes place during the contract period.

Compensation

The Corporation compensates the guaranteed party on the basis
of 85 percent of the incurred loss where the risk is one of infringement on the investor's fundamental rights or one of war, and 90
percent of the incurred loss if the risk is inconvertibility. The
guarantee contracts require that the guaranteed party always bear
the percentage not covered by the guarantee against loss and refrain
from insuring it or transferring it to a third party. The reason for
this is to keep the guaranteed party, through his bearing part of
the loss, cautious in his dealings, giving him a vested interest in
avoiding or reducing losses. The Corporation may also suspend
payment of compensation in cases where such payment requires
issuance of a final court ruling, and until such time as the ruling
is issued. In this case the investor is entitled to receive 50 percent
of the total compensation charged against provision of adequate
insurance. The Corporation is also subrogated, within the limits
of the compensation provided, to the rights of the investor whom
it compensates.

Limits of Insurance

The Corporation applies a number of ceilings when paying compensation during implementation of guarantee operations; these
ceilings are necessary to maintain the Corporation's financial position, as it has commitments and obligations of its own.

- There is a maximum amount for the total cover that is fixed
  by the Corporation; this total may not at any time exceed five
  times the Corporation's total capital plus reserves. (This maximum reached approximately 215 million Kuwaiti dinars ($762
  million) by the end of 1988.)

- There is also a national maximum, imposed by the necessity of spreading operations among the various member states, which the Corporation's Council set at 50 percent of the total insurance transactions, provided that the amount of insurance in every case does not exceed the Corporation's paid-up capital of KD 22 million ($78 million) or the total capital plus reserves of KD 43 million ($152 million), in those special cases requiring the Corporation to make new estimates.
- The third ceiling is the maximum amount of insurance in respect of any single transaction. The Corporation's Convention sets this maximum at about 10 percent of the total amount of capital plus reserves, or KD 4.3 million ($15.2 million). This limit may be doubled, that is, increased to 20 percent, for investments to which the IAIGC gives special priority, and to which attention was drawn earlier in this paper (see section on investments eligible for guarantee, above).

The Experience of the IAIGC

Guaranteed Investments

Total Arab investments guaranteed by the IAIGC through the various types of guarantee discussed earlier amounted to about $293 million for the period 1975–88. Eighty guarantee contracts have been concluded, of which 48 (about 50 percent of total contracts), valued at $140 million (about 48 percent of the total amounts insured), were direct investment and equity participation guarantee contracts. Loan guarantees for investment projects amounted to $123 million or about 42 percent of the total value of contracts (see Table 1). The sectoral distribution of the guaranteed invest-

Table 1. Guarantee Contracts Concluded up to December 31, 1988

Type of Contract	Number	Total Value of Contracts	
		Kuwaiti dinars	U.S. dollars
Direct investment	23	30,898,640	109,569,645
Equity participation	18	8,733,833	30,971,039
Loan	28	34,654,951	122,889,897
Contractors' equipment	11	8,397,803	29,779,443
Total	80	82,685,227	293,210,024

ments shows that most of the guarantees went to the tourism sector, which received 35 percent, followed by industry at 25 percent and services at 24 percent (Table 2). Most of the guaranteed investments were in seven host countries, namely, Egypt and the Yemen Arab Republic (each 20 percent), Morocco (15 percent), Iraq (13 percent), the Syrian Arab Republic (10 percent), Sudan (6 percent), and Mauritania (4 percent) (see Table 3).

Risk Realization

To date, no risks relating to direct investment or equity participation guarantees have eventuated, so that the Corporation has not paid out any compensation in terms of these two types of guarantee contracts. The Corporation did receive notification of the risk of seisin by a host country over a piece of land intended for a guaranteed project, but the Corporation interceded, and the authorities subsequently canceled the measure, thus averting payment of compensation.

However, for loan guarantees, inconvertibility risks were realized in the case of two loans from Arab financial institutions to investment projects in two Arab countries. The amount of compensation paid was $7.6 million, or 90 percent of the total amount guaranteed, but the Corporation was subsequently able to receive that sum. The IAIGC also paid compensation for another loan valued at $3 million; its retrieval is in process.

Table 2. Investment Guarantee Contracts by Sector, Concluded up to December 31, 1988

		Total Value of Contracts		
Sector	Number	Kuwaiti dinars	U.S. dollars	Percent
Industry	14	20,562,402	72,916,319	24.87
Agriculture	8	1,421,944	5,042,355	1.72
Tourism	21	28,976,096	102,752,113	35.04
Animal wealth and fisheries	14	10,365,251	36,756,209	12.53
Real estate	2	1,447,500	5,132,978	1.74
Infrastructure	21	19,912,034	70,610,050	24.10
Total	80	82,685,227	293,210,024	100.00

Table 3.   Geographical Distribution of Operations as at December 31, 1988

Country	Total Value of Contracts Kuwaiti dinars	U.S. dollars	Percent
Bahrain	86,700	307,447	—
Egypt	17,578,637	62,335,592	21
Iraq	11,020,516	39,079,844	13
Jordan	430,000	1,524,823	—
Kuwait	785,953	2,787,067	1
Mauritania	3,447,551	12,225,358	4
Morocco	11,983,129	42,493,365	15
Somalia	844,393	2,994,301	1
Sudan	6,690,003	23,723,415	8
Syrian Arab Republic	8,094,544	28,704,057	10
Tunisia	731,727	2,594,777	1
United Arab Emirates	2,422,000	8,588,652	3
Yemen Arab Republic	17,420,440	61,774,610	21
Yemen, People's Democratic Republic of	1,149,634	4,076,716	2
Total	82,685,227	293,210,024	100

Summary

Arab investment flows guaranteed by the Corporation since it began operations are very modest when compared with the figures for unofficial investment flows[12] between the Arab countries, which were estimated at $9.88 billion at the end of 1988.[13] In our opinion, the smallness of the investments guaranteed in relation to total flows should not detract from the importance of these investments, for they constitute what are called "additional" flows; that is, they appear over and above the natural flows resulting from the presence of good investment opportunities and a conducive investment climate. Their owners do not see the noncommercial risks accompanying the project as so large that they should forgo the invest-

[12]Includes public sector investments managed according to business principles.

[13]See IAIGC, "Inter-Arab Investments: Their Progress, Successes and Failures," research report presented at Eleventh Conference of the Arab Economists Union, Casablanca, October 3–5, 1989, Table (1), p. 6.

ment or seek out ways by which to reduce the risks. This concept is called the concept of "additionality."[14]

Like natural flows, additional flows are essentially products of a good investment opportunity and a reasonable investment climate. But the investor believes there are noncommercial risks, such as the threat of nationalization or confiscation or inconvertibility, that are high enough to warrant his refusal to proceed with the investment. In other words, the high risks raise the net present value, which is the ratio utilized in appraising the financial feasibility of a project, so that all other alternative opportunities appear more attractive to the investor; as a result, the investor decides not to enter the project.

However, if guarantees are provided against the possible realization of these risks, the investor's calculations would change. The net present value would then be lower, increasing the chances of a decision to proceed with the investment. From this we can infer that guarantees against noncommercial risks are not in fact the decisive factor in direct investment flows between countries; the principal catalyst to these flows is in fact the availability of good investment opportunities within a conducive investment climate. International experience bears out this thesis, for we find that most direct investment flows during the eighties were to the newly industrializing countries of southest Asia, where good investment opportunities have emerged and economic and financial policies are conducive to such investment.[15] The same is apparent for the Arab world, where the greatest unofficial direct investments are in those countries that have sought to improve their investment climate by applying more liberal economic and financial policies and by reducing state control of economic activity or in general allowing market forces greater leeway in the determination of prices and the distribution of resources.[16]

[14]A good discussion of this concept may be found in a report by Arthur Young & Co., dated May 28, 1982, to the Overseas Private Investment Corporation (OPIC) as to the impact of OPIC's activities on U.S. investment flows to developing countries. The report defines "additionality" as the net increase in investment flows resulting from the guarantee of a given project.

[15]See article by David Goldsbrough, "Foreign Direct Investment in Developing Countries," *Finance and Development*, Vol. 22, No. 1 (March 1985), pp. 31–34.

[16]For a description of the distribution of Arab investment flows between the Arab countries specifically, see IAIGC, *Report on the Investment Climate in the Arab Countries, 1988* (Kuwait, May 1989), pp. 50–51 (Table 2).

From what has been discussed thus far, it is apparent that the promotion of direct investment flows between countries is not a function of guarantees alone. Guarantees should be part of a complete and integrated package of services including, in addition to guarantees against noncommercial risks, the following:

- Helping the investor to identify available investment opportunities in a host country and to determine a suitable project for investment.
- Helping the parties to the investment process, whether promoters, investors, or official agencies, to become acquainted with one another during the promotion of investment opportunities and the determination of sources of finance.
- Describing for the investor the various aspects of the investment climate in a host country, including project licensing measures, incentives, and exemptions stipulated in the country's investment laws.
- Helping the host country to improve its investment climate (especially its legal and institutional aspects) by providing it with technical assistance in these areas.

Perhaps the officials who drew up the Corporation's Convention had this broad concept of service in mind, for the provision of guarantees to Arab investors is closely tied to the provision of these very services. The Convention expressly states that, "for the purpose of promoting investments among member countries, the Corporation shall undertake activities that are ancillary to its main purpose and in particular the promotion of research relating to the identification of investment opportunities and the conditions of investment in the said countries."

The Corporation has been very active, especially in the last few years, in providing services ancillary to guarantees. It has researched and published studies on all facets of the investment climate in the Arab countries and held conferences and training seminars on various issues and instruments of investment. It has also initiated a promotion service that seeks, within the means available, to acquaint Arab investors with investment opportunities open for financing. The Corporation has also provided technical assistance to member states to help improve the legal and institutional aspects of their investment climate and enhance the efficiency of cadres responsible for foreign investment promotion and administration in the Arab countries.

It is difficult to evaluate the impact of all these services on inter-Arab investment flows, especially over the short run. Being support services, their impact takes place through other measures. However much one may speak of specific achievements in the areas of promotion, legal consultation, or general foreign investment policies, they have had a direct effect on the achievement of specific flows and have contributed positively to improving the investment climate in general. No doubt, intensifying these services and pursuing them with professional competence, in addition to providing comprehensive, flexible, and reasonably priced guarantees, will prove most fruitful over the long run and will improve the investment climate within the Arab countries and thus lead to greater direct investment flows between these countries.

As a postscript, there are a number of objective causes pertaining to the nature of Arab investment flows and the process of developing guarantees that have contributed to reducing the size of guaranteed investments. The first cause is that the most outstanding direct Arab investments in the Arab countries came from public sources.[17] Some were in the form of joint Arab projects, where government participation did not need any guarantees to encourage such participation. Also, it was during the heyday of the Corporation (the latter part of the seventies), when investments were at their peak, that the foundations of the Corporation were laid, its financial status consolidated, and its services defined. Finally, unofficial direct investment flows at both the international and Arab levels became tighter during the eighties. There were a number of reasons for this development, most of which go back to the deteriorating economic situation in most host countries, which, as suggested earlier, has a direct bearing on the weakening demand for guarantees.

To sum up, the role played by guarantees in attracting investments is an ancillary or complementary one, and an improved investment climate, in all its various political, economic, and in-

---

[17]The government share in investment flows managed according to business principles in the seven major Arab countries receiving investments amounted to nearly 87 percent. See IAIGC, "Evaluation of Arab Investment Projects," paper presented at Seminar on Performance Evaluation of Arab Investment Projects, Amman, Jordan, May 22–23, 1989.

stitutional aspects, is really the key factor in attracting direct foreign investments to the Arab world. It cannot be overemphasized
that the process of improving the climate of investment is extremely complicated and fraught with difficulties over the short
run. But there are encouraging signs, not the least of which is that
this question is a leading topic of discussion in international talks
on development problems in general and on the debt question in
particular. The prevailing view appears to be that improving the
investment climate, through restructuring and readjustment of
ailing economies toward greater liberalization, can help to attract
resources, especially direct investments, that will not fetter the
state with additional debts yet introduce new techniques and useful
managerial experience; that is, greater commercial investment flows
are a major avenue for resolving the debt problem and, ultimately,
the problem of underdevelopment. There is no doubt that greater
effort and assistance from the international and regional donor
communities, embodied in their states and institutions, are central
to achieving tangible progress in this area. But, ultimately, it is
the indigenous initiatives of the countries concerned that are the
determining factor.

Comment

Nour El-Din Farrag

The following remarks on the subject of investment guarantees bring together a number of points that seemed worth highlighting, some personal opinions, as well as certain clarifications that can only serve to complement Mr. Abdel Rahman Taha's excellent study on "Investment Guarantees: The Role of the Inter-Arab Investment Guarantee Corporation." Consequently, what follows is more an "annotation" than a "commentary," but one that will hopefully stimulate further discussion.

First, the subject of investment guarantees is tied up with protecting the rights of the investor, as these guarantees are considered a form of property rights protection. In the advanced industrial countries, this matter is not in contention. There, property rights are protected by the nation's constitution; the exercise of them is regulated by laws that acknowledge international conventions, and their application is supervised by fair judicial systems and preserved by impartial executive agencies, before whom the national investor and the foreign investor are equal. This broad system of regulation achieved its stability, permanence, and following after a long time, but it has generated confidence for the investor and has won his trust.

The advanced industrial countries have also instituted political, economic, and social liberties—shaped by the prevailing forms of government—and have adopted the market approach to managing their economies, intervening only in cases of infringement or breakdown resulting from progress and growth. They have long since abandoned the planned form of economy.

For these reasons, international investment capital moves freely between these countries, influenced only by traditional economic and financial considerations, and it excludes from its accounts what has come to be termed "political risk." As the latter is the principal motivation behind the quest for investment guarantees, we do not observe in the developed countries provisions for guaranteeing investments against political risks, nor are there any known bilateral or collective agreements for protecting foreign investment, since there is no need for them. There are, however, regulations designed to encourage investment, both domestic and foreign, and to secure attractive returns commensurate with the extent of economic and commercial risk engendered in certain economic sectors or specific geographic areas that market forces do not reflect to the desired degree. But the investment's source and its adjusted returns are surer than the political risk. This situation is not limited to the developed countries, for certain developing countries, albeit few, have been actively engaged in this process, especially those that have become, or are on their way to becoming, newly industrializing economies.

The question of investment guarantees, particularly foreign investment guarantees, in the sense of protecting foreign investment from political risk, is essentially one of the mobility of investment capital between capital exporting states (mostly the developed countries and a few developing countries) and the developing countries receiving these transfers.

One of the most important economic policy objectives for Arab countries hosting foreign capital is to reach a stage where this capital no longer needs defending against political risk, that is, a stage at which investment guarantee schemes can be dispensed with; and let our starting point be Arab investments within the Arab world.

Second, the importance of foreign investment guarantee schemes against political risk, especially the risk of currency inconvertibility, appeared shortly after the Second World War in response to the call for the reconstruction of Western Europe, whose economies had been ravaged by the war.

The capital exporting states of Western Europe became much more interested in these schemes following the breakup of their colonies in Third World countries, the recovery by these countries of their political independence and legal sovereignty over their own natural resources, the wave of nationalization of foreign investments that ensued in their territories, as well as the apprehensions and political disturbances that accompanied the first stages of independence, and the damage sustained by those foreign investments not subjected to nationalization.

The need of the advanced industrial countries for sustained flows of primary materials from the newly independent countries became intertwined with the corresponding need of the latter for financial resources to develop their economies. This need led to the creation of legal and financial schemes designed to restore confidence in foreign investment for the exploitation of these natural resources, or at least to narrow the margin of distrust prevailing. A series of bilateral international agreements to protect foreign investments were concluded between the capital exporting industrial countries and the developing countries with their sought-after natural resources. At the same time that these agreements were being concluded, national institutions were established to guarantee foreign investments against political risks in the developing countries.

Certainly, the goals of foreign investment guarantee schemes have developed considerably with the accelerating economic growth and prosperity of the advanced industrial countries during the second half of this century. Promoting the economic development of developing countries has become an objective of investment guarantee schemes in these countries. But fear and apprehension over the future of foreign investment in developing countries remain, because their political and judicial systems have not inspired much confidence. Legal and executive instruments are the two principal driving forces of foreign investment in most of these countries.

The profuse literature on the subject of foreign investment guarantees abounds with definitions of political risk, varying in length, limit, detail, and range according to the purpose of the study. But the studies all agree on the inclusion of three conventional categories of risk: (1) seizure, nationalization, and expropriation; (2) nonnatural catastrophes such as wars, civil violence, rioting, and insurrection; and (3) the inconvertibility of currencies or prohibition of transfers abroad. The convention establishing the Multilateral Investment Guarantee Agency (MIGA) introduced another category of risk—the breach of contractual obligations by the state toward the foreign investor where "travesty of justice" is in question, in either one of three forms: the absence of a legal or arbitration board to which the investor may appeal his case; the agency's default in issuing its decision within a reasonable span of time; and the inability of the investor underwritten to implement the decision issued in his favor.

Considering the contemporary history of the Arab world, it is difficult to contend that a period rife with seizures, nationalization, and forced expropriation did not in fact occur in a number of Arab countries influenced by extremist doctrines, doctrines that proved in time to be hollow. On the other hand, it is not difficult to see the beginnings of a new phase within these countries, signaling a fundamental change in political and economic philosophies toward respect for the rule of law and the inviolability of property. Reflecting the roots of the new phase, this category of political risk is bound to wane and eventually disappear.

The remaining three categories of political risk vary in degree and importance from one Arab country to another. But there is no doubt that the risk of currency inconvertibility—in spite of its present inflated importance among many investors—is the least difficult to resolve and the closest to being abandoned in a number of Arab countries that have begun to adopt new structural reform policies for their economies. Moreover, this risk applies mainly to investment in import-substituting industries; no problem arises where the investment is in export-oriented industries—those industries to which capital importing countries are giving priority.

Legislation encouraging investment has been promulgated in a large number of Arab countries hosting such investments, or is presently being promulgated on the basis of the principle of protecting investment from the risks of seizure, nationalization, or expropriation, as well as the threat of currency inconvertibility, already incorporated in their clauses. Thus, legal guarantees against these risks have either already found their way into the legal system governing foreign investment in these countries, or are in the process of doing so.

As for the state's breach of contractual obligations in travesty of justice, it is difficult to find any examples of this in the Arab countries. It is one of those risks that will automatically disappear with the spread of the current drive to respect the rule of law and preserve rights, and with the growing recognition of the need for greater foreign investment flows and of the positive, perhaps even central, role that Arab investments may play in building a new Arab economy.

That leaves nonnatural catastrophes—a political risk of which Arab investment is wary. These risks are without doubt concrete, but they are also limited to a few Arab countries, and their elimination is tied to the success of the current and rapid efforts being waged to restore peace and political stability and to renormalize the path of economic development in these countries.

To sum up, the risks of seizure, nationalization, and forced expropriation are no longer real threats in our contemporary Arab world. The other forms of political risk, though waning, remain, and vary in importance from one Arab country to the next, thus requiring some investment guarantee. However, in my opinion, this requirement is transitory and relates in an inversely proportional way to those long-term political and economic developments that are taking place now in Arab countries hosting Arab and foreign investments, which will be positively affected by the current developments among our neighbors to the north and east, as they are similar in nature and follow a parallel course.

Third, despite the voluminous studies and specialized research conducted on foreign investment guarantees and their role in the economic development of developing countries, one is hard pressed to find a single cogent quantitative study on the impact of the presence (or absence) of these guarantees on investment capital flows to these countries.

On the other hand, a number of recent studies on the subject, based on about two decades of experience in underwriting investments, including Mr. Abdel Rahman Taha's valuable research for this seminar, have, through a qualitative analysis of this experience, reached the following conclusion: That investment guarantees are perhaps mostly a necessary condition for initiating investment flows to developing countries but are insufficient to sustain, increase, or develop these flows.

These studies summarize by stating that "guarantees against noncommercial risks are not in fact the decisive factor in direct investment flows between countries; . . . the role played by guarantees in attracting investments is an ancillary or complementary one, . . . [and that] the principal catalyst to these flows is in fact the availability of good investment opportunities within a conducive investment climate . . . [or] an investment climate that is on the whole reasonable."[1]

The focusing of attention on the importance of familiarity with favorable investment opportunities, their identification and pro-

---

[1]Abdel Rahman Taha, "Investment Guarantees: The Role of the Inter-Arab Investment Guarantee Corporation," above.

motion, and improvement in the investment climate in developing countries that host investments led to initiatives taken in these two fields being assigned a prominent place within the basic objectives of investment guarantee corporations, which were also charged with providing technical assistance and consultancy services in these areas.

It is worth mentioning that as much as these corporations have improved the investment climate in host countries, the need of the foreign investor for guarantees before investing has correspondingly lessened; demand for them is decreasing or has ceased, and this is perhaps the ultimate measure of the success of these corporations in achieving the goals for which they were established.

This conclusion on the role of investment guarantees against political risks, irrespective of the natural financial attraction for the foreign investor that receives direct and effective compensation for material losses sustained, apparently led researchers to argue that the importance of providing investment guarantees through national or international specialized institutions lies more in the positive psychological effect they create for the investor when deciding whether to invest. Moreover, the provision of investment guarantees by multilateral institutions in which both capital exporting countries and recipient host countries participate serves to reinforce this psychological effect, if the host country shares the responsibility of guaranteeing investments against political risk and is committed to showing encouragement and sympathy when dealing with foreign investments.

Fourth, efforts by the advanced industrial countries—and a few newly industrializing countries—to provide protection against political risk for their foreign investments in developing countries led to the formation of a network of investment guarantee schemes comprising bilateral investment agreements that offer legal guarantees for foreign investments, and national institutions that provide financial (compensatory) guarantees against political risks to these investments.

The absence of corresponding schemes, especially financial compensation against political risks endured, for inter-Arab investments, and the dire need to promote these visible investments, were behind the formation in the early seventies of a multilateral Arab scheme to guarantee inter-Arab investments and the dele-

gation of the task of applying it to the Inter-Arab Investment
Guarantee Corporation (IAIGC).

This Arab scheme for underwriting investments is important
because (1) it is the first such multilateral scheme joining together
capital exporting countries and investment-receiving countries in
one institution; (2) all its founding states are developing countries
belonging to a single regional association; and (3) its objective is
to serve as one of the pillars of joint economic development by
encouraging the transnational movement of Arab capital for investment in productive projects, with decisions to invest subject
solely to economic and financial considerations (that is, remaining
free of political risks). Mr. Abdel Rahman Taha has highlighted
the broad features of this inter-Arab investment guarantee scheme,
as applied by the IAIGC since 1975, and his presentation was
outstanding.

He also appraised the experience of this inter-Arab investment
guarantee scheme in terms of the extent of its success in promoting
visible Arab investments. He summarized: "Arab investment flows
guaranteed by the Corporation since it began operations are very
modest when compared with the figures for unofficial investment
flows between the Arab countries, which were estimated at $9.88
billion at the end of 1988."

Actually, the investment flows guaranteed by the Corporation
were not only modest in proportion to total flows; they were small
even in absolute terms. The total value of direct investment guarantee contracts and equity participation, as well as loan guarantees
for financing investment projects, did not exceed $112 million at
the end of 1988; this figure is divided between 7 countries out of
a total of 20 participating countries.

The modesty of what has been achieved to date compared with
what was sought in inter-Arab investment schemes, which Mr.
Taha attributes to "objective causes," may also be due to the
following:

- The discrepancy between the financial resources made available to start the Corporation (10 million Kuwaiti dinars in
  capital) and the requirements that it play an influential role in
  promoting investment capital flows needed to finance many
  new projects that are by their nature large scale, such as in
  petroleum and petrochemicals, energy, mining industries, and
  agroindustrial complexes.

- National investment guarantee institutions in capital exporting countries ultimately rely on the financial capacities of their
  countries; the guarantees they issue are covered by their own
  governments, which is not so with the IAIGC.
- The Corporation works alone in an extremely complicated
  field, for there are no country investment guarantee institutions with which to dovetail when providing supplementary
  financial resources to a disguised insurance cover that can
  affect the investments needed to implement major projects.
- National investment guarantee institutions are permitted, within
  limits, to increase their financial resources by obtaining long-
  term loans guaranteed by their governments; the IAIGC was
  permitted no such opportunity.
- As a result of all these factors, and in the interests of economy
  and caution, the figures for all available project guarantees
  during the first several years of the Corporation's operations
  were greatly dampened. This situation no doubt affected the
  institution's image before investors. Although the Corporation was later able to double its capital and achieve the same
  in reserves, the figures for guarantees available for each project
  continue to range between $15 million for conventional proj-
  ects and $30 million for joint projects, which are still modest
  when considering the investment requirements of large-scale
  Arab projects.
- A few years ago the Corporation began guaranteeing Arab
  export credit facilities against political risks, and the total value
  of contracts concluded reached $350 million by the end of
  1988. This figure represents about 76 percent of total contracts
  concluded up to that time; other contracts amounted to $113
  million, thus making the overall total $463 million.

  If the figures for operations under consideration for the
  same period are included (and these total $381 million, with
  $106 million in investment guarantees and $275 million in
  export credit facilities), a total of $844 million is obtained.
  But this amount exceeds the upper ceiling set by the Corporation's Convention for total guarantees—five times the
  capital reserve, or $762 million. It is also indicative of the
  constraints imposed by the Corporation's financial center on
  the potential expansion of its operations, and suggests that a
  re-examination of its own financial resources and operational

priorities is in order. They should be balanced against the desired growth rate for its operations.

- It may be advisable when conducting such a re-examination for the Corporation to examine the potential financial (and technical) benefits of cooperation with MIGA, now that seven Arab countries have become signatories to the Convention establishing the Agency and thus wield significant voting power—slightly over 11 percent of the total voting power of all member countries—which will doubtless increase, as three other Arab countries are also preparing to endorse the Convention.

- Positive comment is also in order here. The Corporation is to be commended for the great efforts it has made to provide ancillary services, especially in the two areas of identifying available investment opportunities in host countries and specifying the types of projects open for investment, and in providing technical assistance to help host countries improve their investment climate, particularly from the legal and institutional sides. The Corporation has also contributed much to developing human resources in these fields and to promoting and attracting Arab investments to their own countries.

Mention has already been made of the paramount importance attached by research on foreign investment to the question of improving the investment climate, as it is the principal criterion for external investment flows to the developing countries.

In summary, the Inter-Arab Investment Guarantee Corporation has confirmed the operational viability of an Arab system for investment guarantees and its capacity to develop within the available financial means. It therefore truly deserves to pursue these capacities at a level commensurate with contemporary Arab requirements for investment guarantees and thus expand its means and its effectiveness in channeling more Arab investments back into the Arab world.

6

Promotion of Arab and Foreign Investment—General Remarks[1]

Ibrahim F.I. Shihata

The promotion of private investment is being widely discussed at present by officials and intellectuals in most countries, developed and developing, irrespective of their political ideologies or economic philosophies. Developing countries in particular have come to realize that prospects for increased external grants and loans are dim and that funding investment through domestic borrowing, with its adverse effects on the rate of inflation, cannot be sustained indefinitely. Furthermore, governments have learned from experience that expansion and tight control of the public sector require the adoption of policies to protect that sector from competition and funds to meet the mounting budget deficits caused by its losses and subsidization. Such protection further impairs the public sector's ability to compete internationally and reduces the prospects for increased exports. The call for the promotion of private investment has emerged as a practical response to these growing concerns.

Dr. Hazem El-Biblawi and I were among the first to address the topic of inter-Arab investment. Nearly 25 years ago, we pointed out that a distinction had to be made between the Arab countries that would increasingly be accumulating surplus funds and seeking investment opportunities and those that would suffer from severe financial deficits despite the investment opportunities available in their territories.[2] We emphasized the need to create an optimal

---

[1]This is a translation of a paper prepared in Arabic and is based on a paper prepared for presentation at a seminar, "Prospects of Sustainable Development," held in Cairo in March 1990. The paper expresses the views of its author and not necessarily those of the institutions with which he is associated.

[2]Ibrahim Shihata and Hazem El-Biblawi, "Pan-Arab Economic Cooperation," Annex to *Al-Ahram Al-Iktissadi*, Cairo, 1965 (in Arabic).

environment to facilitate the movement of capital, goods, and services among all the Arab countries. Twenty-five years later, only a fraction of overall external Arab investments has flowed among Arab countries for the purpose of direct investment. Worse still, resources seem to be flowing now from some of the poorer Arab states to the developed countries in what appears to be an increasingly widespread phenomenon.

The purpose of this paper is to discuss frankly the factors that would allow for a greater flow of investment funds to and among Arab countries and provide an appropriate framework for the promotion and encouragement of the investment of Arab and foreign capital in Arab countries.

Summing Up the Experience

While working for institutions concerned with investment issues and through my involvement in the establishment of the Inter-Arab Investment Guarantee Corporation (Kuwait) and, more recently, my responsibility for the establishment of the Multilateral Investment Guarantee Agency (Washington, D.C.), I have had the opportunity to gain some familiarity with trends in the movement of foreign investment and to meet with numerous private investors and executives of major corporations that invest abroad. Before discussing the detailed issues facing Arab countries, I would like to present my general conclusions from these experiences (bearing in mind the importance of political and social stability to any comprehensive, long-term investment drive and the specific characteristics of world investment flows in general and Arab investments in particular). Since the following facts represent, in my view, the sum and substance of the practical experience. of many countries, I hope that they will be taken as such, and not as being prompted by ideological considerations or purely personal convictions.

First, it is neither practical nor useful for a country to try to encourage foreign investments by means of tax exemptions and similar financial incentives in the absence of a proper environment for successful investment in general. Such an environment cannot be established solely on the country's natural, human, and financial resources; it depends basically on the degree of confidence in its national economic potential. That confidence, in turn, rests on many factors where facts and illusions sometimes overlap and where rational, political, and at times purely psychological considerations interplay. The greatest influence on that confidence seems to be macroeconomic policies and the extent to which they respond to changing realities. Such policies profoundly affect the balance of payments and the state budget and, consequently, exchange and interest rates and the rate of inflation. Also to be taken into account are policies relating to labor legislation, taxation, and even those that affect the training and productivity of workers. In other words, to address investment promotion one has ultimately to be concerned with the country's management of its economic resources and the overall organization of production, distribution, and consumption, both in the legislative context and, more important perhaps, in practice.

Second, it is essential that the government's role in managing the economy be predictable and that disruptive changes in this role be avoided. From the viewpoint of both domestic and foreign private capital, it is of course important that the government's role, whether as direct investor or as investment regulator, be that of a catalyst and promoter whose scope for intervention is at the same time limited. Perhaps even more important for investors is that the authorities not pursue policies that change abruptly from one government to the next and upset projections and calculations on the basis of which the project's profitability and competitiveness were computed. Although as a general rule foreign investment prospers in countries with liberal economies, private foreign investment may also flourish in countries where state enterprises dominate production so long as the government's positive policies vis-à-vis foreign investment remain stable. Such investment may also disappear from countries where governments are unstable and their detailed policies are constantly changing, despite the pursuit of a generally liberal economic policy.

Third, if a government opts for continued reliance on the public sector as the basis of its national economy, it must adjust its financial and institutional structures to allow that sector to operate successfully without depending on a monopoly position or on benefits that are not available to the private sector. This essentially requires that the public sector be freed of governmental administrative controls and that its profits and losses be treated as relevant and decisive factors. The principal role of the public sector is not

to help the government increase the volume of disguised employment or enforce unrealistic prices. Such practices can only lead to
a huge and irresponsible waste of a country's limited resources,
an elimination of new real employment opportunities, and ultimately to the failure of the public sector. This will be a disservice
to the objective which may, and indeed should, be served by other
means that do not distort the productive process. By virtue of the
public sector's sheer magnitude, its failure in turn adversely affects
the economy as a whole and the prospects for the expansion of
private investment in particular. Should there be well-founded
reasons for retaining a large public sector, it becomes important
also that any further expansion should not be at the expense of
public investment in infrastructure (physical and human). This
latter type of investment, by its very nature, requires a major role
by government (as its financial returns are indirect and unattainable
in the short term). It is also vital in order to increase new productive
investments, be they national or foreign, public or private.

Fourth, an extremely important prerequisite for expanding private investment is the existence of a strong financial sector characterized by flexibility and an ability to innovate and to compete
with external financial institutions. This should not be restricted
solely to modernizing banking institutions. It also requires up-
dating legislative controls and strengthening the agencies responsible for tax collection and financing in general. It further calls for
the introduction of sound legal and accounting frameworks and
innovative instruments to mobilize savings (including those of
smaller depositors) for investment purposes under a reasonable
degree of government control but without excessive supervision
and intervention. The financial sector is a basic and effective mo-
tivator for the development of a satisfactory overall investment
climate; its weakness or backwardness will be reflected in all aspects of investment. It is most important therefore that a developed
and sustainable financial sector be in place without becoming a
financial burden on the government. The sector must play an active
part in transforming growing monetary wealth into new real wealth.

Fifth, in light of the foregoing, there can be no great hope for
increased private domestic or foreign investment if the economy
is marked by a rigidity imposed by inherited rules and procedures
that are for the most part futile. Unfortunately, this may be the

situation in most Arab countries. Historical experience has brought about considerable suspicion of both foreign and local capital. While this may be quite understandable, the world is changing, and economic isolation can only lead to a diminishing ability to compete and a decline of the productive segments of the economy. It is possible to increase foreign investment and open the door to local entrepreneurs and financiers within a framework that provides safeguards against the abuse of resources and power and requires a minimum of social responsibility from investors. Such safeguards would require a certain degree of efficiency and integrity on the part of the supervisory agencies. This may be achieved, in the context of appropriate macroeconomic conditions, by changing, through reform of the educational system and otherwise, the conditions that have led to a decline in government services, to poor labor productivity, and to excessive restrictions and the large number of bureaucrats in charge of implementing them. Restrictions tend to create additional restrictions; officials tend to increase their own numbers. The inevitable result is more intermediaries, rather than investors, and widespread corruption that encourages only the worst type of investor and prevents serious investors from even considering opportunities in the country. One of a government's most important duties is indeed to establish clear limits and to ensure their proper application. But a government cannot succeed in doing so if it establishes exaggerated restrictions and procedures, creating a host of beneficiaries of their existence and continuation.

Finally, if it is true that private investment relies on entrepreneurs who are able to identify and efficiently exploit investment opportunities, it is also true that a proper investment environment in which sound economic policies are practiced is likely to lead to the emergence of such entrepreneurs and to encourage them to stay at home in addition to attracting successful investors from abroad. It serves no useful purpose to say that the people of a given country, by their very nature, lack the qualities required of entrepreneurs. The policies and procedures in force are responsible, to a large extent, for the presence or absence of such qualities. Furthermore, most investments nowadays are made by corporations where decision making depends on specialized professionals of whom additional numbers can always be trained.

Characteristics of Global and Arab Investment

Generally speaking, investors tend to invest outside their own countries when the net financial returns from external investment, adjusted to allow for risks, are greater than those that can be expected from investment at home. This assumes that the risk factor involved is not of such magnitude as to make the overall domestic investment environment unacceptable. Thus, if a private U.S. corporation has the choice of making a particular investment in New York or, for example, in Mexico City, with net annual returns of 20 percent in the former and 30 percent in the latter, the decision may finally rest on whether the difference between the two rates warrants the additional risks involved in investing abroad. Such risks may be related in particular to the decline in the value of local currency relative to the dollar, the extent to which profits can be freely remitted, and the possibilities of government interference in investment issues. There are of course investment opportunities in certain sectors (such as newly discovered oil fields and mines), which will, because of their high rates of return, attract investments despite a poor overall investment climate. And there are investments where a low exchange rate might be an advantage because of the investment's export orientation, especially when production is not heavily dependent on imports and where exporters have the right to retain profits in foreign exchange accounts. There are also cases where bank deposits may move from one country to another solely owing to political risks, or other discretionary factors (particularly in the case of individual investors). Moreover, short-term adverse economic conditions have not particularly affected the flow of funds to the United States because of continued confidence in the stability of the country and in the position of the dollar in the longer term. Many investments are characterized by their search for high rates of financial return in the short term and many are motivated by the "herd instinct" or the tendency to follow the lead of larger investors. As a general rule, however, investors only tend to invest abroad in the expectation of a higher return, duly adjusted to allow for risk factors, including exchange rate and transfer risks.

An investor opts to invest in one country over another on the basis of a comparison of the risk-adjusted returns in each case. Accordingly, there may be a preference for a more modest net return in a particular country because of the strength of its currency and its stability over a higher return from a country where there is a potential for continued currency depreciation, or for drastic and abrupt changes in local conditions. Such preferences are generally shown by individual and corporate investors alike. Larger corporations may however enjoy a greater degree of flexibility because of their ability to diversify their investments, both geographically and in terms of sectors, and hedge against risks through "self insurance." In addition, major corporations are better able to incur losses in the short term. This enhances their ability to take an interest in new projects that require expenditure with no immediate return. Like other investors, however, such corporations may, if they have incurred losses in a given country, be influenced by the experience when they decide on new investments.

The diminishing need for primary commodities in sophisticated industrial production (because of technological advances relying on alternative materials), the gradual reduction in the numbers of workers needed for such production (as against increasing reliance on technical knowledge), as well as the great scientific advances and their impact on the structure of agricultural and industrial production have led some commentators to fear an increasing deterioration of the comparative advantages enjoyed by developing countries in general. They also suspect that these and other factors will foster the tendency in industrial countries to concentrate on production at home, with the possibility of a spread of regional economic groupings adopting protectionist measures for their respective markets. Commentators also note that, notwithstanding these fears, there is an increase of certain types of foreign investment in developing countries that goes beyond the usual exploitation of natural resources, for obvious comparative advantages (such as in industries that require vast numbers of unskilled workers, or which are close to principal consumer markets, or have an adverse impact on the environment). In such cases, investments might increase in developing countries to avoid social problems arising out of importing labor into the developed countries and the complications associated with environmental issues in such countries.

Observers of direct foreign investment flows also note that they are heavily concentrated in geographic terms (with both home and host countries largely being western developed countries), and in terms of developing country economic sectors. (Such flows were formerly directed toward agriculture in equatorial regions and mining or the production of consumer goods in countries with relatively large markets; lately, they have increasingly been directed toward export industries and services that depend on the purchase or leasing of advanced technology.) Observers further note the spread of "institutional investors," such as pension funds and insurance companies that hold considerable liquid funds and seek to invest them in securities in promising and stable markets.

The United States is still the major importer and exporter of foreign direct investment worldwide, although Japan has begun competing as an investment exporter (most Japanese investments being directed to the United States, Europe, and South East Asia). For a long time Latin America, particularly Brazil and Mexico, provided a preferred location for foreign direct investment in the developing world because of its relatively large domestic markets and proximity to the American market. The situation has changed for several reasons, the more important being the deterioration of the macroeconomic situation, with those countries facing severe inflation, a huge external debt, contracting domestic markets, and unfavorable exchange rates. Many foreign investments tend now to prefer South East Asia and China (with the beginnings of an increasing interest in India) where the countries concerned do not face abnormal debt-servicing burdens, are characterized by a more disciplined work force, and where, again, there are large markets and a tremendous ability to compete and export.

Inter-Arab investments (excluding loans) are marked by their paucity (whether in terms of each investment or of the accumulated volume of investments among Arab states) and by a lack of diversification (most are directed toward real estate as well as some small industries and services in the banking, tourism, and transport sectors). Relatively large-scale projects have usually taken the form of joint ventures involving governments (joint investment corporations or joint ventures in a particular production sphere). Their operation has in many cases been assigned to civil servants with no prior investment experience, whose activities have been marked by inefficiency and a pattern of mutual complaints. The governmental nature of the ownership and management of many such joint ventures has been an important reason for their lack of success in several cases. The general difficulties besetting joint Arab action and the little care paid to management techniques have compounded the problem. At the same time, private Arab funds have been typically marked by their search for a quick and easy profit, even if the result is a mere transformation from one to another form of financial resource (without creating real wealth). Initially at least, many Arab investors either acted through foreign corporations owing to shortcomings in their own institutions, or were merely satisfied with portfolio investments (buying up a minority share of stocks in project equity, without trying to exercise management control or play an active part in operations). "Investment" in bank deposits and securities continued to be the prevailing pattern of Arab capital flows even to the western countries, either out of fear of political reaction against direct investment in foreign countries or owing to a lack of adequate knowledge of direct investment in foreign markets. Furthermore, Arab financial markets, which remain limited and weak, were unable to compete against foreign markets in attracting funds to invest in securities, particularly institutional investor funds.

With the exception of the oil and gas sector, investment inflows into the Arab states have been small in comparison to the overall level of investment, which has in each country been predominantly governmental (excluding the agricultural sector). Investments as a proportion of gross national product have been high in many Arab states since 1975, especially in Saudi Arabia, Algeria, and (until recently) Egypt, but unfortunately many such investments have had low rates of (financial and economic) return. Enterprises intended to be market oriented did not always conduct their business in ways that would allow them to be competitive at prices reflecting their production costs and benefits; in many cases, they instead relied on government protection from competition, on employment monopolies, and, ultimately, on direct government subsidization.

Finally, the legal framework for inter-Arab investments has been characterized by a plethora of bilateral and multilateral agreements. The ambitious provisions of some of these agreements seem, however, to have given expression to what should have been achieved ideally, rather than to what is achievable in practice.

Foreign Investment—Incentives and Restrictions

Most countries are at present competing to attract foreign investments. This is particularly true of developing countries and countries in Eastern Europe; yet few have succeeded in attracting useful investments of a magnitude that can materially influence growth rates. Although successful examples include countries that do not grant foreign investors any preferential treatment, most developing countries have resorted to what might be termed the "incentives and restrictions game," which is similar in many ways to the children's board game "snakes and ladders."

Most incentives take the form of customs exemptions and tax benefits. Some countries (particularly those where macroeconomic conditions are not attractive) are extravagant in granting such exemptions instead of ensuring that taxation levels, applicable to all concerned, are not so excessive that they curb new investments or lead to tax evasion by investors. Other countries go so far as to offer grants to foreign investors (as if it were not enough to provide disguised subsidization by means of exemptions and make materials and services available to them at less than their real prices). Others provide preferential treatment in borrowing from local money markets or—what is much worse—ensure protection from competition either by locking markets or imposing excessive restrictions on the importation of comparable products.

While a few incentives may be necessary or useful in some cases, mainly because of competition with other countries, fiscal or similar incentives often represent an unjustified sacrifice by the country's treasury, since they rarely play an important part in investment decision making (although they are naturally welcomed by the investors); they usually merely increase the profits of investments that would have been made in any case. Worse, some of these incentives can be counterproductive, as is the case when a central bank compels commercial banks to lend at lower rates for projects in particular sectors, or to particular investors, leading the banks to avoid funding such projects and to concentrate instead on less important enterprises to which they can lend at higher rates. Furthermore, tax exemptions on bank deposits may result in their being preferred over real investment opportunities that may not enjoy the same exemptions. Incentive approval procedures and the broad discretionary powers wielded in their implementation may also open the way to discriminatory treatment on subjective grounds.

The situation is exacerbated when incentives are coupled with numerous restrictions. Even when restrictions are justified in theory, they may often result in unnecessary bureaucratic interference in investment affairs and an increase in the possibilities of delay and the potential for corruption. Furthermore, the coupling of excessive restrictions with overindulgent incentives sends mixed signals to potential investors that can confuse their evaluation of government's intentions or of the overall investment environment.

Most restrictions can be explained by considerations that are easy enough to understand. The restrictions may be intended to improve the balance of payments position or benefit local industry (for example, performance requirements pertaining to a minimum local component or to the exportation of a proportion of production); to train or increase the employment of nationals (for example, conditions limiting the employment of foreigners); to assign labor an important role in management matters or a share in profits; to develop specific sectors or geographical areas; or to develop local technology or limit the role of foreign companies in the economy (for example, requiring a commitment to a particular volume or proportion of local production).

Many such restrictions, however, ignore the integral nature of a country's economy, the interchange of benefits among its various components, and the response of such components, however disparate they may appear to be, to economic incentives resulting from appropriate overall policies. Certain restrictions may be based on erroneous ideas that give priority to attractive slogans over the needs of competition in the marketplace. Indeed, some restrictions may, inadvertently, have an adverse effect on the economy, for example, because of their possible effects on exchange rates.[3] Gen-

---

[3]For example, Egypt's new Investment Law (No. 230 of 1989, Article 22) provides that the transfer of net profits of invested capital should "be limited to the credit balance of the project's foreign exchange account" thereby making it impossible for a producer distributing exclusively in the domestic market to transfer profits, unless the foreign exchange is purchased from the market (rather than being allowed in an orderly way through the Central Bank). According to an earlier ministerial decree, the additional costs involved in transferring profits in such a manner are deductible from gross project profits, which adds another unwarranted adverse effect on local partners. The situation becomes more distorted when the gap between official and market rates of exchange widens.

erally speaking, excessive restrictions discourage investors and lead them either to turn to other countries where their investments will not be subject to similar restrictions or to overcome such restrictions in other costly or objectionable ways (for example, through reaching agreement with the government for special treatment, resorting to legal or other means to avoid the application of regulations, or corrupting government officials responsible for approval or supervision).

Some investment codes, such as Egypt's 1989 Investment Law, have adopted a procedure requiring approval by successive levels in the government hierarchy. Thus, the Board of Directors of the Egyptian General Investment Authority is required to approve numerous detailed aspects of an investment project, and all of the Authority's resolutions are subject to the approval of the Prime Minister, even though the Authority's Board is chaired by the Prime Minister himself. True, the law provides that approval by the Prime Minister is assumed if no response is made within 15 days,[4] but this is another anomalous solution because of the possible risks implicit in such "tacit" approval. Would it not be more advisable to limit the need for the Prime Minister's approval to decisions of strategic importance and vest the Authority's Board with final authority to approve other general resolutions, leaving decisions on detailed matters to the Chairman of the Authority or his duly authorized associates, in the light of the limits set by the Board? A minimum of restrictions dictated by the public interest that are possible to supervise adequately would seem to be the more sensible practice.

Mobilization and Utilization of Savings: General Status and a Specific Proposal

I have referred to the importance of the financial and banking sector in particular in ensuring increased private investment. Recent studies indicate that, despite its great importance, the sector is marked by severe shortcomings in most developing countries, to the extent that, if sound accounting practices were applied, or constant government subsidization were brought to a halt, most

[4]See Article 48 of Law No. 230 of 1989. Morocco has also adopted (in September 1989) a procedure whereby government approval is assumed of any request by a foreign investor if no reply is received within two months.

local development banks and some commercial banks might not survive bankruptcy procedures. Moreover, there have been certain unfortunate experiences, particularly in Kuwait and Egypt, where some individuals were able to amass enormous amounts of other people's savings in schemes which were, at best, illusory or deceptive. Such schemes ultimately ended in major financial crises and in the loss of payments made by numerous savers who, in the absence of minimum supervision by government authorities, had been misled by a false hope for quick profits.

Experience in many Arab countries confirms that substantial liquid funds are available for investment but are not being tapped owing to the lack of institutions operating prudently in the mobilization and investment of funds within a general framework conducive to successful operations. As already mentioned, most institutions established as Arab investment corporations have assumed the form of intergovernmental joint ventures with all the ills to which this course of action is prone. Such ventures have failed in any case to play a significant part in mobilizing and investing private savings. Conditions have improved with the increasing number of Arab firms specializing in financial matters and the development of Arab experience in banking and fiscal matters. However, the need for further organized training (for example, through an advanced training center, set up by agreement of various banks), and the need to gain further information on the innovative financial instruments constantly being developed in foreign markets should be recognized.

One important institutional deficiency is the scarcity of arrangements whereby savings of expatriate workers and others wishing to invest in a specific Arab state or states may be mobilized with a reasonable degree of security and return. Relevant experience outside the Arab world (for example, in the Republic of Korea, Mexico, Malaysia, Taiwan Province of China, Thailand, the Philippines, India, and lately Portugal and Hungary) resulted in the setting up of so-called country funds for this purpose. The idea is rather simple, namely, to provide a trustworthy mechanism through which investors can convert their monetary contributions into financial papers of real investments. The funds in effect collect private savings from persons willing to contribute acceptable foreign exchange (or from specific institutional investors) and invest such funds in the form of corporate shares negotiable in financial markets and hence available for trading or for use as collateral in banking operations.

The most important feature of this approach is that it requires no funding by the beneficiary state and no sponsorship role on the part of any government. Moreover, no external subsidization is required; only a small contribution by a respected financial institution may be needed as evidence of seriousness and confidence. Such funds have been set up as holding companies or trusts administered by a management company. The initiative for setting up such funds has come in most cases from the International Finance Corporation (IFC)—a World Bank affiliate—sometimes in partnership with private U.S. financial institutions. The operation is preceded by a study of the local investment and financial markets, their potential for expansion, and the risks involved. Also considered are the possibilities of mobilizing savings for this purpose, especially from expatriates or resident nationals who have already converted savings into a foreign currency and deposited them in foreign accounts.

The most suitable legal form for the operation is in addition considered before implementation. If the operation appears to be feasible, the fund or investment corporation is established in the appropriate form (usually registered in a small foreign country to avoid complexities and taxation difficulties). Subscriptions may be limited to certain specific investment institutions, with the IFC or some well-known private financial house subscribing a minor share in each case. The new corporation selects an efficient management team of international stature, issues a detailed prospectus, and chooses the financial market in which its securities will be listed. Upon receipt of contributions, the corporation places them in stocks issued by corporate bodies in the countries concerned (either for existing investments, for expansion or restructuring purposes, or for new ventures). The holding corporation or the private contributors may take out insurance against the political risks involved, including currency exchange risks, through government agencies and private corporations in industrial countries. If needed, the Inter-Arab Investment Guarantee Corporation and the Multilateral Investment Guarantee Agency (MIGA) may also be asked to provide such insurance for investment flows among their members which are directed to a specific Arab country.

The Commonwealth Secretariat is now in the process of setting up a collective fund of this type for the benefit of its developing member countries. Preliminary studies for the fund have now been completed. The fund would be established as a limited liability company, which receives subscriptions from institutional investors only for long-term investment in securities representing equity of projects in developing Commonwealth countries. Arab countries may well consider a similar project to mobilize and invest private savings, and study the format proposed for possible adaptation to their own needs without burdening the budget of any government. Each Arab state whose nationals hold substantial funds abroad and are presumably seeking safe investment opportunities in their own countries may also seek the creation of a foreign-based investment corporation to attract such funds, possibly with the assistance of the IFC, or any private financial institution of international standing, in the preparation of studies and in the implementation of the scheme. The basic requirement is a framework that inspires confidence and convinces Arab and foreign investors of the seriousness of the project and its prospects for success. For purely practical reasons, setting up separate country funds of this type may prove to be a much more feasible undertaking than a joint Arab fund.

In view of the substantial and increasing volume of dollar savings by its nationals, both at home and abroad, the Egyptian Government, in particular, may take the initiative in promoting the establishment of an international financial investment fund for Egypt along the lines just described. The success of any such fund presupposes that the Government will not oppose its participation in existing and future investments on the pretext of protecting the public sector. Full or partial subscription by the fund to the capital of public sector enterprises, after appropriate restructuring, may be needed to allow for the creation of a relatively large financial market where securities may be purchased or sold. It would be useful in this respect to seek the involvement of the IFC in devising the most appropriate techniques and details relating to the funds that may be set up either by one or a group of Arab states, in view of its experience in assisting the establishment of national funds by the other above-mentioned countries.

Conclusion

A significant expansion of private investment, domestic or foreign, in an Arab country requires the creation of an attractive investment climate on the basis of a comprehensive economic strategy adopted by the country concerned. Such a strategy must be based on realistic macroeconomic policies that achieve stabilization at home without overlooking the ever-increasing relationships between local and international economies. This requires

- Economic incentives designed to encourage efficient use of resources based on sound macroeconomic policies and structural, including pricing, adjustments.
- Infrastructure representing the minimum requirements for investment, be it material (roads, communications, etc.) or human (requisite number of workers in the specializations needed, coupled with proper training and discipline).
- A banking system managed by institutions able to mobilize and utilize domestic savings and inflows of funds efficiently and effectively with limited but effective supervision by governmental regulatory agencies.
- An overall stable institutional framework based on (a) up-to-date laws and regulations protecting the public interest and providing stability and protection of private property without excessive restrictions that could adversely affect initiatives and lead to delays and corruption; (b) practical and rapid action to ensure respect for regulations and the settlement of any disputes without delay or complication, either by means of administrative action, domestic tribunals, or conciliation and arbitration; and (c) government agencies exercising duly publicized limited powers, efficiently and impartially.

This paper has pointed out the particular importance of modernizing the financial sector. Establishing a higher Arab institute for research and training may be considered for this purpose. This may also assist in following developments in external money markets and the creation of new mechanisms for the effective mobilization and safe investment of funds. The paper presupposes major economic policy changes which may infringe on the vested interests of limited groups. The principal starting point may therefore be on the intellectual front, and in particular the extent to which new realities succeed or fail in bringing about new economic policies in the countries concerned.

7

Egypt's Investment Strategy, Policies, and Performance Since the Infitah

Heba Handoussa

The rate of capital accumulation is the key variable that determines the rate of growth of an economy in the medium term, while the allocation of investment resources across sectors and activities is critical in determining the pace and sustainability of long-term growth and equilibrium. After experiencing a decade of unprecedented growth in investment and gross domestic product (GDP) (9 percent per annum) from the mid-1970s to the mid-1980s, Egypt is again suffering from all of the symptoms of structural imbalance and stagnation that colored the interwar period, 1967–73. Investment strategy, together with the package of macroeconomic policies adopted since the Infitah of the 1970s, is largely responsible for the suboptimal pattern of investment that has in turn accentuated the underlying problems of disequilibrium in the labor market, the foreign exchange market, and the government budget.

Over the past 15 years, structural change has involved the rapid growth of the nontraded goods and services sectors of the economy at the expense of the traded commodity sectors except for petroleum. The relative neglect of investment in agriculture and manufacturing has in turn led to a wide gap between the rates of growth in aggregate demand and supply with its negative repercussions on reduced exports of agricultural and manufactured goods and increased reliance on the importation of consumer goods as well as capital goods and intermediates.

Ironically, the persistence of an import-substituting strategy has resulted in increased dependence of the economy and especially the manufacturing sector on imports. This trend was reinforced by the gradual overvaluation of the domestic currency (Dutch disease) of the 1970s.[1]

Moreover, the overvalued exchange rate, together with the development of a negative real rate of interest, has encouraged a process of rapid mechanization in the two major sectors of productive employment—agriculture and manufacturing. The result of adopting capital-intensive techniques has been a significant decline in labor absorption, which was exacerbated on account of the Government's shrinking resources and the forced reduction of recruitment in the civil service. Open unemployment thus shot up from 7 percent in 1976 to 15 percent in 1986.

Another salient characteristic of the past decade and a half is the Government's inability to control inflation, which, coupled with price controls on public sector output, has led to the vicious circle whereby the Government's attempt to contain inflationary pressures has itself been responsible for inflationary financing, with the consequent chronic deficit in the budget, growing price distortions, and continuing inflation. The uneven pattern of price increases has had a detrimental impact on the allocation of savings and investments, encouraging speculative activity, hoarding, and capital flight as opposed to investment in the productive sectors of the economy.

It was against this background of structural imbalance that the Government adopted a program of economic reform and macroeconomic stabilization in mid-1986. The key instruments of reform are domestic prices for public sector goods and services, the exchange rate, interest rate, and government expenditure. As far as investment policies are concerned, the Government envisages an increasingly liberalized and competitive environment that will attract additional capital from private domestic and foreign investors. However, the major issue at stake is the extent to which the reform agenda will lean toward expenditure-reducing as opposed to expenditure-switching measures of stabilization. What is of relevance to investment performance is the degree to which credit rationing is implemented and interest rate increases wielded so as to restrict aggregate investment expenditure.

[1] For a discussion of Egypt's version of the Dutch disease, see Heba Handoussa, "The Impact of Foreign Aid on Egypt's Economic Development: 1952–1986," paper presented to Conference on Aid, Capital Flows and Development, Talloires, France, 1987 (revised in 1988).

The purpose of this paper is to survey developments in the legislative, policy, and planning framework that have affected the rate and pattern of investment since the early 1970s and to assess the roles of private and public sector investments in Egypt's recent development experience. The next section gives a brief summary of major changes that have taken place in Egypt's economic system from the 1950s to the present. The paper then focuses on investment legislation introduced since the early 1970s in an attempt to accelerate the flow of private domestic and foreign investment. The following section analyzes the size and structure of private investments and their contribution to the national economy. Then the role of planning in the liberalization era and its impact in the context of structural adjustment is appraised. In the final section, the paper defines the major challenges facing the reform of Egypt's investment climate and suggests some measures for improved resource mobilization and investment allocation.

Survey of Development Strategy Since the 1950s

Throughout the period since 1950, Egypt has experimented with three different approaches to economic development. During the 1950s the private sector dominated economic activity, operating under a relatively protective trade regime. State intervention was limited to the provision of finance or equity participation to those new industrial projects established within the framework of an industrialization program. Investment policies were liberal, and an investment law was enacted to attract foreign capital.

Starting in 1960, a radical shift was made toward socialism, with large-scale nationalization of the private sector in all key activities outside agriculture. State-owned enterprises were now to monopolize all of the formal manufacturing sector, finance, and foreign trade, as well as the bulk of transport and distribution, working within the framework of comprehensive planning and centralized control. Private ownership and operation was restricted to agriculture, real estate, and the informal sectors, but even these sectors were subjected to centralized control of pricing, marketing, and the procurement of raw materials and foreign exchange.

The interwar period from 1967 to 1973 was to drain the economy, as a disproportionate share of resources were diverted to the mobilization effort, while Egypt's complex and reasonably well-developed infrastructure and industrial base were deprived of the necessary investments for maintenance or expansion. Medium-term planning was abandoned, and the Government struggled to finance the minimum requirements of food and intermediate imports.

Ever since the late 1960s, evidence shows that the Government became increasingly aware that it could not meet with the competing demands of current and capital expenditure, and that the public sector alone could not take up the challenge of economic development. A number of measures were taken to reduce centralization and give the private sector some freedom to import and export. In 1971, an investment encouragement law was enacted (Law No. 65) that would attract foreign capital into newly established free zones and invite Arab capital to undertake inland projects.

The Open Door Policy was officially adopted by Sadat in 1973, bringing about a radical reorientation toward a market economy. This comprehensive shift was intended to reinstate the domestic private sector, attract foreign capital and technology, promote exports, and pave the way toward recovery, prosperity, and the maximum use of the country's potential for long-term development.

The package of liberalization measures came in quick succession and covered investment legislation, the trade and exchange rate regime, and the system of centralized control over the public sector. The government monopolies of finance and foreign trade were abolished, and private sector activity could now enter all fields and sectors without exception. However, comparing Egypt's economic environment of the mid-1970s with that of the mid-1950s, two variables seemed to have irrevocably changed. The first was that the large public sector that had spread its weight across the economy was here to stay, and the second was that the bureaucracy had become so large and well entrenched that decentralization would take a long time to achieve. Potential private investors had therefore become highly antagonistic toward and suspicious of government action.

Meanwhile, the petroleum boom in the Arab world meant massive out-migration of Egyptians and significant aid and investment flows to Egypt. Moreover, Egypt's rapprochement to the West brought about the resumption of aid transfers from countries of the Organization for Economic Cooperation and Development (OECD), the growth in trade with OECD countries, and the activation of foreign investment in petroleum exploration. The country's political reorientation, together with the growth in foreign commercial and investment interests in Egypt, was to act as a catalyst in restoring domestic private confidence, and it soon responded with significant investment in various sectors as detailed later in this paper.

Now that business confidence was regained and the Government was able to tap foreign aid and its own petroleum income to rehabilitate the war-torn cities and the infrastructure, it was up to the planners to design an appropriate strategy for the medium- and long-term growth of the economy.

An examination of key macroeconomic variables over the past four development decades serves to emphasize five major themes that have underlined Egypt's recent economic history. The first is the obviously high correlation between the changing share of GDP devoted to investment and the corresponding rates of GDP growth achieved. The second is the limited domestic savings capacity of the private (household) sector, which has been supplemented with workers' remittances since the mid-1970s. The third is the glaring trade-off between government consumption expenditure and resource mobilization for investment and growth. The fourth is the cyclical nature of foreign aid flows as measured by the savings gap and their impact on the size of the investment effort. The fifth is the persistence of an import-substituting investment strategy as exemplified in the small share of manufactured exports as a percentage of GDP.

Investment Policies and the Legislative Framework

Law No. 43 can be considered the cornerstone of Egypt's Open Door Policy, as further amended by Law No. 32 of 1977 and more recently repealed in favor of the more generalized Investment Law No. 230 of 1989. In June 1974, Law No. 43 for Foreign and Arab Investment and Free Zones was issued, replacing the previous Law No. 65 of 1971. The old law had provided incentives such as tax holidays, liberal terms of profit, and capital transfers, and guarantees against noncommercial risks. The main significance of Law No. 43 was its opening the door to foreign, in addition to Arab, capital, its explicit description of all fields of economic activities open to such investors (except petroleum, which is subject to separate legislation), and the provision of firmer guarantees against nationalization.

Law No. 43 clearly distinguished between free zone investments, for which local participation is not required and tax holidays are indefinite, and inland projects, which must be carried out in partnership with local enterprises unless exemption is specifically sought and provided. The income (profit) tax holiday would be 5 years for a typical project, 8 years or more for projects with special value to the economy (for example, export-oriented projects), and 10–15 years for projects in land reclamation or in new cities. The additional privilege of customs exemption on imported capital goods could also be offered by special decree. Apart from the positive incentives of the law, the main attraction of working under Law No. 43 status was exemption from labor laws, exchange control regulations, and from the need to obtain licenses for importing or exporting.

The amendment to Law No. 43, Law No. 32 of 1977, provided an additional impetus to foreign and local private investment. First, it spelled out that the opportunity for private domestic investors to take advantage of the law was available on equal terms to those provided to foreign investors, with the criterion for a project's eligibility being foreign currency rather than foreign nationality. The amended Law No. 43 also redefined the exchange rate applicable to the valuation of foreign capital from the official exchange rate to the highest announced rate, to give the foreign-currency-denominated equity component full advantage of partial devaluations of the exchange rate. It also removed the earlier condition that each project maintain a foreign currency account that could only be fed with export earnings and foreign currency transfers from abroad, which has meant that investors have been able simply to purchase foreign currency on the local market with their local currency earnings, removing the need to export.

During the 1970s, it became increasingly apparent that Law No. 43 could not serve as the all-embracing channel for private investment in Egypt and that it was neither designed nor appropriate for such a purpose. Instead, the company law (Law No. 26 of 1954), which had been subjected to various amendments during the socialist era, would now have to be revised to serve as the basic legislation pertaining to the establishment or expansion of joint stock, limited partnership, and limited liability companies.

The new company law, Law No. 159, was issued in 1981, and by 1989, both it and the new investment law (Law No. 230 of 1989 replacing Law No. 43) have become the two legislative instruments governing private investment in Egypt. The implementing bodies are the Capital Market Authority for Law No. 159 and the General Authority for Investment (GAFI) for Law No. 230.

The salient feature of Law No. 159 is that it has removed all of the restrictive rules that governed private companies under the old company law (Law No. 26). These rules had required private companies, like public firms, to follow rigid rules on the distribution of their profits and the participation of employees in management. According to Law No. 26, up to 25 percent of company profits would be distributed among workers and another 5 percent used in the purchase of government bonds, four members of the board of directors would be elected from among the workers, and the salaries of managers were subject to the ceiling of LE 5,000 per annum. The new company law was successful in abolishing these and many other restrictions that placed existing private companies at a substantial disadvantage vis-à-vis Law No. 43 companies. In fact, the record shows that only 27 joint stock companies had been formed over the 20-year period from 1960 to 1980. In contrast, since its enactment, Law No. 159 of 1981 has seen the establishment of more than 200 such companies.

Law No. 159 is primarily intended for fully local private investments, although foreign investors can participate in joint ventures with a maximum 51 percent share in equity. However, this law makes no provision for the repatriation of profits or capital, and all companies subject to it must abide by the exchange control and licensing regulations for importing and exporting. Since the law does not discriminate among areas of economic activity, it is less generous than Law No. 43 in offering tax and other fiscal incentives. Moreover, the company law abides by a number of labor laws to which Law No. 43 projects are not subject. Until the enactment of the new investment law (Law No. 230 of 1989) the only advantages of Law No. 159 over Law No. 43 were that the prices of major local inputs such as energy were heavily subsidized.

With the enactment of the new investment law in July 1989, investors now have a choice between opting for establishment and operation under either Law No. 159 or Law No. 230. Table 1

Table 1. Comparison of Law Nos. 43, 230, and 159

Law 43/1974 as amended	Law 230/1989	Law 159/1981
Fields of activity (Art. 3) All except petroleum	(Art. 1) Excluded: finance, contracting, consultancy, transport (*)	No specified fields
Egyptian participation in equity (Art. 4) Mandatory but no minimum specified (*)	(Art. 5) Not mandatory(*)	(Art. 37) Minimum 49 percent Egyptian equity
Capital and profit repatriation (Arts. 21, 22) Allowed	(Arts. 23, 22) Allowed	Not allowed
Foreign ownership of land Not allowed	(Art. 6) Allowed (*)	Not allowed
Price controls None	None (*)	Possible
Exchange and trade (Arts. 14, 15) No exchange controls and no import or export licenses	(Arts. 18, 19) No controls No licenses	Subject to controls and licensing
Income tax holiday (Art. 16) 5 years and up to 8 years (*) 10 years and up to 15 years for land reclamation and new cities (*)	(Arts. 11, 12) 5–10 years (*) 0–15 years (*)	50 percent tax relief on shares quoted on stock exchange

	15–20 years (*) on low-cost housing	Projects in "new communities" enjoy tax privilege of Law 59/1977
Customs exemption on capital goods for some projects (*)	No customs exemptions	No customs exemptions
Worker participation in profit At discretion of company	10 percent of profit with no ceiling	10 percent of profit up to ceiling of one year's wages

NOTES: The relevant article of the law is given in parentheses; asterisk denotes GAFI discretion in recommending special status.

summarizes the major changes between the old and the new investment encouragement laws (Law Nos. 43 and 230) and compares them with Law No. 159.

A number of observations can be made on the rules and incentives provided by Egypt's investment legislation for the private sector. One is that the provisions of Law No. 230 are significantly more generous than those of Law No. 43, especially to foreign investors who are no longer required to have an Egyptian partner, and who can now own land and real estate in relation to their project. Additional profit tax exemptions have also been extended for projects in medium- and low-cost housing and for other projects that GAFI may deem to deserve a longer than typical tax holiday. Another important change is that certain fields of activity including finance, consultancy, contracting, and transport are no longer subject to the investment encouragement law. This change is welcome in view of the proliferation of these service activities, which are no longer a priority area of investment from the point of view of the economy.

Two new rules in the investment law have been criticized by Egypt's business community: Article 20 of Law No. 230, which stipulates that companies must distribute a minimum of 10 percent of their annual profits to workers with no upper limit (as exists in Law No. 159). Another complaint is about Article 9, which gives the Council of Ministers the right to impose price or profit ceilings on necessities if the need arises. Given that Law No. 230 was intended to reduce the extent of the difference between Law Nos. 43 and 159, it is difficult to explain why legislators have increased rather than reduced the gap between the rules governing profit sharing by employees. Again, output price controls (even on necessities) should have no place in an environment that is being liberalized, especially when Article 9 itself mentions that price discrimination on the provision of inputs is being phased out for all private producers.

A final comment on the new investment law is that it maintains and perhaps even increases the discretionary power of GAFI in awarding special privileges to projects. As Table 1 shows, this is true of key elements of the legislation: area of activity, domestic participation, tax holidays, and foreign ownership of land. This feature of the law is disturbing, since it may encourage abuse of such power by GAFI officials and/or result in all investors ob-

taining the maximum of privileges available under the law, without offering the economy extra benefits. It is a known fact that
the tax contribution of all Law No. 43 projects (more than 700)
in operation is still insignificant because of the overindulgence of
the authorities in awarding tax concessions. It would therefore
have been wise for the new investment law to have become more
specific on areas of economic activity subject to the law and on
the duration of the concessions to be awarded.

All in all, Egypt's new investment code (Law No. 230 of 1989)
can be considered most generous and flexible when compared with
similar codes ruling in other semi-industrialized economies, especially in the treatment of foreign investors. So far, it is Egyptian
capital that has responded to the generous terms offered by the
previous law (Law No. 43), and it remains to be seen if foreign
investors will now be attracted by the additional concessions offered by Law No. 230. In the next section, an appraisal is made
of the impact of Law No. 43 on inland projects. Free zones are
excluded from the analysis for lack of space and because they have
had a negligible impact on the economy to date.

Investment Response of the "New" Private Sector

By mid-1989, the Investment Authority reports that a total of
1,427 inland projects had been approved since the early 1970s,
with a cumulative value of authorized capital of LE 7.5 billion and
total investment costs (authorized capital plus loans) of LE 14.0
billion. However, these totals include figures for the financial sector—banks and investment companies—of LE 2.4 billion of authorized capital and LE 2.6 billion of investment costs, and these
figures should be deducted because they otherwise involve double
counting since most placements and credits from the financial
sector appear in the authorized capital plus loans item of the nonfinancial sectors. The adjusted figures for the aggregate authorized
capital of inland nonfinancial projects of LE 5.1 billion and for
aggregate investment costs of LE 11.4 billion are therefore a more
accurate representation of the size of actual and prospective investments over the period from 1974 to the early 1990s as approved
under the status of Law No. 43.

The data for mid-1989 also show that 721 projects in the nonfinancial sector were in operation out of the total of 1,158 projects

approved (or two thirds of the total), with total investment costs of LE 6.5 billion out of the total of LE 11.4 billion approved (57 percent of the total). Another 194 projects, worth LE 1.9 billion of total investment costs, were under execution. The proportion of projects that are either in operation or under active implementation together account for 79 percent of total approved projects and 74 percent of total approved investments to date. The absolute number of projects and the total value of investments are impressive, reflecting that Law No. 43 has indeed been successful in attracting substantial capital flows toward various sectors of economic activity.

In current prices at which all projects are valued at the time of approval, the estimated growth in annual investment under Law No. 43 is also high. Taking three-year averages, annual investment expenditure by Law No. 43 projects grew from LE 65 million during 1975–77, to an estimated LE 300 million in 1978–80, to about LE 800 million during 1981–83, and close to LE 1,320 million during 1984–86. The figure reported by the Investment Authority for 1987 is LE 1,562 million.[2] Valued at constant prices, the annual growth rate of investments is of course much less significant, given the domestic rate of inflation and the successive devaluations of the rate of exchange at which imported capital is valued.

The share of foreign currency in total investment is well over half, which can be expected, given that the basic criterion for eligibility for Law No. 43 status is foreign capital, irrespective of the nationality of the investor. The predominance of foreign as opposed to domestic currency in the equity capital and total investment costs of projects is also due to Egypt's heavy dependence on imported capital goods that themselves account for the major proportion of assets in most projects.

In relation to aggregate capital formation in the economy, it can also be shown that Law No. 43 investments account for a significant share of gross fixed investment in the economy since the beginning of the Infitah. There are at least two ways of estimating the contribution of these investments to aggregate investments.

---

[2]For 1975–80, the annual investment figures were estimated by the Economic Studies Unit in the Study on Law No. 43 Investment Policies, Ministry of Economy and Economic Cooperation, December 1979, Table 11 of appendix. Investment figures for the 1980s are from an unpublished World Bank report. These figures include investments under Law No. 159 of 1981.

The first is to compare aggregate capital costs of Law No. 43 projects over the decade 1977 to 1986/87 with the investment figures reported for the same period in the first and second Five-Year Plan (see Tables 2 and 3). The second and perhaps more reliable method is to calculate the proportion of total dollar imports of capital goods to Egypt undertaken by Law No. 43 projects.

The first estimate puts Law No. 43 investments over the decade 1977 to 1986/87 in current prices at LE 5,276 million,[3] compared with the achieved gross fixed investments for the same period as reported by the Five-Year Plan documents (for 1982/83–1986 and 1987/88–1991/92) of LE 54,100 million (in current prices) for the economy as a whole. As a proportion of gross fixed investments in the economy, Law No. 43 projects have thus accounted for about 10 percent, which is a small but significant share. As a proportion of gross fixed investment in the private sector in the economy at large, these projects have accounted for 41 percent, which shows how important the new private sector has been to capital formation in the aggregate private sector. In the non-agricultural private sector, Law No. 43 projects (excluding projects in agriculture both from Law No. 43 figures and from plan achievements) have accounted for 47 percent of gross fixed investment. It is therefore clear that Law No. 43 investments have become a most significant force in resource mobilization in the economy and that these investments have played a leading role in reasserting the vigor and initiative of a liberalized private sector.

The second methodology used to calculate the share of Law No. 43 investments in aggregate investment in the economy is to focus on expenditure as reported in customs statistics on imports of capital goods and their dollar value. Egypt has no capital goods industry to speak of, and import statistics therefore give a reliable picture of the value and distribution of investment in machinery and equipment. Over the decade 1975–1984/85, aggregate imports of capital goods to Egypt reached $25.4 billion, of which $3.3 billion or 13 percent are accounted for by Law No. 43 projects (Table 4).

---

[3]This estimate is obtained by subtracting 1978 figures from 1988 figures for capital costs of nonfinancial projects in operation only. This estimate is conservative, with an implied lag of only one year in implementation, while the flow of investment was in fact growing over time. All figures on Law No. 43 projects in production can be found in Appendix Table 2.

Table 2. Public Sector Gross Fixed Investment by Sector, 1977–92
(In million Egyptian pounds)

	1977–1981/82 (Current prices)		1982/83–1986/87 (Current prices)[a]				1987/88–1991/92 (Current prices)[a]	
	Actual	Percent	Target	Percent	Actual	Percent	Target	Percent
Agriculture	1,171	8	782	3	771	3	852	3
Irrigation			1,652	6	1,373	5	1,435	5
Manufacturing and mining	3,910	26	5,955	23	6,051	22	5,791	21
Petroleum	476	3	1,425	6	1,387	5	1,115	4
Electricity	1,293	9	2,508	10	2,625	10	4,761	17
Contracting	449	3	529	2	762	3	631	2
Total commodity	7,290	49	12,851	50	12,968	48	14,585	52
Transport and communications	4,259	29	5,133	20	7,219	27	4,703	17
Suez Canal			328	1	368	1	240	1
Distribution and trade			348	1	430	2	233	1
Finance	430	3	126		88		143	
Tourism			284	1	271	1	208	1
Total productive services	4,718	32	6,219	24	8,376	31	5,528	20
Housing	473	3	218	1	263	1	167	
Public utilities	1,135	8	2,627	10	2,894	11	4,017	14
Education			834	3	745	3	1,629	6
Health	1,230	8	659	3	468	2	798	3
Other and unspecified			1,061	4	1,412	5	1,094	4
Total social services	2,837	19	5,399	21	5,214	21	7,705	28
Grand total	14,845	100	25,854	100	27,126	100	28,500[b]	100

Sources: Figures for 1977–1981/82 are from Five-Year Plan 1982/83–1986/87, Table 36. Figures for 1982/83–1986/87 and for 1987/88–1991/92 are from Five-Year Plan 1987/88–1991/92, Tables (6) and (80).

[a]The plan document (1987/88–1991/92) does not specify what prices were used for valuation. It would seem, however, that current prices are used for both five-year intervals.

[b]Includes a contingency fund of LE 683 million.

Table 3. Private Sector Gross Fixed Investment by Sector, 1977–92
(In million Egyptian pounds)

	1977–1981/82 (Current prices)		1982/83–1986/87 (Current prices)[a]				1987/88–1991/92 (Current prices)[a]	
	Actual	Percent	Target	Percent	Actual	Percent	Target	Percent
Agriculture and irrigation	488	14	1,332	15	1,187	13	2,650	15
Manufacturing and mining	967	28	1,332	21	1,723	19	6,400	36
Petroleum	—		4,400[b]					
Electricity			54		42			
Contracting	143	4	237	3	270	3	500	3
Total commodity	1,597	46	3,397	40	3,221	35	9,600	54
Transport and communications	150	4	326	4	372	4	1,400	8
Distribution			50	1	43		80	
Finance	76	2	24		22		—	
Tourism			239	3	181	2	220	1
Total productive services	226	7	648	8	617	7	1,700	10
Housing	1,377	40	4,331	51	5,284	57	6,600	37
Education			18		21		35	
Health	260	7	33		33		50	
Other and unspecified			154	1	110	1	15	
Total social services	1,636	47	4,409	52	5,358	58	6,700	37
Grand total	3,460	100	8,581	100	9,285	100	18,000	100

Sources: Figures for 1977–1981/82 are from Five-Year Plan 1982/83–1986/87, Table 36. Figures for 1982/83–1986/87 and for 1987/88–1991/92 are from Five-Year Plan 1987/88–1991/92, Tables (7) and (80).
[a]See note a to Table 2.
[b]Foreign private investment in petroleum is excluded from totals.

Table 4.   Imports of Capital Goods, 1975–1984/85

	(In billion U.S. dollars)	(In percent)
Foreign petroleum companies	5.53	22
Law No. 43 projects	3.28	13
Other private sector companies	4.74	19
Public sector	<u>11.87</u>	<u>46</u>
Total	25.42	100

Source: Heba Handoussa, "The Impact of Foreign Aid on Egypt's Economic De-velopment: 1952–1986," paper presented to Conference on Aid, Capital Flows and Development, Talloires, France, 1987 (revised in 1988), p. 44.

The figures in Table 4 clearly show that the share of Law No. 43 projects in capital accumulation has been dramatic and im-pressive, accounting for 41 percent of total private sector (exclud-ing petroleum) imports of capital goods. The figures also show that the aggregate share of the private sector (total of Law No. 43 plus non–Law 43 and petroleum) during the boom decade of the mid-1970s to mid-1980s was more than half of the economy's total expenditure on the import of capital goods. It is therefore of par-amount importance for policymakers to direct their attention to improving the investment climate and to giving the appropriate set of incentives to secure the continued flow of valuable private investment resources into the most productive sectors from the point of view of the economy.

Sectoral Composition of Law No. 43 Projects

The distribution of Law No. 43 projects across sectors of eco-nomic activity shows that the dominant sectors in terms of num-bers and investment value are manufacturing, finance, and tour-ism. The manufacturing industry is responsible for about 44 percent of total approved projects and their total investment costs. The share of manufacturing is also rising; it accounts for 56 percent of the number of projects under execution as opposed to 40 percent of those in operation, and for 54 percent of authorized capital of projects under execution as opposed to 35 percent for projects in production (see Appendix Tables 1, 2, and 3).

To date, it seems fair to say that the bulk of investments in Egypt's formal private sector is undertaken by Law No. 43 projects. Our estimate of the cumulative value of Law No. 43 investments in manufacturing for 1977–1986/87 is LE 2,298 million, which is equivalent to as much as 85 percent of the value of aggregate private sector investment in manufacturing as reported by the plan documents over the same period (see Table 3). Law No. 43 investments in manufacturing also account for a respectable share of aggregate investment in manufacturing (public plus private) over the 1977–1986/87 period with a share of 18 percent. Given the target of the current Five-Year Plan (1987/88–1991/92) of raising the share of private manufacturing to as much as 52 percent of total investment in manufacturing (see Tables 2 and 3), a great deal of effort must be exerted by authorities to motivate the formal private sector to accelerate its rate of growth in manufacturing.

The finance sector has been the second largest in terms of the number of investment companies and banks that have been attracted to operate under Law No. 43. By mid-1989, 269 finance projects had been approved by the Investment Authority, of which 210 were operating (143 investment companies and 67 banks) and another 19 were under implementation (17 investment companies and 2 banks). In spite of the many criticisms of the proliferation of banks and investment companies and of the recommendations made for discouraging the entry of more such projects since the late 1970s,[4] the annual number of new approvals for finance projects has continued (see Appendix Table 4). The nature and magnitude of the problems created by many of these risky or unsound ventures are too extensive to deal with in this paper but have recently received special attention and new legislation by policymakers (Law No. 146 of 1988).

The third largest sector in size is the Law No. 43 tourism sector, which numbered 121 approved projects by mid-1989 worth LE 1,955 million in investment costs. Half of these projects in terms of both number and investment cost were in operation, and another 27 projects worth LE 484 million were under implementation. It is important to note that a significant number of investments in tourism have been approved and executed under separate legislation for the promotion of tourism projects (Law No. 1 of 1973), so that Law No. 43 investments in tourism sig-

[4]See Study on Law No. 43 Investment Policies (cited in fn. 2).

nificantly underestimate total investments undertaken in that sector since the early 1970s.

Tourism has been by far the big success story of the Infitah era. Hotels, transport, and other projects servicing the tourism industry have proliferated and multiplied over the past 15 years, and the expanded capacity of the industry has enjoyed high rates of return. The contribution of the sector to the balance of payments has made it compete with petroleum and workers' remittances as one of the key earners of foreign exchange. The tourism sector also plays an essential role in the direct and indirect generation of employment opportunities and in creating linkages with the small-scale informal sectors in manufacturing and services.

The Size Distribution of Projects and Their Implications

In assessing the role of Law No. 43 in attracting investments, it is important to analyze the size distribution of projects to evaluate the extent to which the law discriminates against small investors. Although the law does not stipulate a minimum amount of equity, it is clear from looking at the size distribution of projects that small-scale investors stand no chance of obtaining the privileges of the law. Appendix Table 5 was prepared carefully, using the actual balance sheets of all projects in production for 1984 to distinguish between different sizes of projects according to capital employed (defined as fixed assets plus working capital). In the smallest category, only 5 projects had capital employed of less than LE 100,000, the smallest project having capital employed of LE 64,000. The next category of LE 100,000–500,000 of capital employed had 46 projects, and another 40 projects employed between LE 500,000 and LE 1 million. The size LE 1–10 million had 221 projects and that of more than LE 10 million had another 111 projects.

The above results imply that only large projects have obtained Law No. 43 status, so that medium- and small-scale investors have been deprived access to the same attractive rules offered to large firms. In a situation where unemployment is high, where small savers are the rule, and when opportunities for setting up viable small-scale enterprises are plentiful, it seems unwise to ignore the potential of private sector initiative and its likely response to legislation that offers it similar incentives to those provided to large-scale investors.

If one looks at the savings profile of the Egyptian private sector, one finds that small savers predominate. The bulk of savings are generated from the windfall incomes earned from working for an average of two to four years in petroleum-rich countries. The small saver is looking for a safe investment that will yield a secure return to complement his modest income from employment in Egypt when he returns home. The proportion of small savers who will seek an independent "Mashroo" (project) that they will personally operate or consign to a member of their family is still limited but finds no support from the policy environment.

Unfortunately most savers end up allocating their "one-time" savings in one of three ways: a housing unit, a foreign currency account, or an investment company. The first two are a hedge against inflation but do not yield the kind of productive returns of which the economy is in dire need; the third has proved to be not only unproductive but also highly risky for the depositor. The result of neglecting the need to develop effective savings instruments and of ignoring the negative repercussions of inflation is that policymakers now face the unenviable situation in which a significant proportion of Egypt's private savings are tied to unproductive assets or have been lost to the depositor altogether. The 1986 census thus puts the number of unoccupied housing units at 1.8 million, while estimates of foreign currency deposits placed abroad range from $10–75 billion. The latest figures on the ratio of recovered assets to deposits at the "Rayan" investment company that collapsed two years ago is only 17 percent. Such scandals are far from confidence raising among the saving public and have doubtless had a negative impact on the savings effort of the typical saver.

The Shares of National Private and Public Capital

Although Law No. 43 was initially promulgated to benefit foreign and Arab investors, it was soon interpreted to include domestic capital, as long as it participated with foreign currency in the equity of a project, even if no nonnational took part in the investment. The amendment to Law No. 43 (Law No. 32 of 1977) gave the equal treatment of Egyptian capital explicit recognition, and the result was that fully Egyptian-owned projects began to multiply. Whereas 102 projects out of a total of 505 approved projects (20 percent) by the end of 1978 had between 90 and 100

percent of their equity share contributed by Egyptians, the proportion of approved projects that are 100 percent Egyptian owned
had grown to 42 percent by mid-1988 (Appendix Table 1).

The distribution of authorized capital (Appendix Table 6) shows
that the share of Egyptian capital in the total authorized equity
capital of projects is even more striking. By the end of 1978, more
than half of aggregate capital (54 percent) was Egyptian, and this
share reached as much as 68 percent or more than two thirds of
the total by mid-1988. The allocation of Egyptian capital is highest
in manufacturing, housing, and tourism, which together account
for 82 percent of total Egyptian equity capital. Although Egyptian
equity participation accounts for more than half of the equity
capital of all sectors other than petroleum services, investment in
sectors such as agriculture, mining, and other services is small in
absolute value. The share of national capital in the equity of banks
and investment companies is also important, with 75 percent and
57 percent Egyptian equity in these two sectors, respectively, by
mid-1988.

Turning to the distinction between private and public domestic
capital (Appendix Table 7), one of the most striking observations
is on the significance of the role public enterprises have played in
initiating and contributing to the capital of Law No. 43 projects,
in cooperation with domestic or foreign partners, and sometimes
with public capital alone contributing all of the equity of a project.
As of June 1988, public enterprises were contributing to 18 percent
of total projects approved in all sectors of economic activity, and
these projects represented 23 percent of total authorized capital.
In the nonfinancial sector, the public sector was represented in as
many as 156 projects worth LE 921 million of equity capital. Out
of these projects, 85 were in manufacturing, 19 in agriculture, 16
in tourism, and 21 in services. The public sector was also participating in 42 banks and 52 investment companies.

Information on the status of total approvals as of June 1989
enables a direct comparison of the contribution of the public and
private domestic participation in Law No. 43 projects. The authorized capital of the public sector stood at LE 1.5 billion, compared with LE 3.5 billion for the private sector, implying a contribution of 30 percent by the public sector in aggregate domestic
capital of these projects. When the financial projects are excluded,
the respective contributions of public and private national capital

were LE 830 million and LE 2,682 million, implying a contribution of 24 percent by the public sector in aggregate nonfinancial domestic capital of Law No. 43 projects. Although, as stated earlier, the addition of the financial sector may overstate the size of overall investments under this law, it must be remembered that we are here working with figures on equity capital rather than total investment costs. In any case, since we are interested in this section in identifying the overall contribution of the public sector in financing Law No. 43 projects, it is fair to consider that the major part of the credit obtained by these projects comes from wholly owned public sector banks or joint venture banks with majority participation of the public sector.

The above information and reasoning lead us to conclude that at least one third of the total cost of domestic investment under Law No. 43 has been contributed by Egypt's public sector, either in the form of direct equity participation or in the form of long-term loans from public sector banks. This highly significant contribution by the public sector raises two important questions: first, to what extent have public sector resources drawn into Law No. 43 projects meant a sacrifice in terms of the alternative investments that could have been made to rehabilitate Egypt's traditional public sector? Second, to which extent has this obvious form of privatization through expansion of the joint venture sector undermined the competitive position of the old, established public sector enterprises?

The major issue at stake is the pervasive dualism in the legal framework and in the degree of centralization that governs public as opposed to private sector operations. Joint ventures set up under Law No. 43 status with public sector participation are treated as fully private enterprises with all of the privileges and autonomy described in the previous section of this paper. Attempts at reforming the legislation ruling public sector enterprises to achieve autonomy and decentralization have so far been unsuccessful insofar as the old public sector firms still suffer from considerable constraints on their potential for competitive behavior. The key problems relate to wage and salary scales for skilled workers and management personnel, the controls on the pricing of output, product mix, and marketing strategy of public enterprises, and the rigid rules that interfere with investment and financing decisions. As long as this excessive discrimination against the public sector continues, the answers to the two questions raised earlier can only be negative.

In a liberalized and truly competitive environment, decisions made on setting up joint ventures between public and private firms can be expected to benefit the economy, as public and private capital join forces in what is a nonzero sum game. Both partners stand to gain from drawing on each other's resources of technology, experience, skills, and market access at home and abroad. On the other hand, given the nature of the advantages available to private companies alone, it would be no surprise to find that in a number of cases the establishment of a Law No. 43 joint venture has been motivated by the desire of top management in a given public sector firm to improve their own prospects with no regard for the health of the enterprise as a whole. In such cases, the joint venture has only served the limited personal gains of those public sector managers and employees absorbed into the joint venture. While the old public enterprise is drained of its best skills, what is even more important is that it also loses to the new joint venture a significant share of its market because of the discrimination that limits its competitive behavior.

Fortunately, the majority of joint ventures established under Law No. 43 are viable projects with high returns and healthy prospects for expansion, especially in manufacturing and tourism. Their output of goods and services has served to raise quality competition and make the old, established public enterprises strive to improve their management skills and become more conscious of consumer preferences. The increasing number of enterprises operating in each field of economic activity from the private and public sectors has not only raised competition but has also created such an increase in the total capacity of individual subsectors that enterprises are now being forced to search for foreign markets in which to sell their products. This shift away from the captive domestic market situation of the 1960s and 1970s is still in its very early stages, but the drive and potential for export are now clearly present.

The Contribution of Foreign Investment

The major contribution of foreign investment in Egypt's economy over the period since the Infitah has been in the petroleum sector, which operates outside Law No. 43.[5] In spite of the generous terms offered by this law to all investors, the economy has attracted only small but nevertheless significant flows of direct foreign investment in such sectors as tourism, manufacturing, and finance. By mid-1988, the cumulative value of authorized capital (for the total number of approved projects) of foreign nationals stood at LE 1.6 billion, or 31 percent of the aggregate value of authorized capital in the nonfinancial sector (Appendix Table 6). In annual dollar terms the flow does not seem to have increased over time although it is difficult to make a precise estimate, since the Investment Authority considers all capital denominated in foreign currency as foreign, without distinction between nationalities.

Arab capital has its largest concentration in the tourism sector, accounting for 26 percent of total authorized capital of the sector. Non-Arab capital has its largest concentration in manufacturing, with 21 percent of the sector's total authorized capital. In the finance sector both Arab and non-Arab capital have been evident, with shares of 17 percent and 19 percent, respectively. Between the end of 1978 and mid-1988, the share of Arab capital in the nonfinancial sector was almost constant (13 percent in 1978 and 12 percent in 1988), whereas that of other foreign nationalities declined from 33 percent to 19 percent. Even so the experience across subsectors is uneven. The share of non-Arab capital has thus declined in tourism (from 53 percent in 1978 to 18 percent in 1988) but has been maintained in manufacturing at 21 percent over the decade. The reverse is true of Arab capital, whose contribution in manufacturing has declined from 17 percent in 1978 to only 9 percent in 1988, while its contribution in tourism has risen from 7 percent in 1978 to 26 percent by 1988. These percentages in fact understate the extent of the changes because they refer to cumulative values of capital rather than increments.

What the above trends seem to indicate is that Arab capital made a slow and cautious entry into the Egyptian economy and was subsequently discouraged from increasing its relatively small stake as a result of disrupted political relations following Camp David in 1979. On the other hand, non-Arab capital made an important start in the mid-1970s but decelerated its investment effort,

---

[5]All entries pertaining to petroleum in the appendix tables are for petroleum services.

following the general slowdown in the economy starting in 1984/85.

There are two major criticisms that may be leveled at the investment legislation as it pertains to foreign investment. The first is its lack of priorities with regard to sectors of economic activity as indicated by the absence of either a positive or a negative list identifying specific investment areas. This lack of selectivity is in sharp contrast to the very precise foreign investment codes of successful semi-industrialized countries such as the Republic of Korea, where the Government maintained tight control over those fields available to foreign investment, thereby maximizing the benefits of technology transfer and export promotion in those areas where Korea had the least experience.

The second serious criticism concerns the laxity of Egypt's investment code with regard to exchange control and export commitments. Although, initially, Law No. 43 stipulated that each project maintain a foreign currency account that could be fed only with export earnings or transfers from abroad, the amendment of 1977 (Law No. 32) made it possible for projects to buy foreign currency in the domestic market. This in turn reduced the need for projects to export either for the purpose of importing intermediates or for repatriating profits. The Investment Authority can also be criticized for not exerting pressure on Law No. 43 projects to fulfill their export commitments as stipulated in the initial approval of the project.

The Impact of Investments on Employment and Exports

In comparison with labor absorption throughout the economy, Law No. 43 investments have made a very small contribution to employment generation. Taking the decade 1978–88, the number of jobs created by Law No. 43 companies over the period was about 145,000 jobs (Appendix Tables 2 and 3), or only 10 percent of the total number of jobs created by the aggregate private sector.[6] However, if one excludes the private small-scale informal activities and agriculture, it becomes evident that the share of Law No. 43 projects in employment creation has been significant.

The manufacturing sector has been responsible for employing

[6]See Five-Year Plan 1986/87–1991/92 for estimate of increase in employment of private sector of 767,000 over the period 1981/82–1986/87. For period 1977–1981/82, estimate is made by author of another 700,000.

more than two thirds of the work force engaged by Law No. 43 companies, with 98,000 jobs created between 1978 and 1988. This figure compares favorably with the total increase in manufacturing employment for the economy as a whole of 671,000 (Law No. 43 manufacturing equal to 15 percent). If we exclude the number of jobs created by public enterprises in manufacturing over the same period (about 120,000 jobs), Law No. 43 manufacturing projects are responsible for 18 percent of jobs created in Egypt's private sector manufacturing industry. Although this ratio may seem acceptable, one can say that it is too small in comparison with the very much larger share of Law No. 43 projects in total private manufacturing investments, estimated at 85 percent. The example of manufacturing is symptomatic of one of the major weaknesses of Law No. 43 investments, which is their very high capital intensity, a characteristic shared by all subsectors.

As early as 1979 it was clear that the incremental capital to labor ratio of Law No. 43 projects approved to date was about LE 15,000, which was more than twice the overall average for the economy.[7] By 1988/89, the average capital intensity of these projects had increased to LE 41,000, implying an even larger increase in the incremental capital to labor ratio. The problem of using relatively capital-intensive techniques of production in a country that boasts an abundant, relatively skilled, and low-wage labor force is especially disturbing given that unemployment has been accelerating since the early 1980s. Reform of the package of macroeconomic policies, including the rate of interest and the rate of exchange, could do much to promote investments that are more labor intensive.

The export performance of Law No. 43 projects has also been very weak over the decade 1974–84. As late as 1984/85, exports of Law No. 43 firms in operation were only $26 million in contrast to imports of $609 million over the previous year.[8] Although the trade regime is partly to blame because of its strong anti-export bias, the Investment Authority could have played a more assertive role in coaxing Law No. 43 firms to export.

Fortunately, the devaluation of 1987 has made Egypt's manufactured exports more competitive on the international market, and Law No. 43 firms have made significant progress toward

[7]Study on Law No. 43 Investment Policies (cited in fn. 2), p. 15.
[8]H. Handoussa (cited in fn. 1), p. 46.

achieving their export potential. Figures for 1987 show that exports worth LE 200 million (about $100 million) were made in that year by Law No. 43 manufacturing projects, a large improvement over the previous decade. Even though two textile projects alone account for more than half of these exports, the figures give optimism in the sense that a large number of enterprises (64) have taken part in export marketing, which should help them acquaint themselves with foreign markets and step up their export targets and achievements.

Plan Strategy: Targets and Achievements

In the context of a liberalized economic system, a plan is only useful insofar as it makes available official data on the actual performance of the economy over the previous period, gives clear guidelines on the strategy to be adopted over the medium to long term, and provides consistent forecasts of trends in the broad macroeconomic variables that the economy must deal with in the next plan period. Accurate figures on the growth in GDP, employment, exports, imports, and sectoral value added are all essential to policymakers in appraising performance and designing appropriate policies for the future. Moreover, the confidence of the business community, both local and foreign, can only be gained if statistics on key variables are perceived as reliable and timely. Recent experience with Egypt's plan documents demonstrates a degree of inconsistency that gives rise to much concern and skepticism.

Examples of glaring inconsistencies can be found in the plan estimates of employment and unemployment and of aggregate and sectoral growth rates for the economy, when compared with data available from separate official sources. Another perturbing feature of the most recent second Five-Year Plan (1987/88–1991/92) is that it fails to specify the prices used (constant or current) in valuing past and future investments. Subject to these major reservations, an attempt is made here to analyze the overall strategy and structural changes as presented in the first and second Five-Year Plan documents.

Main Features of the First and Second Five-Year Plans

The strategy of import substitution is still the basic feature that characterizes both Five-Year Plan strategies. In spite of the Government's pronouncements about export promotion, the package of policies as well as the range of projects actually selected and the goals of self-sufficiency by product are all to satisfy the domestic market without due regard to the notion of comparative advantage.

Both Five-Year Plans have targeted an increasing role for private investment in the economy. The second Five-Year Plan hopes to raise the share of private sector investments to 39 percent of gross fixed investment, up from its estimated share of 24 percent in the previous plan period (1982/83–1986/87). Another common feature of both plans is that public investments are confined to infrastructure and utilities and investment in public enterprises is restricted to rehabilitation and renewal.

Given the sharp decline in investment resources available to the Government over the current Five-Year Plan, the plan document rightly focuses on the need to raise capacity utilization and efficiency rather than to create new capacity in the public sector.

Public Sector Investment and Planning

In spite of the many calls made for decentralization and increased autonomy for the public sector, state-owned enterprises continue to conform to rigid centralized planning procedures. The Ministry of Planning and the National Investment Bank together coordinate public investment across sectors of economic activity according to the Government's budget constraint. What this means is that individual enterprise investment goals are almost invariably tampered with by the Ministry of Planning, and once the final size and composition of the investment budget are approved for an enterprise, the room for change in response to changing conditions becomes virtually impossible.

Not only do public enterprises have to abide by the rigid investment targets specified in the plan documents but their production must also conform to the strict physical output targets according to detailed commodity plans. This planning approach is totally unsuited to the spirit of liberalization, and its negative repercussions permeate the entire decision-making apparatus of public enterprise. This Soviet style of centralized decision making is being abandoned in socialist countries, and it is high time that Egypt discards it in favor of giving public enterprises full autonomy in their investment, finance, and output decisions. Unfortunately, until today, most public enterprises still measure their own productivity in terms of quantity of output at the expense of quality and marketability.

Sectoral Distribution of Private Investment

The private sector's share in gross fixed investment is to increase from the 19 percent achieved in the five-year period 1977–1981/82 and that of 24 percent over the first Five-Year Plan 1982/83–1986/87 to as much as 39 percent of gross fixed investment during the current Five-Year Plan. This targeted increase seems overly optimistic given the economic recession the country is experiencing, with its accompanying decline in domestic absorption. Unless policies can be introduced to shift the incentive regime that now guides trade and investment away from nontradables back toward tradables and away from import substitutes toward exports, it is unlikely that the size of private investment resources envisaged by the plan will materialize.

What is more important, the second Five-Year Plan target of radically transforming the structure of private investment toward the commodity sectors (see Table 3) will be even more difficult to achieve under present conditions. As much as 57 percent of actual private gross fixed investment had been allocated to housing in the first Five-Year Plan. The current Five-Year Plan hopes to reduce the share of housing to 37 percent, in favor of an increase in manufacturing from the 19 percent achieved in the first Five-Year Plan to as much as 36 percent.

What is implied by the sectoral distribution of gross fixed investment in the current plan document is that the private sector's share in manufacturing gross fixed investment will be able to jump from the 20 percent achieved in 1977–1981/82 and the 22 percent achieved in 1982/83–1986/87 to an unrealistic 53 percent during the second Five-Year Plan. In absolute terms, investment undertaken by the private sector in manufacturing is expected to multiply to 3.7 times its value over the previous plan period. The plan document gives no indication of how this dramatic leap is to be achieved.

In policy and strategy terms, the only way these ambitious goals for the private sector can be realized is for the country to adopt a radical package of trade, exchange rate, and tax measures and incentives for export promotion in the style of Turkey in the early 1980s. Given the present untapped potential that exists, for example, in Egypt's textile industry with its comparative advantage, a turnabout from modest performance to dynamic growth can perhaps be envisaged only if a dramatic increase in exports is achieved.

Structural Adjustment and Macroeconomic Policies

Investments since the mid-1970s have been biased toward services rather than the commodity sectors, whose share in gross fixed investment fell from 61 percent during 1966–73 to 49 percent in 1974–81 and to 45 percent in the first Five-Year Plan. This bias has resulted in unbalanced growth, with agriculture and manufacturing suffering the most neglect. Gross fixed investment in agriculture and irrigation as a proportion of gross fixed investment in the economy actually fell from 16 percent in 1966/67–73 (excluding investments in the High Dam) to 7.3 percent in 1974–1980/81 and to 9 percent in the first Five-Year Plan. In manufacturing and mining, their share in gross fixed investment fell from 28 percent to 27 percent to 21 percent over the same time periods.[9] The outcome has been the relatively poor performance of these two sectors as well as the increased dependence of the economy on windfall earnings such as petroleum and workers' remittances.

Consequently, when petroleum prices were hit and all other windfall incomes stagnated, the economy found itself with no fallback position, and a serious economic crisis ensued. Structural adjustment became mandatory to redress the balance between the commodity-producing sectors and other sectors of the economy. It is now clear that Egypt's investment strategy must not only shift from import substitution to export orientation but that this new strategy must be backed by a total package of appropriate macroeconomic policies. These policies should include not only a reformed investment regime but also a revision of the trade and protection regime and of price, employment, and fiscal policies.

Major Issues and Recommendations

This paper has reviewed the investment record of the Infitah and shown that liberalization of the legislation and policy environment has been successful in bringing the private sector back to the fore, with a share of 24 percent of gross fixed investment in the national economy, up from less than 10 percent throughout

---

[9]Figures for 1960–76 are from *Report on Investment Policies over 1959/60 to 1982/83 Period*, Economic and Financial Affairs Committee, Shura Council (Cairo, 1984). Figures for 1977–1986/87 are from Five-Year Plans 1981/82–1986/87 and 1987/88–1991/92.

the 1960s and early 1970s. Law No. 43 has been the major instrument of legislation, and projects executed under it are responsible for about one half of aggregate private investment outside
agriculture.

Two major criticisms of the investment encouragement laws
have been made. One is that they cater only for the large-scale
projects and ignore the medium- and small-scale investor; the other
is that they do not distinguish between high-priority and low-
priority fields of economic activity. The negative result is that
small, labor-intensive investments have been discouraged and that
highly protected consumer goods industries have taken an unduly
large share of total investment resources. The laxity of the Investment Authority in implementing Law No. 43 has also been
responsible for poor achievements in export performance, in spite
of the export target being one of the major goals of the investment
law.

Another important conclusion of this study is that public sector
resources have made a significant contribution to Law No. 43 joint
ventures, with a share of about one third of the total investment
costs of projects approved to date. Yet because the traditional
public sector is still subject to a high degree of centralization and
rigid legislation as regards finance, pricing, and wage determination, this excessive discrimination has meant that public enterprises may sometimes make investment decisions of low priority
to the economy, simply as a way of obtaining favored treatment
under Law No. 43. Immediate reform of public sector legislation
is required to remove the present dualism in the policy environment and to enable an autonomous public sector to make the
necessary improvements in its competitive behavior.

The role of planning in the economy is also in need of revision,
toward reduced centralization and better coordination between
plan targets and the package of macroeconomic policies. Planning
cannot achieve results unless all policies are geared to a clearly
chosen and clearly stated strategy. The import-substitution strategy followed by Egypt since the 1930s must be abandoned in favor
of a bold strategy of export promotion, with far-reaching changes
in the trade and price regimes that until the present imply a strong
anti-export bias.

The reforms suggested for the trade regime include a reduction
in tariff protection, a review of domestic indirect taxes, and re-

moval of the serious price distortions that currently discriminate in favor of production for the domestic market. Reforms of the interest rate and capital market must also be implemented to mobilize domestic savings and channel them into productive investment. One important option would be to allow public enterprises to sell their shares on the stock market, a step that would relieve enterprises of their financial constraints and attract private sector savings into high-priority public investment.

In concluding this paper, it seems fair to say that despite the serious economic crisis that Egypt is experiencing, there is much room for optimism if the Government undertakes its adjustment program with determination. This optimism is based on the fact that much of Egypt's potential is still untapped, so that adjustment policies could bring about dramatic growth based on the export sector leading the economy toward fuller utilization of its rich resources of manpower and manufacturing capacity.

Appendix: Developments in Law No. 43 Projects, 1978–88

Appendix Table 1. Profile of Total Projects Approved, End-1978 and Mid-1988

Projects	Number 1978	Number 1988	Authorized Capital Plus Loans (million Egyptian pounds) 1978	1988	Projects with Egyptian Equity of 90–100 Percent 1978	1988
Manufacturing	243	567	1,047	7,237	49	203
Textiles	*33*	*82*	*295*	*976*	*4*	*29*
Food	32	93	67	678	12	52
Chemicals	*70*	*129*	*113*	*1,610*	*12*	*32*
Wood	*11*	*13*	*16*	*56*	*3*	*5*
Engineering	*40*	*64*	*282*	*1,120*	*6*	*14*
Building materials	*27*	*104*	*222*	*1,535*	*6*	*44*
Metals	*21*	*49*	*36*	*825*	*5*	*17*
Pharmaceuticals	*9*	*33*	*16*	*333*	*1*	*14*
Mining	—	7	—	101	—	3
Agriculture	33	106	251	764	9	52
Tourism	86	112	570	1,867	20	53
Housing	35	85	243	1,210	10	68
Contracting	57	107	570	270	6	39
Services	51	120			8	43
Transport	*10*	*10*	*61*	*76*	*1*	*1*
Health	*13*	*36*	*52*	*252*	*6*	*27*
Consultancy		*26*		*20*		*1*
Petroleum	*9*	*4*	*9*	*176*		
Others	*19*	*42*	*139*	*351*	*1*	*14*
Nonfinancial	505	1,104	2,410	12,167	102	461
Finance	86	265	324	2,347		107
Banks	*37*	*72*	*130*	*690*		*32*
Investment companies	*49*	*193*	*195*	*1,656*		*75*
Grand total	591	1,369	3,450	14,514	102	568

Appendix Table 2. Profile of Total Projects in Production, End-1978 and Mid-1988

Projects	Number 1978	Number 1988	Authorized Capital Plus Loans (million Egyptian pounds) 1978	1988	Estimated Employment 1978	1988
Manufacturing	83	340	64	3,359	6,937	93,912
Textiles		55		867	982	51,256
Food		55		328	1,439	9,002
Chemicals		83		421	2,488	10,351
Wood		12		54	134	2,243
Engineering		32		234	818	4,056
Building materials		47		566	85	6,389
Metals		42		762	961	8,603
Pharmaceuticals		14		127	30	2,010
Mining		3		16	—	368
Agriculture	7	45	37	358	541	6,529
Tourism	22	66	84	880	2,505	6,192
Housing	4	25	124	271	31	87
Contracting		79		206	2,106	29,761
Services	26	85	13	332	872	10,587
Transport	3	8	8	65	453	1,035
Health		19		23		2,041
Consultancy		24		18		417
Petroleum	5	4	6	117		349
Others		30		108	419	6,745
Nonfinancial	150	643	336	5,612	12,992	147,434
Finance	41	210	144	1,823		
Banks	29	67	91	678		
Investment companies	12	143	53	1,145		
Grand total	191	853	479	7,435	12,992	147,434

Appendix Table 3. Profile of Total Projects Under Execution, End-1978 and Mid-1988

Projects	Number 1978	Number 1988	Authorized Capital Plus Loans (million Egyptian pounds) 1978	Authorized Capital Plus Loans (million Egyptian pounds) 1988	Estimated Employment 1978	Estimated Employment 1988
Manufacturing	100	93	614	639	31,046	12,244
Textiles		3		54	15,924	8,849
Food		19		116	1,560	1,337
Chemicals		23		124	3,369	1,712
Wood		12		539	455	
Engineering		10		65	1,576	1,650
Building materials		14		134	6,966	1,989
Metals		1		1	916	35
Pharmaceuticals		11		144	280	2,672
Mining		2		81		
Agriculture	17	18	165	177	2,960	3,668
Tourism	48	25	327	449	14,947	8,016
Housing	22	21	83	202	161	623
Contracting		14		35	7,867	6,962
Services	39	14	86		3,090	5,911
Transport	4		27		355	
Health		8		85	2,057	3,702
Consultancy		3		1		750
Petroleum	2		1			
Others		3		13	678	1,459
Nonfinancial	232	187	1,303	1,683		28,072
Finance	27	13	131	156		
Banks	5	2	32	7		
Investment companies	22	11	98	149		
Grand total	259	200	1,434	1,839	60,071	28,072

Appendix Table 4. Developments in Approved Projects, 1979–89
(In million Egyptian pounds)

Years	Industrial Projects			Services Projects			Finance Projects			Agricultural Projects			Construction			Total		
	Number	Equity	Investment costs	Number	Equity	Investment costs	Number	Equity	Investment costs	Number	Equity	Investment costs	Number	Equity	Investment costs	Number	Equity	Investment costs
6/30/79	199	758	1,935	105	693	1,379	96	1,026	1,126	18	116	249	60	78	266	478	2,671	4,957
1979/80	45	134	300	18	73	143	21	242	362	7	12	20	26	51	100	117	513	927
1980/81	54	472	1,315	22	43	144	54	316	317	16	53	149	18	34	88	174	221	2,014
1981/82	58	399	1,234	20	92	161	25	91	91	11	18	44	16	22	41	130	634	1,568
1982/83	25	82	183	11	62	139	13	24	24	9	29	55	13	89	144	71	288	543
1983/84	49	163	312	20	93	183	5	55	55	23	64	134	13	107	185	110	485	870
1984/85	40	132	294	3	8	19	6	26	26	10	26	41	17	95	201	76	288	581
1985/86	43	166	511	10	44	101	1	3	3	2	2	3	13	76	185	69	292	803
1986/87	34	194	415	13	121	312	16	88	88	6	21	51	12	91	199	81	517	1,068
1987/88	27	323	734	10	61	101	18	253	253	4	13	18	4	35	68	63	685	1,174
Grand total	574	2,823	7,233	232	1,290	2,682	265	2,126	2,345	106	353	764	192	680	1,481	1,369	7,284	14,514
Increase, 1980/81–1983/84	186	1,116	3,044	73	290	627	107	486	487	59	164	342	60	252	458	485	1,628	5,000
Increase, 1984/85–1987/88	144	815	1,954	36	234	533	41	370	370	22	62	113	46	297	473	289	1,782	3,102

Appendix Table 5. Projects Classified by Size of Capital Employed and Capital Intensity per Worker
(Projects in production as of mid-1984)

Projects	Number					Average Capital Employed per Project (In million Egyptian pounds)				
	Less than LE 100,000	LE 100,000– 500,000	LE 500,000– 1 million	LE 1– 10 million	More than LE 10 million	Less than 100,000	100,000– 500,000	500,000– 1 million	1– 10 million	More than 10 million
Manufacturing										
Textiles	—	6	5	13	13	—	0.318	0.748	3	60
Food	—	4	2	19	10	—	0.131	0.680	4	40
Chemicals	1	5	5	38	14	0.064	0.356	0.780	3	21
Wood	1	1	1	3	4	0.088	0.303	0.760	5	20
Engineering	—	6	—	13	7	—	0.300	—	4	22
Building materials	—	—	1	12	7	—	—	0.860	4	97
Metals	—	—	4	18	6	—	—	0.700	3	16
Pharmaceuticals	—	—	1	1	1	—	—	0.980	2	25
Mining	—	1	—	2	—	—	0.400	—	4	—
Agriculture	—	1	1	18	11	—	0.150	0.570	5	42
Tourism	1	5	7	15	17	0.084	0.300	0.700	4	38
Housing	—	—	1	1	2	—	—	0.690	2	22
Contracting	—	3	6	42	10	—	0.400	0.700	3	20
Petroleum	—	—	—	1	3	—	—	—	7	92
Services										
Transport	—	—	1	1	1	—	—	0.800	3	43
Hospitals	—	2	3	8	3	—	0.400	0.900	3	23
Consultancy	2	10	1	6	1	0.078	0.300	0.900	3	14
Others	—	2	1	10	1	—	0.300	0.600	3	61

Appendix Table 6.   Participation of Egyptians, Arabs, and Foreign Countries in Authorized Equity of Total Approved Projects as of End-1978 and Mid-1988

(In million Egyptian pounds)

Nationality	1978 Egyptian Capital	Percent	Arab Capital	Percent	Foreign Capital	Percent	Total	1988 Egyptian Capital	Percent	Arab Capital	Percent	Foreign Capital	Percent	Total
Manufacturing	263	61	75	17	95	21	433	2,004	72	260	9	524	21	2,792
Textiles	66	63	10	9	30	29	105	204	68	47	16	47	16	298
Food	18	72	4	15	4	14	25	212	71	30	10	56	19	298
Chemicals	44	54	24	30	14	17	81	405	68	55	9	136	23	597
Wood	7	76	2	23	1	5	9	24	67	9	25	3	8	35
Engineering	39	44	17	19	32	36	88	297	69	31	7	102	24	431
Building materials	70	82	6	6	10	12	85	500	78	54	8	90	14	644
Metals	12	42	14	49	3	10	29	251	75	29	9	55	16	335
Pharmaceuticals	7	71	1	7	3	26	10	111	72	5	3	38	24	154
Mining	—	—	—	—	—	—		33	94	1	3	1	2	35
Agriculture	75	70	13	12	19	17	106	260	73	57	16	36	10	354
Tourism	170	50	22	7	179	53	336	468	56	219	26	154	18	833
Housing	166	77	43	20	7	3	216	505	91	47	8	2	—	554
Contracting	18	61	1	4	10	34	29	96	76	11	9	17	14	123
Services	42	22	15	8	135	70	192	245	60	19	5	145	35	410
Petroleum	5	56	—	2	3	40	9	17	36	—	—	29	64	46
Nonfinancial	738	55	170	13	444	33	1,342	3,626	69	614	12	978	19	5,217
Finance	168	54	100	32	45	15	314	1,341	63	372	17	412	19	2,126
Banks	74	57	23	13	33	25	130	520	75	49	7	122	18	690
Investment companies	94	51	77	42	13	7	184	822	57	323	22	291	20	1,435
Grand total	906	54	270	16	490	29	1,664	4,970	68	987	14	1,327	18	7,284

Appendix Table 7. Participation of Public Sector in Approved Projects as of June 1988

Projects	Number			Authorized Capital (In million Egyptian pounds)		
	Public sector[a]	Total	Percentage of total	Public sector[b]	Total	Percentage of total
Manufacturing	85	567	15	765	2,793	27
Textiles	*8*	*92*	*10*	*105*	*297*	*35*
Food	*18*	*93*	*19*	*33*	*299*	*11*
Chemicals	*14*	*129*	*11*	*190*	*597*	*32*
Wood	*3*	*13*	*23*	*4*	*36*	*10*
Engineering	*11*	*64*	*17*	*93*	*431*	*22*
Building materials	*19*	*104*	*18*	*135*	*644*	*21*
Metals	*6*	*49*	*12*	*83*	*335*	*25*
Pharmaceuticals	*6*	*33*	*18*	*21*	*154*	*14*
Mining	2	7	29	27	35	77
Agriculture	19	106	18	70	354	20
Tourism	16	112	14	80	839	9
Housing	3	85	4	14	554	3
Contracting	8	107	7	9	126	7
Services	21	116	18	42	310	14
Petroleum	2	4	50	17	46	36
Nonfinancial	156	1,104	14	921	5,057	18
Finance	94	265	35	638	2,126	30
Banks	*42*	*72*	*58*	*249*	*691*	*36*
Investment companies	*52*	*193*	*27*	*389*	*1,435*	*27*
Grand total	250	1,369	18	1,661	7,184	23

[a]Refers to number of projects with public participation.
[b]Refers to total value of authorized capital of projects in which public sector participates.

Comment

Ahmed El-Ghandour

The author successfully presents a lucid and detailed review of Egypt's investment strategy and policies and surveys the legislative and planning framework that has affected the rate and pattern of investment since the early seventies. The paper, however, mainly emphasized issues related to the private sector and in particular investment under Law No. 43. Moreover, from the beginning of the paper the author did not hesitate to confirm that the investment strategy, together with the package of macroeconomic policies adopted since the Infitah of the 1970s, is largely responsible for the suboptimal pattern of investment.

The core of the paper, as the author defines it, is to examine factors responsible for the gap between the optimal pattern of investment—that is, the pattern of investment that should have prevailed if the right strategy, the right policies, and the right performance had been secured—and the suboptimal pattern that actually materialized.

To that end, the paper focuses on two major themes: the first is related to volume, pattern, policies, and performance of private investment during the liberalization era of the early seventies. The second theme is concerned with the nature of the planning process within the context of a liberalized economic system and how much it is responsible for the suboptimal pattern of investment that has already occurred.

While the major part of the paper deals with the analysis of private investment during the Infitah era, the attention paid to investment in the public sector is relatively small. In fact, the preponderance of the share of public investment in the overall investment effort, together with the set of macroeconomic policies related to it, determines the final impact of the plan on the economy as a whole.

In that context, it may be useful to remember that the share of the public sector in total production assets has grown quite large. Public enterprises dominate industry, transport, and financial sec-

181

tors. Even in agriculture, public investment in land reclamation companies, in agricultural marketing, and sometimes in direct production of agricultural commodities is also quite significant. Thus, it is clear that if present research is targeted at investigating factors responsible for the suboptimal pattern of investment of the economy as a whole, it should mainly concentrate on analyzing the system of public investment.

Let us remind ourselves of the present economic situation in Egypt and how it is linked to the performance of public enterprise. This situation may be summed up as a set of serious imbalances and distortions that led to an inefficient system of investment and production. The deficits on the balance of payments and budget have attained critical levels; the current account deficit rose from $2,350 million in 1982/83 to $5,325 million in 1985/86. Recently, the fiscal deficit increased from LE 4,748 million to LE 8,844 million. The external debt was 112.5 percent of gross domestic product (GDP), and the debt-service ratio (related to GDP) was more than 16 percent in 1986/87. Domestic production of commodities has been losing weight in the overall structure of the economy, with the result that the country is becoming more dependent on the outside world for a major part of its consumption and investment. Distortions of price, trade, and foreign exchange regimes are partly responsible for the above-mentioned imbalances and are the root of inefficiencies of production and resource allocation.

There is a general consensus that the investment and performance of the public sector contributed significantly to the forces leading to the present impasse of the Egyptian economy. This is true whether we refer to the overall deficit of the public sector or to the excessively low rate of return on investment in public enterprises.[1]

The above facts may lead one to reject the eminent author's declared contention at the start of her analysis that ". . .the large public sector that had spread its weight across the economy was here to stay. . . ." Such an "ideological" position constitutes a

---

[1] World Bank, "Egypt: Review of the Finances of the Decentralized Public Sector," Vol. I (unpublished, March 1987). See also Said El-Naggar, "Prospects and Problems of Privatization: The Case of Egypt," paper presented to Thirteenth Annual Symposium, Center for Contemporary Arab Studies, Georgetown University, Washington, April 1988.

serious and rigid constraint on the scope and content of the author's analysis of investment in Egypt. Had investment of the public sector been given its due weight in the author's analysis, the diagnosis and policy messages of the paper would have been otherwise.

Regarding the general content of the paper one may also argue some of the author's assumptions. Among those assumptions is the one related to the nature of Sadat's economic system. From the start, the author emphasized that Sadat's Open Door Policy brought about a "radical reorientation toward a market economy" and that "this comprehensive shift was intended to reinstate the domestic private sector. . . ." In fact, it is difficult to accept the author's proposition that Sadat's regime was radically different from Nasser's regime and to pursue the analysis as the author did on the assumption that it is the change of regime that is responsible for all the evils of the present economic situation in Egypt.

In fact, the essence of both systems is statism; a huge and dominant state sector in industry and in services was the fundamental feature of both Nasser's and Sadat's economic and political systems. Liberalization measures brought about by Sadat did not envisage the establishment of a liberal system mainly based on private ownership and initiative. Thus, in explaining economic performance during the liberalization era, the main issue is whether or not the measures above could cope with the inefficiencies of the state-oriented regime as defined by public sector predominance and central planning. Actually, superimposing Sadat's Open Door measures on Nasser's regime deepened the inefficiencies of the latter.

Relevant to this remark is what the author points out about the magnitude of the public sector's contribution to the investment effort through joint ventures under Law No. 43. According to her estimate "at least one third of the total cost of domestic investment under that law has been contributed by Egypt's public sector either in the form of direct equity participation or in the form of long-term loans from public sector banks." Such a dominant share for the public sector clashes with the main logic and basis of a blueprint of a liberal economic system as envisaged by Sadat's Open Door Policy. Whereas such logic entails giving more room to private sector and initiative, the public sector, on the contrary, crowded out investment opportunities available to the private sector. In so doing, the public sector stood against a radical change toward

establishing a liberal economic system. Thus, it may be difficult
not to reject the author's conclusion that the expansion of public
sector enterprises under Law No. 43 is a form of privatization.
Alternatively, it seems more reasonable that expansion of the public sector under Law No. 43 is a sort of "publicization" that stood
against a radical change in the statism of the sixties.

Moreover, extending the previous analysis, one is rather tempted
to reject the paper's stipulation that "expansion of public enterprises under Law No. 43 undermined their competitive position."
Indeed, it seems more plausible to state that such an expansion
extended the monopolistic status of the public sector, thereby
threatening the competitive tendencies in the economy.

In the relatively small part of the paper that deals with plan
strategy, the author examines briefly the performance of public
enterprise and emphasizes decentralization as the means of improving that performance. The paper thereby explicitly discards
privatization as an instrument that could improve the functioning
of public enterprise and could also help the economy rid itself of
a part of the burden that affects, as mentioned earlier, its overall
economic and financial performance. This view may be partly
attributed to the author's a priori value judgment position in favor
of the public sector. In fact, the author focuses on central planning
as the source of all evils for the poor performance of public enterprise in Egypt. Thus, the paper emphasizes that

> In spite of the many calls made in favor of decentralization and in-
> creased autonomy for the public sector, state-owned enterprises con-
> tinue to conform to rigid centralized planning procedures. This plan-
> ning approach is totally unsuited to the spirit of liberalization, and its
> negative repercussions permeate the entire decision-making apparatus
> of public enterprise.

Though one would not disagree with the author over the shortcomings of the planning process in Egypt, it is difficult to accept
her argument that decentralization should be the core of a program
for public enterprise reform. In fact, analysis of measures and
procedures for decentralization that have taken place throughout
the liberalization era, and of those measures and procedures undertaken by Nasser's regime itself clearly shows that they failed
to bring about a tangible improvement in the performance of
public enterprises. On the contrary, some of these measures were

mainly responsible for a part of the negative aspects of the present public sector situation. A World Bank study emphasizes that the freedom given to nonfinancial public enterprises to contract foreign loans induced many enterprises to borrow excessively from abroad without regard to their debt-service capacity.[2]

Apparently, in connection with privatization, the paper may not have made a sufficiently clear distinction between decentralized planning procedures for the public sector (where, given the nature of public ownership, central authority bureaucratic directives are indispensible) and liberal market forces based on private initiatives and expectations. Indeed, a private company facing competitive conditions must be efficient to survive and grow. The transfer of property rights from the public to the private domain creates new attitudes and incentives capable of raising standards of efficiency. More important, in explaining the attitude toward decentralization versus privatization, the paper does not sufficiently examine investment and performance of the public sector within a wider framework that takes into account the difficulties of the economy as a whole and that establishes a comprehensive reform program.

Earlier discussion of difficulties facing the Egyptian economy and their interrelationship with the poor performance of public enterprise made privatization an important ingredient of any viable reform program. The impact of privatization on productivity and on budget and balance of payments deficits should appear here as a major issue.

The author quite appropriately pointed out that the role assigned by the current Five-Year Plan to the private sector is overly optimistic. She notes that according to the plan's estimates the share of the private sector in gross fixed investment has to increase from 24 percent during the first Five-Year Plan to the high percentage of 39 percent during the current Five-Year Plan. In fact, one notices on reading the plan documents that they do not reveal how such a large share is calculated. The feeling is that this estimate is a residual left after the planner has exhausted all potential government finance of the overall public investment package. Nevertheless, given this ambitious target for the private sector, one should entirely agree with the author that for this goal to be realized it is

[2]World Bank, "Egypt: Review of the Finances of the Decentralized Public Sector," Vol. I (unpublished, March 1987), p. iv.

necessary for the country to adopt a radical package of trade, exchange rate, and tax measures and incentives, and a reformed investment regime. Relevant to the author's conclusion, one might ask whether the new investment regime in Egypt has sufficient potential as a positive step forward and in particular whether the new law succeeded in making at least a partial breakthrough in overcoming the obstacles to establishing an appropriate investment climate.

One cannot disagree with the author's emphasis on the need for an export promotion drive. Nevertheless, it is difficult to accept export promotion investment as an alternative to import substitution. Both are strategies that are not mutually exclusive.

A successful import–substitution strategy may have the double advantage of improving the balance of payments deficit in the medium term, while at the same time paving the road for the newly developed industries to become important exporters to the international market.

In fact, the problem with the import–substitution policy in Egypt does not reside in the concept itself but rather in the way the strategy has been conceived and adopted. At the conceptual level, import substitution does not imply development of activities to "satisfy the domestic market without due regard to the notion of comparative advantage."

In so saying, one erroneously identifies import substitution with self-sufficiency. In other words, while the import-substitution policy may be looked at as a corollary of List's infant industry argument, self-sufficiency is a corollary of the autarky planning of the Soviet bloc. Given the very large range of industries and activities that a developing country could launch, there is no need to start import-substitution strategy in the fields in which the country cannot have a comparative advantage in the long run. In the light of the above argument, earlier investment in the textile industry proved successful in paving the way for Egypt's textile exports to the international market, while investment in iron and steel, automobiles, aluminum, and the like is a self-sufficiency device that deprived Egypt of investing in quite a broad range of activities in which it would have had a comparative advantage in the long run. Moreover, taking into account direct and indirect effects, the investment in the automobile industry and the like did not result in net savings of foreign exchange.

The paper calls for reform by introducing a comprehensive package of "appropriate" macroeconomic policies including reformed investment, exchange rate, trade, protection, price, employment, and fiscal policies and regimes, together with an export promotion strategy. That reform package should be able to "bring about dramatic growth" and tap a significant portion of Egypt's potential that is "still untapped."

In this respect the eminent author accepts the consensus among economists and policymakers that there is dire need for macroeconomic reform. It is the job of economists to derive the stylized formula and specific mechanics of such an "appropriate" package.

8

Investment Process in the Gulf Cooperation Council States

Abdullah Al-Kuwaiz

Development is in essence a series of changes in the socioeconomic structure, namely, in areas of manufacturing, agriculture, infrastructure, and services, such as education and health. The investment process itself generates these sectors' output, whether direct (industry and agriculture) or indirect (infrastructure and services).

At the outset it may be appropriate to point out that years before the establishment of the Gulf Cooperation Council (GCC), joint work was undertaken officially and privately on both bilateral and multilateral levels. Thus the establishment of the Council has served to institutionalize joint work and to organize it within the framework of endorsed agreements and documents. In other words, rather than being haphazard and seasonal, work is now being carried out within a collective institutionalized framework that provides a suitable environment for conceptualization and development.

With this perspective in view, the first part of this paper briefly addresses the investment dimension of the work objectives delineated in the Council's documents, whereas the second part investigates aspects inherent in their implementation, and the third part deals with the investment factors dictated by the economies of the GCC states. The final part presents recommendations for augmenting the effectiveness of the joint investment activity in the Council.

The Investment Dimension of the Council's Objectives

Article 4 of the GCC Charter summarizes the institutional aspect as finding an appropriate and balanced environment for investment in the GCC states through establishment of identical regulations in the areas of:

- economic and financial affairs;
- commercial, customs, and communications affairs; and
- legislative and administrative affairs.

The article also calls for "enhancing scientific and technological advancement in areas of industry, mining, agriculture, animal and marine resources, establishment of scientific research centers, joint projects and encouragement of private sector cooperation . . . ," within the framework of "realizing coordination, integration and interdependence among the member states in all fields."

The Consolidated Economic Agreement was concluded to determine and detail those objectives, as it urges the member states to agree upon a number of arrangements to achieve coordination and integration among their economies. By reviewing the Agreement's articles, we find that the most significant of the arrangements that are directly related to investment are the following:

- Freedom to import and export products of national origin without imposing tariff or nontariff barriers thereon;
- Establishment of a uniform customs tariff with the objective of protecting national products;
- Granting all facilities to transit trade and exempting it from duties;
- Coordination of export and import policies and regulations;
- Creating a collective negotiating power to support the negotiating status of the GCC states in the area of importing their basic needs and exporting their major products;
- Freedom of movement of individuals and capital and freedom to own and operate businesses and real estate;
- Encouraging the private sector in member states to establish joint projects;
- Coordinating industrial activity and setting up policies and procedures for realizing industrial development, consolidating industrial legislation and regulations, locating industries according to their relative characteristics, and encouraging the establishment of basic and complementary industries among member states;
- Stressing the establishment of joint projects in industry, ag-

riculture, and services with public, private, or mixed capital
to achieve economic integration;

- Cooperation in areas of applied and technological research
  and sciences, including the conclusion of consolidated agreements for technology transfer;
- According the same treatment to transportation owned by
  other member states' nationals when passing through or toward each other's territories as to its own;
- Cooperation in areas of transportation and communication
  and in coordinating construction of infrastructure;
- Unification of investment laws and regulations; and
- Coordination of financial, monetary, and banking policies.

The document on the objectives and policies of development
plans adopted by the GCC states included a number of comprehensive objectives relating to human development by upgrading
the citizens' social, health, academic, and cultural levels, as well
as developing and diversifying the production base and completing
the required applied and technological infrastructure among member states. The objectives gave special significance to the private
sector by encouraging it to interact positively with government
policies by

- Using the opportunity to operate, manage, and maintain some
  of the utilities run by the state;
- Participating in appropriating and managing some industries
  established by the state;
- Encouraging the establishment of joint stock companies;
- Finding means of trading company shares with the objective
  of encouraging investment;
- Contributing to the development and execution of training
  programs;
- Conducting further studies on investment opportunities and
  on the economic feasibility of projects in production sectors;
- Giving the private sector priority in implementing contracting
  activities; and
- Encouraging the establishment of national companies to invest
  funds locally.

The document on a consolidated strategy for industrial development was in line with the document on the objectives and policies of development plans. It concentrated on expanding the pro-

duction base and its influence on the role of industry in realizing balanced development in all the GCC states and in increasing its contribution to the gross national product (GNP).

Investment Process in the GCC

The initiative for encouraging investment focuses on the institutional structure and on creating legal and administrative conditions appropriate for carrying out investment activities. It is therefore consistent with the prevailing economic philosophy in the GCC states and represents the implementation of the objectives discussed in the previous section. From this standpoint the most prominent landmarks in GCC history with a direct bearing on investment can be summed up as follows:

- To cancel customs duties on natural resources and industrial, animal, and agricultural products of national origin. Among the objectives such an action can accomplish is that national products will be better able to compete with foreign ones.
- To allow producers (whether persons or corporate bodies) to export their products direct to any of the member states without the need for a local agent. This action will free national products from any extra costs such as an agent's commission and hence they will become better able to compete.
- To give priority to local products and products of national origin in government projects. This will be an extra incentive in the area of marketing that was not applicable in most of the GCC states before establishment of the GCC.
- To treat the means of transportation owned by GCC nationals on an equal basis with national ones when passing through any of the member states' territories and to endorse consolidated transit regulations. This action will increase competition and decrease transportation fares among the GCC states.
- To grant the required facilities to ships and vessels owned by any of the member states or their citizens and treat them the same as national ones. This action will enable shipping companies to compete and will therefore encourage investment.
- To allow GCC nationals to engage in retail trade. Practice in the wholesale trade will be allowed as of March 1, 1990, and it is to be hoped that this action will expand the marketing

outlets for national products and increase competition, with the aim of creating suitable bases for investment.

- To give GCC nationals the right to obtain loans from industrial banks and funds. The objective behind such a procedure is to provide investment opportunities to all GCC nationals and not to confine them to nationals of certain states. This will augment competition and provide investors with more flexible options.
- To allow GCC nationals to appropriate shares of joint stock companies and to transfer them in conformity with the relevant controls, with the objective of encouraging investors to invest in all GCC states without the need for any arrangement except a project feasibility study.
- To accomplish equality of taxation among GCC nationals. This action is intended to fulfill the rights of citizenship in the area of investment and to encourage investors to invest locally.
- Studies on joint projects. The GCC Secretariat-General has studied a number of projects; some proved to be economically feasible and are now being carried out (a company to produce pure breeds of fowl, a company for the production and marketing of seeds and seedlings, and a reinsurance company). Moreover, national airline companies established a mutual company for supplying aircraft from their companies at London's Heathrow Airport. The shareholders' base has been expanded in a number of joint stock companies in the GCC states (such as Saudi Cables and a telephone manufacturing project) to which a number of the Council's nationals have subscribed. Arrangements for establishing a company for manufacturing poultry and dairy equipment in the United Arab Emirates are now under way.

The Secretariat-General in collaboration with the Gulf Investment Corporation has completed preliminary feasibility studies for 20 projects; the Corporation will promote a number of them and establish them in cooperation with private sector companies in member states.

The Secretariat-General also completed a study on the institutional and organizational aspects of the joint projects and the policies adopted by the GCC states to encourage such projects. This study deals with issues relating to financing and the incentives required for activating investment in these projects. It proposed specific policies, and the possibility of their being adopted by member states will be discussed.

- Joint corporations. At its third session the Council agreed on establishing the Gulf Investment Corporation (GIC) with a capital of $2.1 billion. Among its objectives are the promotion and incorporation of industrial, agricultural, mining, and other projects. The GIC is currently taking part in four production projects while studying investment opportunities in a number of other projects, some in collaboration with the Secretariat-General.

  The GCC standards and specifications authority was established to contribute to standardizing the specifications for national industries and imported commodities, with the intention of expanding the market to make it more attractive to investors as well as to satisfy standards of excellence, quality, consumer protection issues, and environment preservation requirements.

  To protect industrial patents, the GCC states are currently studying the establishment of a patent office. They are also investigating the possibility of establishing an arbitration center to handle, among other issues, any disputes that may arise from investment activities. This action will further enhance investors' confidence.

- Consolidation of procedures and regulations. To improve the legal atmosphere for investment, to provide more confidence, and to bring the legal systems in the GCC states closer to each other in legal provisions, it was agreed to consolidate a number of systems with a direct relationship to investment and economic activities in general, such as guidelines for commercial agencies and trademarks; the system for investment of foreign capital; the system to protect industrial products of national origin; rules for coordinating and encouraging the establishment of industrial projects; and general principles of a consolidated industrial system.

  The Secretariat-General has also completed the draft of the commercial law and the model insurance law for GCC states. Owing to the circumstances of the administrative systems in member states and their desire to complete suitable frameworks to guarantee the successful application of these systems, most of the arrangements are in the form of guidelines.

- Monetary and banking areas. Most developing countries are suffering a shortage in their foreign currency assets and a weakness in their banking system, which in most cases is either a branch of a foreign bank or state owned, which curbs their ability to contribute effectively to encouraging investment for administrative or technical reasons. But in GCC states it is different, owing to the abundance of their foreign currency assets, the fact that money transfers among them are not subject to restrictions, and the relative stability of the exchange rates of their currencies. This solves a major problem normally faced by interstate investment, as the exchange rate risks become less acute and the presence of a modern net of commercial and specialized banks with connections to international markets makes the investor's task easier.
- Infrastructure. The GCC states enjoy modern infrastructure, including roads, ports, communications, and power stations. The GCC programs are directed toward continuous development and interconnection of this infrastructure to encourage communication, provide low-cost energy, and cut down transportation expenses between production and distribution areas locally or abroad.
- Investment incentives. In past years the GCC states have established a number of incentives with the aim of expanding the production base by offering loans and industrial estates and providing the necessary services at subsidized rates, as well as exempting from customs duties industrial inputs (such as equipment and raw materials) while increasing the customs tariff on similar imports, provided that certain conditions are satisfied by local products.

     The GCC states are currently taking the action necessary to consolidate these incentives, by permitting loans and government purchasing policies and by consolidating services and fuel prices.

Investment Factors in the GCC States

The preceding parts of this paper have reviewed the investment aspect of GCC objectives based on the documents issued and on the objectives accomplished so far that have a direct impact on the activation of investment and the creation of a suitable environment for it.

Nevertheless, the institutional and legal aspects are only a part of the components that should be available for the establishment of effective service and production investments. A review of the structure of the GCC states' economies brings out a number of adverse factors that hinder the positive aspects in these economies (that is, the availability of purchasing power, financing, and low-cost energy sources, in addition to the availability of infrastructure, a variety of incentives, and market expansion that has occurred since establishment of the GCC). The presence of such factors prevents these positive aspects being utilized in the short and medium term. In other words, the expansion of the market and the accomplishment of the institutional and legal frameworks will take longer to achieve at national and regional levels.

In my estimation the major negative factors are the following:

- The structural composition of the GCC economies is characterized by the fact that they have a single source of income—oil—which forms about 90 percent of export revenue. Moreover, GNP growth is significantly dependent on demand for oil and on prices that are subject to international market conditions.

- Besides the availability of economic, environmental, legal, and institutional requirements, the success of any investment activity is attributed to the presence of a successful business organizer who is capable of selecting investment opportunities and is willing to bear the risk. While we appreciate the efforts exerted by businessmen who are first of all merchants, and while we appreciate their attempts in the fields of services and industrialization, the movement in this direction is still limited. In the field of natural resources, the national labor force is scarce, and there is a marked dependence on foreign labor. On the other hand, the nonhydrocarbon raw materials needed for industrial purposes are limited, the absence of a well-established technological base, and the limited size of the market do not justify the establishment of a large number of industries.

- Despite the unanimity that in the long run collective economic action serves the best interests of the community, the situation is different in the short run. There is tension between the pole

of collective action as laid down in the Charter of the Council
and the pole of local national interests. This is not unusual
under circumstances of weak collective organizations and inadequate joint action.

There is no doubt that in recent years we are beginning to
face this phenomenon and its ramifications. Member countries
are jealous of their sovereignty and national interests. At the
same time the process of restructuring at the national level
still lags behind the institutional and legal requirements of
integration.

The slowdown of economic growth following the decline
in the demand for oil as well as in its price and the value of
the dollar checks the progress toward integration and puts an
additional responsibility on the private sector not only as the
leader in development but also as a driving force for joint
action.

Recommendations

To enhance the joint work within the GCC framework requires
employing all approaches and possibilities to break the deadlock
of the factors mentioned above. However, investment and development in general are considered the means of realizing such
a goal, as the only alternative to expansion of the production base
is to submit to external conditions that are beyond the control of
the GCC states and therefore serious work in this direction does
not depend only on a single component. For example, the legal
and institutional circumstances provided by the establishment of
the Council have not resulted in essential changes in the problems
facing its members' economies.

Even if we are aware that solving some of these problems falls
within a long-term perspective, we should not yield to this justification. Many contemporary serious development experiences
have proved that a strong will is capable of combating hardships
or at least of mitigating them.

Academic and field studies have proved that, from the perspective of appropriate and pragmatic solutions, joint work in the
long term will result in a net increase in the aggregate income of
the parties without it being necessarily at the expense of any of
them.

The importance of seriously considering the development issue in the GCC states from a comprehensive perspective that mobilizes all possibilities stems from this belief. The following is an attempt to explore such possibilities.

Expansion and Diversification of the Production Base

This goal can be achieved through conventional or modern methods. For instance, joint projects are an instrument in several selected industries to realize positive interconnection with established industries or to establish new ones. This method, in addition to contributing to the expansion of the production base, contributes to accomplishing an interconnection between the economies of the GCC states, particularly if we take into consideration the similarity of their production structures, which do not conform with the classical approach to integration that is based on an exchange of commodities.

There is also the economic balance approach, where the foreign supplier counterbalances his contracts with projects in which the private sector takes part. This approach will achieve the transfer of foreign technology as well as contributing to the expansion of the production base. We believe that the collective adoption of this approach is a positive contribution toward the realization of development and integration.

A free trade zone was established in Dubai, United Arab Emirates, and attracted many foreign companies. The GCC states have to evaluate the positive aspects of this experiment in terms of its impact on the production base.

Support for the Role of the GIC and the National Lending Institutions

The GIC is the investment arm of the GCC. The establishment of or participation in production projects in the GCC states is one of its objectives. Any step in this direction requires a more objective evaluation of the GIC business outlook on investment opportunities in the GCC states at present. With regard to national lending institutions, GCC nationals have been allowed to borrow for industrial projects on an equal basis with nationals of the state concerned. Intensification of meetings between these institutions may result in increasing lending opportunities.

Suitable Mechanism for Effective Government Contribution in Joint Work

There is an apparent hesitation concerning the contribution of government to joint projects based on a belief in the free economy principle and the major role the private sector should play, but, in practice, concerns about economic development and national security may contradict this principle even in countries where it originated. National security is often closely related to development. It should not be taken as an invitation to establish a bureaucracy of public enterprises. But if matters are left to a free economy, it could have only negative consequences in an area that lacks a diversified national resources base (including the private sector) and depends on a single depleting source of income.

Linking Lending and Development Aid with Trade Policy

The GCC states are still playing a major role in granting loans and development aid. It is obvious that lending relations are connected with trade relations by stimulating the response of the borrowing countries to their imports from GCC states or by paying part of the loans in the form of manufactured or intermediate goods (an agreement on trade policy is assumed here).

Relations with Neighboring Countries

Relations with neighboring countries should be regulated through agreements and a number of joint projects should be established that can be individually executed and that can contribute to solving the problem of the limits of the market in the GCC states.

Consolidating the Customs Tariff

Among the incomplete steps in GCC joint work is the consolidation of the customs tariff in conformity with Article 4 of the economic agreement. Since one of the objectives of tariff consolidation is to protect national products against competing foreign products, the construction of a customs wall through tariff consolidation becomes an important requirement of joint work.

Mechanism to Solve Disputes

As a result of canceling tariffs on interstate trade, increasing the exchange of trade, and allowing the practice of economic and professional activities, it is inevitable that some disputes will arise in the beginning. The containment of such disputes entails the establishment of an effective mechanism to solve them, which will then be followed by an increase in joint work.

Incentives

We have indicated above the numerous incentives provided by the GCC states with the intention of expanding the production base, and because such incentives differ from one state to another within the GCC, the provision of a balanced environment requires the consolidation of these incentives.

Comment

Mahsoun Galal

Before presenting my comments I should like to thank Mr. Abdullah Al-Kuwaiz, the Assistant Secretary General for Economic Affairs in the Gulf Cooperation Council (GCC), for undertaking this study on the investment process in the GCC states. I am sure all of you agree that he is perhaps the best qualified to discuss the subject of the joint effort, given his familiarity with, and active involvement in, this initiative.

Mr. Al-Kuwaiz subdivided his research paper into four main parts. In the first he addressed the institutional, legal, and organizational aspects of the Council, which are mainly, if not entirely, guidelines gleaned from the cooperative experience of the Council states. Many of the agreements reached by the Council owe their success to the provisions and aspirations of these guidelines; prime examples are the Consolidated Economic Agreement and the Articles of Association of the GCC. If anything is to be said of this, it is that we fully agree that applying these clauses or agreements would definitely promote the progress of the joint economic effort within GCC states generally.

As the author pointed out in his paper, while these organizational, legal, and institutional aspects are important, they remain an aid or a guideline, without the power to implement or enforce provisions (which, of course, is only natural). Thus, to strengthen cooperative ties or the joint effort, individuals, institutions, and society at large must acknowledge the need to translate aspirations and agreements into concrete and practical action.

The similarity between the regulations and laws governing investment and economic transactions in general is certainly an important factor influencing the progress of cooperation and coordination. However, there is an insufficiency or even absence of these laws—as well as mechanisms for their enforcement—in certain GCC states, which therefore requires intensified efforts in this field.

The second part of the paper sheds light on the investment

process within the GCC, most of which is regulated by the documents and agreements of the Council, and there are indications of some achievements in this area. If these achievements seem modest, the reasons are understandable: GCC cooperation is a relatively recent development and the economies of its countries are very similar. As the paper indicates, an intensive joint effort is lacking. This similarity, and the lack of integration, in many ways augments the difficulty of coordinating the joint effort and achieving a common collective interest. But it also provides opportunities for coordination, particularly in dealings with the outside world and in avoiding duplication of domestic investments.

When discussing joint project studies or the establishment of joint institutions, the author notes that pre-feasibility studies have been completed for 20 projects; also, the Gulf Investment Corporation was established as the "investment arm" of the GCC, and this Corporation has participated in 4 productive projects since its establishment. That is, of course, a modest achievement, particularly when compared with the thousands of active productive projects in the Council states, or with the hopes attached to such joint GCC institutions and the means available.

In general, despite the recentness of this experience, one may legitimately ask about the extent of social welfare achieved in the course of the GCC's joint effort. Would it have been possible to achieve what was achieved by employing or merging available resources if they had been disposed of differently? In other words, what is the "alternative opportunity cost"? These questions are difficult, and their answers are elusive; nevertheless, they are legitimate.

In the third part of his paper the author addresses the limits to investment in GCC countries. A close examination of these limits leaves no doubt as to their reality, and one must acknowledge that they are formidable challenges that cannot be made easier except through serious concerted effort. These challenges include

- Structural imbalances in the economies of the GCC;
- Limited markets;
- The lack of intensity in the joint effort, which may be described as weak linkages in the integration of GCC economies owing to their similarity;
- The dichotomy between national sovereignty and joint effort.

To overcome these and other challenges, the author proposed some valuable scientific recommendations. I would like to add the following:

- The need to avoid duplicating active economic projects in the various GCC countries, which only serves to provoke more intense competition in markets that are already narrow and limited, in spite of the considerable purchasing power enjoyed. The introduction of a coordinating body may be required.

- A number of industrial projects that emerged during the boom period later faltered and now suffer from the problems of the post-boom phase. As these projects contain national resources, I would suggest that a "GCC shareholding company" be formed to manage and assume ownership of companies and projects in default. Joint companies can play their part in salvaging the situation by adopting a long-term development perspective—precisely the reverse of the commercial perspective, which calls for rapid and immediate profits.

- The paper drew attention to the need to unify incentive schemes for industrial development in GCC countries in a bid to achieve equal investment opportunities. Prominent among these incentives are development loans provided by financial lending institutions. It may be appropriate to call for the reappraisal of the lending policies of these funds and to request that they refinance active projects in default with additional or medium-term loans, thus helping to revive these projects.

    Such an initiative provides an opportunity to preserve public funds previously lent and to preserve private resources invested with them, in addition to playing a part in redressing the structural imbalances discussed in the paper.

- In confirming the contents of the paper, and to contribute to resolving the structural imbalances in GCC economies, projects need to be established in other productive sectors. An intensification of joint efforts to identify additional investment opportunities will be required, and joint GCC institutions could play a prominent part in this effort.

- It is imperative that investment opportunities in attractive projects be opened for the GCC countries' private sectors, without limiting their choices by making promising projects the monopoly of joint GCC companies. Such monopolization would create unjustifiable delays in implementation and cause the private sector to compete for less feasible projects.

- Abundant financial and energy resources (including their basic outputs) are the most important comparative advantages enjoyed by the GCC region, and it is natural for these advantages to be reflected in investment opportunities in the region. Therefore, there is no apparent reason why basic materials and energy should not be provided to local industries, with subsidization, especially where higher value added is achieved than can be obtained from the sale of these materials in external markets.

Finally, it is noteworthy that the establishment of the GCC was followed by the formation of other Arab associations. We hope that the precedent thus set will lead to greater and wider Arab economic integration and coordination, an objective that has unfortunately met with failure over the past three decades. It is also hoped that this experience will expand and unify the Arab market as a whole and increase the volume of inter-Arab visible trade and not split into small economic blocs or coalitions within the Arab world that could be swept away by the rapid globalization of the world's major economic blocs. The importance of Arab economic cooperation and coordination rests on (1) national security considerations, (2) the presence of opportunities for integration, and (3) the need to expand markets.

9

Investment Policies in Iraq, 1950–87

Abdel-Monem Seyed Ali

The emphasis on investment as a basic and strategic component of a country's economic and social development should perhaps not be overdone. It is not, of course, the only component, for there are other strategic factors, such as entrepreneurial ability, the required skills and know-how, the efficient utilization of resources, political and social stability, and other elements that complement the factor of capital. But investment remains one of the most important determinants of a country's economic growth. An examination of Iraq's investment policies at this point is thus quite timely, particularly in view of the special conditions the country is currently experiencing after its emergence from a war that proved long, costly, and far-reaching in its economic and social ramifications.

Naturally, macroeconomic policy (financial, monetary, trade, price, and wage), as well as foreign exchange, plays a major part in investment policy and in determining general investment trends. They also have important implications for development strategies and thus for investment strategies in general.

Our aim in this study is to examine the investment policies of Iraq and their evolution from 1950 to the present, focusing on volume of investments, their sectoral distribution and impact on development, the relative share of the public and private sectors, the position taken regarding foreign investment in the country, and the role of macroeconomic policies and their effectiveness in this regard.

It will become apparent in the course of this discussion that three strategic variables were most influential in the determination of

Iraq's investment policy and trends for the period under consideration. These are

- The oil factor, or more specifically, oil production, exports, and revenues, and the foreign exchange generated. (Iraqi investments, which contain a high foreign component, were heavily dependent on this factor.)
- The social imperatives of the ruling party.
- Political changes that have occurred in the country since the fifties and seventies.

These three variables directly influenced general trends in the country's investment policies in terms of the role of the public and private sectors, the role of domestic investment, and, finally, in terms of the nature and impact of international monetary, financial, and development policies on these national investment policies.

Perhaps the most important activities reflecting such policies were the national construction and development plans announced by successive governments during the four decades since 1950. It is both natural and logical to turn to these primary sources for basic information on the evolution of investment policies in Iraq during this period. But the emphasis will ultimately be on contemporary investment policies, that is, those of the late 1980s. However, this period is marked by Iraq's recent emergence from a hard and protracted war that dragged on for some eight years. The war was a major factor behind the reconsideration of a number of economic and social imperatives that had prevailed in the seventies and the first half of the eighties. It will become apparent in the course of this study that political changes in 1958 and in the decade that followed led to basic changes in the country's investment policy. Oil was also pivotal in inducing change during the fifties, and then again in the seventies. However, at every stage, the social and political perspectives of the ruling party tended to color the general direction of these changes, because the process of development in Iraq—and thus Iraq's investment policies—was not subject only to economic considerations but also to other, noneconomic considerations. These noneconomic considerations nevertheless permit one to gauge the achievements of the policies, their performance, their shortcomings, and their evolution in terms of size, direction, and impact in every sphere—economic, social, and political.

Given these (noneconomic) considerations, which were linked in turn with the economically and politically strategic factor of oil, our examination of the evolution of Iraq's investment policies over the past four decades will be within the framework of the economic and political changes that occurred during that period. The first stage is from the early fifties up to 1958, the second is 1958–64, the third, 1964–68, and finally, 1968 to the present. A significant part of the long stretch from 1968 to the present was dominated by the war between Iraq and the Islamic Republic of Iran, which continued until August 1988. This phase witnessed important economic developments that began in 1982 and acquired practical importance for Iraq's investment policies as of 1987. These developments will continue to have a major impact on investment policy well into the next decade.

In this context, our investigation of Iraq's investment policies has been divided into four parts. The first part considers the evolution of these policies in terms of the development plans approved during each phase, namely, the decade of the fifties up to 1958, the sixties up to 1968, the seventies up to 1980, and finally the war years of the eighties up to the present. For each phase, we shall consider the volume of investment and sectoral allocations after discussing briefly the economic and noneconomic factors influencing every aspect of investment policymaking.

The second part of this study considers the status of these policies vis-à-vis the public sector, private sector, and the role of each in the national economy.

The third part considers briefly the position adopted regarding foreign investment in the country, while the fourth part attempts to examine the role of macroeconomic policies in the national economy generally. This includes the effectiveness of financial, monetary, price, and trade policies, foreign exchange, wages and salaries, and the impact of these variables on the size and mode of capital formation, on economic resource utilization and distribution between the various productive sectors, on the amount of foreign exchange earned, on the balance of payments, and, finally, on the level of economic performance in general and economic growth in particular.

This examination should enable us to arrive at definite conclusions regarding investment policies in Iraq and to forecast just what can or cannot be achieved during the next decade, within the limits of uncertainty that such forecasting entails and the relative conservatism of our estimates.

Investment Policies, 1950–58

Oil began to play a significant role in Iraq's economy during the early fifties, helping to finance the Government's budget as well as development projects. The starting point was the increase in oil revenues that began in 1951, following the fifty-fifty profit-sharing agreement on royalties, which had motivated the Government to establish Iraq's Development Board in 1950. The Government assigned 70 percent of these oil revenues to the Development Board to finance major capital development projects in the country. The Board was charged with preparing development plans that the Ministry of Development, established in 1953, proceeded to execute and finance, passing both responsibilities on to the ministries concerned once the process was under way. However, the Board's tasks did not include economic policymaking for the country as a whole, nor were the institutions directly concerned with the development process, such as the Industrial Bank and the Agricultural Bank, subject to the Board's authority. Neither was the Board permitted to manage the investment of private sector savings or interfere in the preparation of the government budget or guide financial and banking institutions or even control the supply of foreign exchange earnings. Its functions were restricted to preparing development programs and executing only the programs assigned to it with the oil revenues so allocated.[1]

Be that as it may, the large increase in oil revenues during the early fifties, and the establishment of the Development Board with its assignment of 70 percent of these revenues to investment objectives, marked the advent of a new economic policy based on large-scale government planning and involvement, and with that a dynamic and highly centralized investment policy. These developments were preceded in the period immediately following the Second World War by the establishment of the Industrial Bank and the Agricultural Bank. Both provided long-term loans for investment and development ventures, clearly illustrating the trend

---

[1]Jawad Hashim and others, *Appraisal of Economic Growth in Iraq, 1950–1970*, Part II, "Developing Commodity Sectors," pp. 196–97.

toward encouraging private sector participation in government investment ventures, especially in industry. The subsequent emergence of the Development Board served to reinforce this trend further.

During this time, the Government was influenced by a number of reports and studies undertaken by specialized foreign missions. These also contributed to an explanation of the Government's economic and investment policies, whether aggregate, sectoral, or geographic. The reports were placed at the disposal of the Development Board, and a brief description of each follows.

- The International Bank for Reconstruction and Development (IBRD) report, *The Economic Development of Iraq.*[2] This 1952 report called for establishing a balanced government investment plan and improving the country's irrigation potential, dams, roads, agriculture, health, and education; in other words, investing in infrastructure and utilizing agricultural output and oil to establish industries that were tailored to meeting basic domestic requirements. The IBRD mission urged the Government to encourage private investors rather than to assume ownership of projects. The mission's report became the basis for the Development Board's investment policies and the development work that followed.[3]

- The Danish economist, Carl Iversen's *A Report on Monetary Policy in Iraq*, 1954.[4] Iversen emphasized the need for a monetary policy that can secure the maximum possible economic balance and stability, expanding in a stable fashion to avoid inflation while maintaining adequate foreign exchange reserves. He underscored the need for coordination between monetary policy and investment spending by the Development Board, and the need to base this spending on coordinating expenditures and earnings on the one hand and expenditures and resources available for project implementation

[2]International Bank for Reconstruction and Development, *The Economic Development of Iraq*, Report of a mission organized by the IBRD at the request of the Government of Iraq (Washington: IBRD, 1952).

[3]Kathleen M. Langley, *The Industrialization of Iraq* (Cambridge, Massachusetts: Harvard University Press, 1962), p. 83.

[4]Carl Iversen, *A Report on Monetary Policy in Iraq* (Baghdad: National Bank of Iraq, 1954).

on the other. His conclusions prompted the Government to take seriously the threat of inflation that was expected, and in turn impelled it to adopt a free import policy consistent with the continuous spending on development typical of development programs at that time.[5] The report also argued that industrialization was not a strategic factor in development, although Iversen did appreciate the importance of industrialization over the long run.

- Lord Salter's report (1955), *The Development of Iraq: A Plan of Action*.[6] Salter emphasized the importance of the country's natural resources, especially arable land and abundant water, and the need to give greater attention to irrigation, drilling, and agricultural development. He also drew attention to population growth and the constant increase in the demand for food. Agricultural development was necessary for both meeting domestic demand for food and increasing exports. He did not regard industrialization as urgent and called for limited industrial growth, which was both desirable and inevitable, affirming that the Development Board should invest some of its resources in projects leading to rapid and substantial returns, in particular large-scale housing ventures. Salter's report prompted the Board to form a special division for housing affairs, in addition to irrigation projects and the provision of immediate assistance to farmers, all of which would benefit every stratum of society.[7]

- Arthur D. Little report (1952), *A Plan for Industrial Development*.[8] This company drew up an industrial scheme that would provide, at a cost of 43 million Iraqi dinars, direct employment for 35,000 workers and indirectly employ 25,000 others, over a period of five to six years. The plan would be implemented in four stages. The company's report emphasized the need for industrial credits to finance long- and medium-term invest-

[5]Langley (cited in fn. 3), p. 84.

[6]Lord Salter, *The Development of Iraq: A Plan of Action* (Baghdad: Iraq Development Board, 1955).

[7]Langley (cited in fn. 3), pp. 84–85. Also, Thomas Balogh, *Economic Development Policy in Iraq* (translated by Mohammed Hasan, Baghdad, 1958), pp. 40–42.

[8]Arthur D. Little, Inc., *A Plan for Industrial Development* (Cambridge, Massachusetts, 1952).

ments as well as to provide the needed capital for pioneer enterprises.

Thus, 1951 marked a turning point for Iraq's investment and development policies, thanks to revenues from oil. Since then, oil has become a crucial and dynamic component of economic activity, emerging as the principal source of investment spending in the country and of foreign exchange to finance imports, whether consumer goods to counteract the anticipated inflation from large-scale spending or producer goods needed for the development process. The Government of that time gave thoughtful and due consideration to the modes of spending, the management of the country's expanding oil resources, and their allocation at the central government level.

The Development Board was founded in 1950 (by Law No. 23) to formulate economic and financial plans to develop Iraq's resources and raise its people's standard of living. At first, the Board enjoyed considerable administrative, legal, and financial autonomy, and all oil revenues were assigned to its budget. But the volume and flow of these revenues became so large that the Government subsequently reduced the allocation to 70 percent, leaving 30 percent for financing its own general expenses. In 1953 the Ministry of Development was created and charged with executing the Board's investment schemes, which served to limit the Board's authority and in time led to the Government assuming full control of development policy.[9]

The most serious problem facing development programs in those early years was project implementation. Total annual allocations to investment schemes during 1951–58 amounted to ID 418.5 million, but only ID 225.1 million was disbursed. The ratio of investments implemented to investments targeted was therefore no more than 54 percent, with significant variations between sectors; the largest difference (63 percent) occurred between the building and services sectors.[10] This rendered the state's executive agencies unable to fulfill their mission of placing the program's projects under implementation, whether to the Government (ministries,

[9]Balogh (cited in fn. 7), p. 32.
[10]Hashim and others (cited in fn. 1), Part I, pp. 66, 267, and 268.

government agencies) or to contracting parties or agencies charged with monitoring the implementation of the plan.[11]

Apparently, the Development Board did not expect such a large inflow of oil revenues over the short term, which was the cause of its failure to utilize the funds made available to it. The result was that development planning lacked the boldness to match the means available. According to Lord Salter, the Board was in a state of perpetual confusion as to how to implement fully the projects assigned to its budget. Balogh believes that the widening permanent gap between planning and implementation was due, above all, to vacillation in spending, perhaps for the same reason cited by Salter. This view is supported by the fact that the Board was unable to implement even one sixth of the funds earmarked for industrial projects. The Board increased its loans to municipalities and various projects established by other agencies in a bid to compensate for this inadequate spending, but in fact these were more like assistance outlays rather than true lending. Moreover, most of the projects financed were long term and thus could only mature over the long run, except perhaps for housing, dams, and reservoirs, which helped save the country from the destructive threat of floods. As a result, the substantial spending that the Development Board undertook was not matched by comparable growth in production.

Much criticism was leveled at the Development Board and its investment schemes. Among the major criticisms were the following:[12]

- The conservatism of its policy, as the Board shied away from projects that might affect the prevailing social order, particularly in the agricultural sector; that is, programs were planned within and on the basis of the prevailing system, with no attempt to change that system.
- The Board did not endorse a policy of dynamic industrialization or strive to develop manufacturing for the purpose of achieving industrial independence and self-reliance.
- The financing of projects was not undertaken within the framework of a unified economic development plan for the econ-

[11]Ibid., pp. 166–67.
[12]Ibid., pp. 46–48.

omy as a whole, nor did the Board establish clear-cut development strategies or study the potential consequences of its
projects, whether direct or indirect.
- The Board's programs were based solely on economic considerations. Long-term investments were given precedence
  over projects with a direct impact on production, even though
  the latter could have borne fruit over the short term and may
  have shown tangible results much sooner.

However, in all fairness, now that four decades of continuous
development have elapsed, and given the economic, social, and
political conditions that prevailed in the fifties, the Board per-
formed rather well. It may even be regarded as a success, considering all the constraints encountered: more specifically, its lack of
experience in planning, the shortage of technical skills, unsuitable
economic and political conditions, the lack of the complements to
capital development, the national economy's limited absorptive
capacity, and the absence of adequate infrastructure. Moreover,
to give the agricultural sector the necessary attention required that
efforts focus on projects in irrigation, dam construction, and water
storage, installation of roads, bridges, and electricity and water
networks on a large scale, in addition to building houses, schools,
and hospitals. For this reason, the Board could not implement its
programs in full. Spending could not keep up with the growth in
oil revenues, which was itself the principal engine of developmental investment during that period.

Investment Policies, 1958–68

If oil revenues were the principal factor influencing investment
policy during 1950–58, political transformations in the subsequent
phase, 1958–68, were a key factor in the formation of these policies, in the size of investment, in direction, and in allocation of
funds. This second phase was characterized by four basic changes,
the last of which occurred in 1968. Among the consequences of
the first three was the deterioration of relations between the Government and the foreign oil companies operating in Iraq, which
were genuinely prejudicial to Iraq's sovereignty over its own oil
resources, resulting, as we shall see, in modest growth in oil revenues. Official negotiations with these companies failed to reach
a mutually satisfactory agreement, which prompted the Govern-

ment to enact the famous Law No. 80 of 1961. By this law, Iraq was able to recover 99.5 percent of its territories previously subject to the oil concessions. This act impelled the oil companies to pursue a policy of blatant pressure by manipulating the rate of oil production, sometimes increasing and sometimes reducing it, throughout the period under consideration. This policy naturally affected oil returns, which fluctuated accordingly, declining in some years and rising in others, though by no more than 0.3 percent. Although output in 1968 was increased by 54.5 percent, in 1969 it declined by 1.8 percent.[13] The vacillations in revenues generally coincided with political changes that occurred during this time, resulting in a comparative deterioration in the role of oil revenues in financing investments while augmenting the political transformation in investment policy trends (volume, financing, and sectoral distribution).

As for investment policy, emphasis shifted from agriculture to industry, on the grounds that the latter yielded quicker results and more widely distributed benefits, than the agricultural sector, from which only a minority of large landowners had thus far profited.[14]

At the same time, the proportion of oil revenues assigned to investment development objectives was reduced from 70 percent to 50 percent. The remaining 50 percent was transferred to the Government's regular budget, which was normally directed to public consumption expenditures.[15]

The most significant modification in the planning process during this period was the enactment of Planning Board Law No. 18 of 1966, which endorsed the principle of comprehensive planning for the national economy and affirmed the need to avoid restricting it to economic considerations alone. The text proclaimed in no uncertain terms that among the tasks of the Board was "coordination between economic, financial, monetary and trade policies to ensure the implementation of the plan . . . and to submit comments on the annual budget proposal of the State within the general framework of the plan, in addition to orienting the private sector

[13]OPEC, *Annual Statistical Bulletin, 1970,* Tables (13) and (78), pp. 24 and 118.

[14]Hashim and others (cited in fn. 1), Part I, p. 50.

[15]Ibid., p. 87.

toward the plan's development objectives."[16] Perhaps this was the first indicator of the need for coordination between development and investment plans on the one hand, and the Government's macroeconomic policies on the other.

Another important development that affected investment policy during this period was the rather sudden move toward national-ization that occurred in July 1964, when 27 private companies in the following sectors were nationalized: weaving and textiles, food products, chemical industries, tanning and leather, and building materials. All commercial banks and insurance companies were also nationalized; these, along with cement and cigarettes, became confined to the public sector. On the other hand, only large in-dustries were nationalized; small and intermediate projects re-mained in the private sector. The total capital of the industrial enterprises nationalized amounted to nearly ID 17.5 million.[17]

The Detailed Economic Plan for 1961–65, which followed the change of government of 1958, is the plan on which our analysis of new investment policies is based. There are several reasons for this choice. For one, the plan was indeed detailed; for another, the greater part of it continued to be implemented up to the middle of 1968. Moreover, it rested on specific principles, in terms of objectives and priorities, which in turn were linked with macro-economic policies. It was also based on a fairly extensive economic analysis of current and projected ends, means, and realities.

Total investment funds assigned through this plan amounted to ID 556.3 million, 30 percent of which was absorbed by the in-dustrial sector. The agricultural sector obtained no more than 20.3 percent, which reduced its standing to fourth place, as the building and housing sector received 25.2 percent, and transport, com-munications, and storage, 24.5 percent. The industrial sector thus gained precedence, an aim that was in keeping with the over-whelming desire of the new generation generally, and intellectuals in particular, to transform the industrial sector into the principal engine of development. Their motive goes back to the belief pop-ular at that time: industry is the basis for economic development

[16]See Paragraphs 2, 3, and 4 of Article (7) in Planning Board Law No. 18 of 1966.

[17]For a good, detailed study of the nationalization decisions, see Safa' Al-Hafez, *The Public Sector and the Scope of Socialist Development in Iraq* (Beirut: Dar Al-Farabi, 1971), p. 79 ff.

generally, and to overcome backwardness and poverty requires developing this sector, even at the expense of agriculture. It was a widespread belief common to all developing countries, impelling them to apply development strategies geared principally to industrialization.

The Detailed Economic Plan for 1961–65 adopted the concept of comprehensive planning at the national economy level. It sought to strike a balance between economic development in all sectors, with due regard to the mutually reinforcing effect of growth in all these sectors and growth of the economy as a whole. It aimed at an annual growth in national income of no less than 8 percent and at reducing dependence on oil by developing the productive capacities of industry and agriculture and increasing their contribution to national income generation by no less than 7.5 percent annually in the agricultural sector and no less than 12 percent in the industrial sector. It also considered the need for balance between the size of national expenditures and their rate of growth on the one hand and between the available productive capacity and its rate of increase on the other; this was to guard against the effects of inflation or recession and to achieve short-term monetary and economic stability. The plan did not fail to link its projects to the broader objectives of Arab economic integration and sought to achieve full employment and expand social services (such as education and health).

Perhaps one of the most important points emphasized in the new plan was the need to coordinate investment policies and macroeconomic policies (that is, financial, monetary, credit, trade, and wage policies). It was the first time that mention was made of these policies and the need for such coordination.[18]

According to the plan, it was most significant that in the list of revenues oil revenues did not comprise more than 69.5 percent of the total. Two other important sources for the plan were external loans (16.9 percent) and domestic borrowing (5.3 percent). This was an important development in sources of financing development plans for Iraq, marking a departure from the decade of the fifties, when planning depended almost exclusively on oil revenues.

[18]See Law No. 78 of 1965 Regarding Five-Year Plan 1965–69.

Investment Policies, 1968–80

The period 1968–80 was characterized by important and decisive political and economic developments. In July 1968 a party came to power that had definite social imperatives, and its economic and political objectives were very different from the forms of government that had prevailed in the fifties and up to the end of the sixties. It was socialist in orientation and did not acknowledge individual decisions on production, allocation, and pricing, in view of the glaring inequality in the distribution of income and wealth. These considerations conditioned the investment policies of the time and were manifest in the political changes initiated by the new Government on the one hand, and in the social orientation of that Government on the other. The new Government was also nationalistic, raising the slogan: "Arab oil for the Arabs." Thus, it believed in the need to free national wealth from the domination of the foreign investor, which was personified then by the foreign oil companies. A major confrontation occurred with the oil companies, which culminated in the 1972 decision to nationalize these companies, a process that was completed the following year.

This situation continued until September 1980, at which time the war between Iraq and the Islamic Republic of Iran broke out. This signaled the start of a new phase whose influence on investment policy continues to this day. We shall discuss this phase in more detail in the next section.

The current phase ended, therefore, as it had begun, with important political developments exercising a decisive impact on investment policy in Iraq throughout the seventies and eighties.

The general national development objectives were as follows:

- To achieve an advanced economic level and increase the Iraqi individual's income to raise his standard of living and realize prosperity and social justice.
- To develop the agricultural sector by increasing productivity and diversifying output, applying modern methods in production technology, in addition to transforming productive and social relations into advanced socialist productive relations; also, to complete horizontal growth and work more toward vertical expansion.
- To increase industrial production, focusing on light industries for the production of consumer goods to meet local demand,

directing any surpluses into export, in addition to developing the national oil sector in terms of production, marketing, and processing.

• To maintain full control over external and internal trade and to expand and diversify exports.
• To support the public sector in all economic branches, as it constitutes the basis for the socialist transformation, and to support the private sector within the limits prescribed; also, to employ all available means to help this sector fulfill its developmental role.
• To link investment policy with savings policy and concentrate on encouraging national saving, with the assurance of full employment for all able-bodied persons in all productive sectors.
• To coordinate regional development projects in Iraq and productive projects in the Arab countries in light of the requirements of Arab economic integration.

One of the most significant results of these developments was that oil revenues increased substantially and at an accelerating rate throughout the seventies, especially after the price adjustment of 1973, increasing from about $521 million in 1970 to nearly $26 billion in 1980. The greatest increases occurred in 1979 ($21.3 billion in 1979, up from $10.9 billion in 1978), and in 1980 when the per barrel price of oil reached its peak.[19] Naturally, this increase affected the volume of investments, reflected in the two Development Plans of 1970–74 and 1976–80, which were, until then, the largest in Iraq's history. The total allocations of the Revised Five-Year Plan for 1970–74 were about ID 1,169 million; the percentage share of each productive sector was 16 percent for agriculture, 19 percent for industry, 10 percent for buildings and services, and 15 percent for transport and communication. Total allocations to commodity sectors were thus about 60 percent. The remaining 40 percent was channeled into large-scale ventures, loans to government departments and institutions, as well as international commitments. In commodity sector allocations, industry came first, receiving 31 percent, or ID 710 million, followed by

[19]Arab Monetary Fund, General Secretariat of the Arab League, Arab Fund for Economic and Social Development, and Organization of Arab Petroleum Exporting Countries, *Joint Arab Economic Report, 1981* (Dubai: Arab Monetary Fund), Table (6–10), p. 236.

agriculture at 27.6 percent, transport and communication at 25 percent, and, finally, buildings and services at 17 percent.[20]

One observes in this pattern of investment a definite shift of emphasis from agriculture to industry, with industry now acquiring absolute priority, compared with a lower degree of precedence in the previous Five-Year Plan (1965–69). The emphasis on communications remained the same, indicating continued concern for infrastructure in the Iraqi economy. The plan's allocations to the various sectors show that the relative importance of each sector for realizing the country's development goals was kept in mind during formulation of the new development policy, as was the sector's maximum potential for implementation.[21]

However, the largest Five-Year Development Plan in Iraq's history till then (the Explosive Plan, as it was then called) was for 1976–80. It was labeled "explosive" because of the massiveness of its macro allocations, which were nearly ID 15.1 billion.[22] This amount was ten times the figure for the previous plan (1970–74) and was followed by what was called the Big Push strategy for development, which sought to eliminate backwardness on every economic front—goods and services, economy, and society—and was motivated by optimistic projections of continued increases in crude oil prices in the international market and therefore in revenues. These revenues did indeed increase throughout the years of the 1976–80 plan, reaching nearly $77 billion.

The industrial sector continued to hold its lead position in terms of volume of allocations and, therefore, relative importance, which came at the expense of the priorities in the Government's investment policy. Meanwhile, despite agriculture's very large allocations, in absolute terms, this sector continued to occupy fourth place. Buildings and services came in second, and transport and communications third, meaning that the two sectors received the lion's share of commodity sector assignments (45 percent) and 35.7 percent of total assignments, confirming the Government's commitment to expand infrastructure and improve social services.

[20]Ministry of Planning, *Progress in Planning* (Baghdad, 4th ed.), p. 57.

[21]Ibid.

[22]Ministry of Planning, Central Statistical Organization, *Annual Abstract of Statistics, 1982* (Baghdad), Table (2–6), p. 126.

Investment Policies During the War Years, 1980–87

From September 1980 until August 1988, Iraq endured one of the longest and harshest trials in its history: the war with the Islamic Republic of Iran and the subjection of Iraq's economy and every other aspect of life to armed assault, subversion, and destruction. The war brought oil exports through the Persian Gulf to a standstill, and oil pumped through the Syrian Arab Republic for export from Mediterranean ports also ceased to flow. Thus, Iraq's oil interests suffered badly. As the export of crude continued to diminish, oil revenues deteriorated from just over $26 billion in 1980 to $9.7 billion in 1983, and then to $7 billion in 1986. As of 1987, however, they began to increase again, after new and strategic pipelines were laid to pump oil, first through Turkey and then through Saudi Arabia. This secured for the country $11.3 billion in oil revenues during that year.[23] The decline in Iraq's oil exports, and therefore revenues, was not due solely to these causes. There was also the accompanying decline in demand for oil in the industrialized countries, a consequence of the general economic stagnation that pervaded the first half of the eighties; this not only led to reduced oil exports,[24] but also to the deterioration of its nominal and effective prices from $34 a barrel in 1981 to $13.5 a barrel in 1986.[25] As oil and oil revenues are essential sources for financing economic and social development plans in the country, and for defining their size and scope, the process of development was the first to be affected by the adversities in the oil sector during the war years. The war also had an impact on the labor force, as a large portion of the manpower was enlisted into the armed forces. The overall result was suboptimum utilization of available productive capacity on the one hand and decline in production and investment performance in other economic sectors on the other.

[23]*Joint Arab Economic Report, 1988* (cited in fn. 19), Statistical Annex, Table (4–3), p. 259.

[24]For oil production for 1979–82, see Organization of Arab Petroleum Exporting Countries, *Ninth Annual Report of the Secretary General, 1982*, Table (2–5), p. 45. For 1983–87, see *Joint Arab Economic Report, 1988* (cited in fn. 19), Statistical Annex, Table (4–15), p. 271.

[25]See, in this regard, *Joint Arab Economic Report, 1988* (cited in fn. 19), Statistical Annex, Table (4–2), p. 258.

Government Policy Toward Public and Private Investment

The public position toward private investment since the thirties and up to the sixties can generally be described as one of continuous support. The Government enacted legislation to promote private investment in the industrial sector generally. In the mid-forties it established the Industrial Bank and Agricultural Bank to help industrialists and agricultural producers, providing them with customs and tax exemptions, land, and financial facilities. The Government also participated in industrial projects, through its industrial expenditures, in a further token of encouragement and support. Its role until the early fifties was largely one of patronage, seeking to help the private sector establish itself and lay the groundwork for expansion. It adopted free trade and liberal economic policies and did not interfere in private ventures except to a very limited degree. Private enterprise dominated all productive sectors, including the foreign oil sector and manufacturing, however modest, simple, and limited in scope in the latter; meanwhile, agriculture was almost completely under private sector control. The Government's role here was minimal, restricted to providing credit facilities as well as the necessary infrastructure in the form of roads, bridges, and dams. The public sector was therefore circumscribed and did not extend beyond public utilities, railroads, ports, and airports,[26] except to include a few specialized banks and one of the commercial banks.

Then came the fifties. Government revenues increased following the revision of the 1950 oil agreements, as described earlier. Its investment role grew, and the sector expanded side by side with the private sector. We noted earlier that the Government's position on private investment did not change, remaining one of support and encouragement, while the general trend in investment policy was liberal and supportive of the private sector. The Government's role in economic activity remained limited to a few industries that the private sector was reluctant to enter into, either because of its limited means, or the intimidating effect of its inexperience in such ventures, or skepticism about their feasibility and potential for success, or the lack of entrepreneurs willing and able to undertake

---

[26]For a highly detailed review, see Langley (cited in fn. 3).

them. Thus, during the fifties, the Planning Board devoted most of its effort to channeling government investment into infrastructure, in particular for the agriculture sector (dams and aqueducts), transportation sector (roads and bridges), and transport (railroads, ports, and airports). Government activity extended to the oil sector in the areas of petroleum products (distillation plants) and distribution of production (filling stations, which were commissioned to the private sector until 1958). It is also apparent that most of the expansion in public investment benefited private enterprise and always supported it; the same applies to the many financial laws that were promulgated, which served to support the private sector through tax exemptions, financial grants, land allocations, the provision of low-priced energy, and exemption of primary material imports from customs duties, in addition to providing loans and credit facilities.

As a result, the private sector came to dominate economic activity during the fifties. The public sector's contribution to GDP in 1953 and 1956 did not exceed 11.7 percent and 14.3 percent, respectively, while its contribution to gross fixed capital formation was about 49 percent for both years. By 1960, its share of GDP was still no more than 18.6 percent and its contribution to gross fixed capital formation, 42.1 percent,[27] which is indicative of the primacy of the private sector during the fifties. The share of the private industrial sector in economic activity and in value added to industry, for example, was about 88.3 percent in 1953 and 88.2 percent in 1956, with an increase in absolute terms from ID 17.4 million to ID 28.3 million. Private capital invested in industry amounted to about ID 4 million in 1953, rising to nearly ID 20 million by 1956;[28] these figures reflect the Government's investment policy during this time, which was consistent with the recommendations of the foreign experts drawn upon by the Planning Board.

The beginning of the republican era in July 1958 saw no change in government investment policy toward the private sector. The new Government provided every form of support and encouragement, especially for the industrial sector, resulting in an ex-

---

[27]Hashim and others (cited in fn. 1), Part I, Statistical Annex (21), p. 288, and Statistical Annex (30), p. 298.

[28]Ibid., Part II, pp. 283–84.

pansion in private industrial enterprises and a relative increase in capital investments therein.

However, an important change occurred in government policy toward public investment during July 1964, when 27 industrial, commercial, banking, and insurance companies were nationalized, and a central Economic Organization was created to manage the nationalized companies. The Government drew a dividing line between the public and private sectors in certain definite areas:

- The banking and insurance sectors were incorporated into the public sector;
- The cement, asbestos, and cigarette industries were placed under the exclusive control of the public sector;
- In other industries, such as weaving, textiles, and foodstuffs, only the larger industrial projects were nationalized, with small and medium-sized projects remaining within the private sector.

The nationalization laws thus played a decisive role in expanding and consolidating the public sector. Although they curbed the scope of the private sector, they did not oppose it; on the contrary, it continued to play an important role in every economic activity. In the industrial sector, where the impact of nationalization was more strongly felt, the number of industrial corporations increased by nearly 40 in the year after nationalization. This trend continued throughout the second half of the sixties despite the partial stagnation of the sector immediately after the decision to nationalize and the trend toward expansion in relatively small industries.[29] The period 1965–68 witnessed a significant increase in private industrial activity, whether in terms of the number of companies, the amount of production, the value added, or the number of personnel, but this expansion was most noticeable in the small business sector.[30]

Among the most important factors contributing to this expansion was the enactment of a new development law that improved conditions for developing private industry. Moreover, the private sector was regarded as a national capital asset with important economic and social functions in the development of the national economy; the public sector was not to replace it, but both were

[29]Ibid., p. 441.
[30]Ibid., p. 443.

to complement one another in a joint effort to bolster the economic and social development of the country.[31]

Thus, the private sector continued to hold a relatively important place in industry by the end of the sixties, although the public sector controlled the largest industrial projects. The share of the private sector in value added to industry was about 45 percent, and the sector continued to dominate agriculture, transportation (excluding railroads), air transport, contracting, and construction, and no less than 50 percent of trade and imports. Meanwhile, investment in the financial and banking sector became state controlled. Despite this, the share of the public sector in GDP and in gross fixed domestic capital formation did not exceed 26.1 percent and 58.6 percent, respectively, for 1968,[32] suggesting that the private sector continued to play a relatively large role in the Iraqi economy—four years after nationalization.

However, an important change occurred in investment after 1968. It followed a fundamental political change that resulted in a Government with openly socialist leanings, inclined toward expanding the role of the state in the national economy generally (including reduction of individual forms of agricultural production, placement of all foreign trade under state jurisdiction, centralization of internal trade, and bolstering the leadership role of the public sector in industry). The objective was to transform Iraq into a socialist society, and these imperatives were reflected in the changes that followed the socialist public sector's participation in all economic sectors.[33]

Public investment thus dominated the manufacturing field, especially in the leading strategic and heavy industries, while private investment was assigned to small consumer goods industries. The public sector also prevailed over foreign trade sectors and achieved extensive control of internal trade. However, the private sector has retained a certain importance within the Iraqi economy even up to the present, for it now participates actively in economic activity to the extent of 40 percent of non-oil GDP and about 25

[31]Ibid.

[32]Ibid., Part I, Statistical Annex (21), p. 288, and Statistical Annex (30), p. 298.

[33]For details, see Arab Baath Socialist Party of Iraq, *Central Report of the Ninth National Conference* (June 1982), pp. 106–108 and 130–47.

percent of gross fixed domestic capital formation—a 5 percent increase compared with 1975.[34]

In contrast to the trend in the late sixties, investment policy during the latter part of the eighties, and especially since the beginning of 1987, was directed to supporting and promoting the private sector. Certain businesses in the public sector were transferred to the private sector, and the latter was permitted to initiate similar ventures within certain areas so far reserved to the public sector, as well as to invest in agricultural, industrial, and trade activities that were competitive with that sector. The Government also granted the private sector numerous tax exemptions, discarded the upper limits on company capital, and permitted the provision of concessional credit facilities to the sector. It provided a number of incentives for Arab investment in the country[35] and deregulated agricultural commodity prices and the prices of many other manufactured commodities. A move was made to develop the financial market by increasing its capacity to handle domestic investments and expedite the circulation of private and joint venture stocks, removing the obstacles to these operations, in particular by modifying legal stipulations to make them compatible with the new changes in investment policy toward the private sector.

In this context, the Government dissolved the Planning Board and replaced it with an Advisory Planning Authority. Development plans became indicative, to be ratified as general indicators and trends.[36]

One may regard these developments in the investment climate in Iraq as part of a more general trend that has swept the Arab region generally in recent years, with the aim of revitalizing the

[34]On the role of the state in economic activity in Iraq from the fifties to the present, see "Evaluation and Future of the Role of the State in Economic Activity in Arab Countries Promoting Social Justice and Redistribution of Income," paper submitted to Seminar on the Role of the State in Economic Activity in the Arab World, Arab Planning Institute, Kuwait, May 27–29, 1989.

[35]See, in this regard, Ibrahim Al-Khafagi, "The Private Sector in the Post-War Era: Prospects and Future Trends," paper submitted to Seventh Conference of the Iraqi Economists Union on Basic Economic Trends in Iraq After the War, Baghdad, January 17–19, 1988.

[36]For a summary of these developments, see Inter-Arab Investment Guarantee Corporation, *Report on the Investment Climate of the Arab Countries*, 1987 and 1988 issues (Kuwait, 1988 and 1989), in particular the sections on Iraq.

private sector and assigning it a greater role in Arab national economies.

Policy Toward Arab and Foreign Investment

We turn now to an examination of policy toward foreign investment, which has been absent from the Iraqi scene since the nationalization of the foreign oil companies in 1972 and 1973. Moreover, the attitude toward foreign investment has by no means been favorable since the revolution of July 1958. Nor does it seem to be changing, even today, except for specifically Arab investments.

In 1988, Arab Investment Law No. 46 was issued to encourage this form of investment to assist in the economic and social development of the country. The law grants Arab investors the right to participate with Iraqi investors in the initiation of Iraqi investment projects, provided that Iraqi participation docs not exceed 49 percent of the project capital. In other words, the law permits Arab investors absolute shareholder majority as a form of encouragement. Furthermore, the law sets the paid-up capital of the investment project at the equivalent of half a million dinars and allows Arab capital in the form of capital assets; it also stipulates customs and tax exemptions, facilities, and guarantees for the project. Iraq's Ministry of Planning has defined the main areas of Arab investment to be in industry, agriculture, livestock, tourism, and mining; outside these sectors, foreign investment is strictly prohibited.[37]

This position on foreign investment in the country may be regarded as official up to the present. We believe that it represents the national consensus on this type of investment, and one that derives originally from the bitter experience with the Western oil companies that had operated in Iraq since the 1920s. It should be borne in mind that Iraq has never felt the need for foreign investments, thanks to the ample domestic funds at its disposal during the fifties, and then again in the seventies. Thus, investment flows to Iraq have been negligible since the forties. Moreover, foreign investments in the past (in the thirties, and even in the seventies) were confined to the oil sector, to the currency exchange

[37]Ibid.,1988, pp. 258 and 270–72.

sector, and to transport and ports. In 1936 a foreign-owned railway project was purchased; in 1952, ownership of the Basra seaport was transferred to the Iraqi Government; in 1951, the Government recovered its crude oil fields for direct exploitation, as well as the concession to distribute petroleum products in the Iraqi market, thus giving it a monopoly over oil distillation and distribution within Iraq.

All these nationalization measures occurred through agreements arrived at amicably. But the first severe blow directed at the foreign oil companies was the famous Law No. 80 of 1961, which recovered for the Government 99.5 percent of the land area formerly subject to the oil concession; this concession had in fact encompassed the whole of Iraq's territory, from the north to the south. Nevertheless, the companies continued to control the largest oil fields, which did not become completely nationalized until June 1972.

As for currency exchange, foreign investments were estimated at ID 2.3 million until July 1964, when they were nationalized. The value of foreign investments nationalized during that year was generally estimated at ID 4.5 million, all of which was compensated.[38]

With the nationalization of the foreign oil companies in 1972 and 1973, the role of foreign investment in Iraq effectively ended. To this day it has not made a comeback, nor is it likely to do so in the foreseeable future.

Macroeconomic Policies and Investment

Iraq is, of course, an oil country, and its oil revenues, as we have seen, finance the country's public investments; 90 percent of total investment allocations committed since the fifties and up to the present have been based on oil revenues. These revenues generally exceeded planned investments and actual expenditures during the fifties and the seventies, encountering some difficulty during the sixties. Thus, public investment policy tended to operate on the assumption of limitless financing for Iraqi development, an assumption apparently backed by the continuing increase in oil exports and thus in the volume of oil revenues accrued. These two

[38]For more details, see Al-Hafez (cited in fn. 17), pp. 80–99.

variables remained high and increased in parallel—although oil revenues grew more rapidly during the latter part of the seventies and early eighties as oil prices increased steadily up to 1982. This increase took place as the oil market began to show signs of weakening (the early eighties) and the industrial capitalist countries encountered economic stagnation. The result was a severe blow to the oil countries generally and to their expectation of continued demand for high-priced oil along the lines prevailing in the late seventies.

Despite all the setbacks that have been encountered, oil and oil revenues are likely to be the paramount sources for financing economic and social development, even though policymakers are now aware that oil is a nonrenewable and unstable resource that cannot be relied upon indefinitely.

If we return once again to the seventies, and before that to the fifties, we find that in the various historical phases through which Iraq passed, macroeconomic policies did not command much attention, thanks to abundant financing from oil. After reviewing the conditions of developing countries generally, one finds these policies acquiring special importance in countries where financial resources are scarce, or which suffer from fluctuations and instability in financial revenues, whether from domestic sources (taxes, production surpluses) or external sources (exports, foreign loans). These conditions differed, both qualitatively and quantitatively, from those that prevailed in the oil countries (including Iraq) since the mid-seventies and, in the end, in the fifties as well. Moreover, the effect of such policies becomes most apparent where the economy is characterized by a private sector that dominates the public sector in both size and impact and obtains its financing from local sources, of which the most important are private savings, bank loans, and accumulated profits rechanneled into productive enterprises. In this case, financial and monetary policies have a direct, tangible, and active impact, or even an indirect impact, on the productive activities of the private sector, in terms of size, sectoral trends, output cost, and prices and profits, and thus in terms of the general composition, size, and direction of private investments.

The private sector in Iraq was the dominant sector during the fifties, when its contributions to GDP and gross fixed capital formation averaged 75 percent and 50 percent, respectively. These ratios are comparatively high and are indicative of the importance of this sector at the time. Thus, macroeconomic policies had an important effect on the sector's productive and investment activities, and monetary policies tended to encourage and support it through the extension of banking, industrial, agricultural, and trade and credit facilities, and by permitting interest rates to shift in response to the supply and demand for credits, though within a legally prescribed ceiling.

The exchange rate of the dinar was relatively stable and was at first pegged to sterling (as Iraq was at that time a member of the sterling area) but was later pegged to the dollar, following Iraq's signing of the agreement establishing the International Monetary Fund (1945). The stability of the exchange rate contributed to the stability of prices, especially of imported goods, and to reducing the risk factor for private investors. Oil revenues provided the needed foreign exchange for meeting the import demands for both investment and consumption. Relatively liberal trade policies also helped to stabilize prices somewhat, as well as to counter the inflationary pressures that followed from development spending, which increased substantially in the wake of accelerating oil revenues.

Because the Government at that time assigned 30 percent of revenues to its general expenses, this helped redress the deficit on current expenditure in the budget but, at the same time, it reduced dependence on taxes. Thus, personal income increased while tax rates remained fixed, and government consumption expenditures increased side by side with the increase in personal consumption expenditures, compounding the inflationary pressures of development spending in the public sector. These pressures were countered by opening the door to imports on the one hand and by encouraging investment in the private sector on the other, to provide the economy with a supply of goods and services; this cushioned the inflationary effect of the large expansion in public and private spending in the face of a relatively small production potential and limited absorptive capacity.

The Government tried to encourage private investment in industry by adopting a protectionist policy and sought to create import-substitution industries for consumer goods. It did not rely on taxes to counter inflation, as the share of revenue from income tax to GNP in 1953 was no more than 0.8 percent and remained effectively unchanged through 1959, when it amounted to 0.9 percent. Thus, taxes were not among the Government's effective and available monetary tools for sustaining the progress of the Iraqi economy in general.

As for wages and prices, the Government left these to market forces and did not interfere in the operation of the market, pursuing a liberal import policy with full freedom for the private sector in productive activities—industrial, agricultural, trade, transport, etc.

It may be argued, therefore, that the general imperatives of government development spending policy at this time were what determined, for the most part, the patterns of growth in economic activity and gross capital formation, as well as their forms, and the extent of utilization of available economic resources and their mode of allocation between the various productive sectors. Spending policy was generally conservative despite the relatively huge sums expended and despite the increase in imports; the balance of payments remained in favor of the national economy and thus led to positive accumulations of foreign exchange.

The macroeconomic policy followed by the Government in the fifties maintained a secure external position for the country. A contributing factor was that actual expenditures were always lower than investment commitments or the oil revenues obtained. This was reflected in the continuous increase in accumulated foreign financial reserves throughout the fifties, rising from $113.7 million in 1951 to $180.9 million in 1953, and to $257 million in 1958.[39] The country enjoyed a balance of trade surplus during this time except for 1958, when Iraq retaliated against the tripartite aggression against Egypt by suspending its oil flows from Mediterranean ports.

The relatively stable rate of exchange alone led to stability in domestic prices, because of the importance of importables for Iraq, but externally the effect on the volume of exportables in general was limited. Oil prices are determined in the global market, so that changes in the exchange rate of the dinar do not affect them. For other, non-oil exports, however, their size and their quality— whether as raw materials or as agricultural commodities— together with the price elasticity of demand, reduce the importance of exchange rate variations. As a result, the effectiveness of the foreign exchange rate as a monetary measure is limited as far as

[39]International Monetary Fund, *International Financial Statistics Yearbook* (Washington, 1981).

exports are concerned; it is also limited for importables because of the low elasticity of domestic demand for them. Being important investment or consumer goods, local demand for them is not price sensitive, particularly when development expenditures are large and there is a continuous rise in personal income, leading to increased demand because of an increase in the marginal propensity to import and consume.

We have already mentioned that the share of general government expenses from oil revenues was raised from 30 percent to 50 percent after the emergence of the Republican Government in Iraq in 1958. Thus, 50 percent of oil revenues were assigned to financing development plans during the sixties, of which the most important was the Five-Year Development Plan for 1965–69. It was observed in these plans that the available financial resources were below optimum for financing target investments. The resource deficit was corrected with a shortfall in actual expenditures against planned allocations on the one hand and by resort to external borrowing on the other. This development is important because it suggested a willingness on the part of the Government to look abroad at that time more than ever before. The Government also planned to draw on internal bank credits to finance part of its planned investments. However, it is clear that the Government was most reluctant to rely on foreign borrowing; actual external loans did not exceed ID 16 million, or 17.5 percent of the original amount planned (that is, ID 91.5 million). Tax policy during this time could not compensate for the drop in oil revenues that ensued from differences with the foreign oil companies, as proceeds from taxes were extremely low, whether in absolute terms or as a percentage of national income.

Among the consequences of the increase in the share of the general budget to 50 percent of oil revenues was a rate of growth in government consumption expenditures exceeding growth in national income. General government expenditures increased between 1953 and 1956 by 273.5 percent, but the percentage increase in national income was no more than 170.2 percent.[40] Direct and indirect taxes—excluding the tax on income of the oil companies—rose by 132 percent.[41] This meant greater reliance of gov-

[40]Hashim and others (cited in fn. 1), Part I, p. 87.
[41]Ibid., p. 89.

ernment consumption expenditures on oil revenues, and at the expense of public investment and development expenditures, as confirmed by the decline in the ratio of the latter to national income from 16 percent in 1957 to 9 percent in 1969.[42] It was only natural that this would lead to a decline in the rate of growth of national income generally, unless the non-oil sector could compensate for the shortfall in public investment expenditures—which did not occur. The private non-oil sector concentrated more on investment in buildings, especially residential, than on productive machinery and equipment, which was to be expected, given the uncertainty in economic policy trends in general, and it remained so throughout the sixties.

All these developments suggest a lack of coordination between the Government's financial and development policies. Monetary policy was also weak despite government control of the banking sector and the financial sector. There was no clear or convincing evidence for the effectiveness of interest rates as a monetary tool, given the atmosphere of uncertainty that prevailed, especially after the nationalization decisions of July 1964. Nor were the other quantitative measures of monetary policy very effective without an organized and developed financial market and the high liquidity that banks usually enjoyed. Consequently, the Central Bank sought to follow a selective and qualitative monetary policy, imposing direct credit controls to influence the trend in bank credits away from the trade sector and toward other productive sectors, especially industry and agriculture.[43]

No change occurred in the exchange rate of the dinar, which was pegged to the dollar, and here the ineffectiveness of the exchange rate policy referred to becomes apparent. It applied to the most important exportables, namely oil, whose price is determined by international market forces, but not to non-oil exports, which are small and vary in availability for export; nor did it apply to importables for which the price elasticity of demand is low because of the great need for these goods whether for development or consumption. Thus, the role of exchange rate policy was for the

[42]Ibid., Statistical Annex (6), p. 270.

[43]On the effectiveness of monetary policy in Iraq, see *The Economics of Money and Banking in Capitalist and Socialist Developing Countries* (Baghdad: Mosul University Press, 2nd ed., 1986), in particular section on Iraq (Part II-1986, Chap. 40).

most part restricted to achieving stability in domestic prices along the lines discussed earlier.[44]

Although the Government was more restrictive and protectionist than before, maintaining control over most foreign trade, it established a monopoly on certain food imports, such as sugar and tea, as well as the import of automobiles, medicines and medical supplies, and agricultural and food products. It also competed with the private sector in certain trade activities and established the General Organization for Trade. However, the imports of this Organization were only 28.1 percent of Iraq's total imports in 1969, while its exports in 1968 were only 10.9 percent of total exports, suggesting that the private sector continued to play a relatively large and important role in Iraq's foreign trade.[45] Owing to the modest increases in oil revenues, imports increased slowly between 1960 and 1966, and subsequently declined to reach a trough in 1968. Eight years later, they were still no more than 15 percent higher than the 1960 level.[46] The balance of trade (non-oil) encountered a perpetual deficit throughout the fifties and sixties, and even to the present. If oil is included, however, a continuous surplus in this balance is obtained, though it varies from year to year with the fluctuations to which oil exports were always subject.

As for wages, the Government set them for personnel in its economic sectors but kept them open for workers in the private sector and did not attempt to intervene except to ensure adherence to the minimum wage laws of the country. The same applied to commodity pricing; those commodities that the Government handled were subject to price control, while others were left to the private sector to determine, in accordance with supply and demand in the open market. The policy of the Government was generally one of competition with the private sector, except in the major consumer goods mentioned earlier, whether basic, such as food, or nonbasic but in high demand, such as automobiles, or for construction, such as cement; these commodities were subject to strict price controls.

Perhaps the most significant aspect of this period, as far as in-

[44]See Ministry of Planning, Central Statistical Organization, *Annual Abstract of Statistics, 1974*, Table (145), p. 209.

[45]Ministry of Planning, *The Provisional Detailed Framework*, pp. 196–98.

[46]Ibid., Table (75), p. 197.

vestment policy is concerned, is the shift toward making the public sector the leading sector in the economy in general, and in investment in particular. The 1964 decisions to nationalize were a turning point toward that end. The share of the public sector in gross fixed domestic capital formation rose from 56.2 percent in 1963 to 63 percent in 1964, even though it subsequently declined to 57.5 percent in 1969; the percentage share of the private sector, on the other hand, rose from 37 percent in 1964 to 42.5 percent in 1969.[47]

The decade of the seventies was characterized by a very aggressive government investment policy. Development spending increased to an extent that overwhelmed the limited production capacities available and the inelastic supply of goods and services; its utilization increased, leading to greater scarcity in available manpower and the large-scale import of Arab and non-Arab labor. This increase was particularly noticeable in the second half of the seventies, especially from 1977 onward. There were signs of shortages in labor and commodities in the services sector (for example, transport), building materials, and infrastructure, where scarcity in services cannot be met by imports from abroad. The interplay of these factors led to increasing costs, wages, and prices. The growth in personal income contributed, which in turn led to greater demand and persistent pressure on prices, compelling the Government to intervene to curb inflation through subsidies or through price determination, fixing, and control policies for most goods and services. Residential and office rents were fixed, as were transportation fares, medical fees, and tourism fares. Prices were set for essential consumer goods, primary materials, and production requirements, in addition to quasi-essential commodities. Luxury commodities were left to the open market. The prices of essential commodities could not be manipulated by the authorities concerned, while an increase in prices of quasi-essential commodities by up to 10 percent was permissible provided prior approval from those authorities was obtained.

It is important to note that this price policy could not establish industrial commodity prices in the private sector in a sound or accurate manner owing to the absence of the unified cost accounting system in the sector's projects. Moreover, the policy was com-

[47]Ibid., pp. 115–17.

mitted to a standardized profit margin for all similar products irrespective of differences in quality. Also, keeping luxury items open to market pricing mechanisms encouraged the private sector to invest in such industries instead of in centrally priced essential commodities.

The Government did not try to intervene in wages, except in setting the minimum, which it continually tried to raise as prices and inflationary pressures have been climbing since the mid-seventies. The purpose was to improve the standard of living of the working class. As of 1974, the Government provided its workers and employees with basic increases in wages and salaries in a bid to increase purchasing power. The precedent was actually set by the private sector, which had increased its wages, impelling the Government to improve its workers' wages to keep up. This step may have contributed to narrowing the gap between wage incomes.

The Government continued to adhere to its trade and protectionist policies, whether through customs duties or by adopting a quota system. High import duties were imposed on consumer goods while customs duties on capital and intermediate goods remained moderate, thus encouraging private sector expansion of consumer industries and the application of capital-intensive, creative production measures, given the scarcity of labor in the latter half of the seventies. The quantitative protectionism, or quota system, was more effective in protecting national industries, which increased substantially the number of commodities prone to protection during the seventies in comparison with the previous decade.

The Government also subsidized exports through a subsidy fund and through a customs reimbursement scheme for duties imposed on inputs that went into the production of export commodities, to help make them competitive with similar foreign commodities.

However, it is an accepted fact that excessive and prolonged protectionism undermines healthy competition between domestic and foreign commodities. It also reduces the efficiency of domestic projects and prevents them from attaining economic maturity, leading to expansions that have no market basis. This creates (a) a surplus production capacity that adds to the costs of their output and makes them uneconomical; (b) a wastage of resources, and thus the imposition of high prices that the consumer has to bear;

(c) the production of commodities of inferior quality; and (d) the emergence of monopolies and the disappearance of healthy competition.

On the other hand, the financial policy pursued tended to encourage private investment in various productive fields, especially those that hitherto discouraged private capital flows because of the risks involved, the paucity of anticipated profits, or reluctance to invest in specific geographic locations. As a result, legislation was enacted that exempted industrial projects from certain taxes and customs duties that either added to the costs of their output (such as taxes and duties on required inputs) or curbed their profits (income tax on profits). These exemptions were necessary for industrial projects whose production was directed to meeting domestic demand or exports, making their output competitive with foreign products, locally and abroad, since the exemptions reduced project costs and increased profits.

Monetary policy remained aggressive. This was true of the credit policies of the Bank of Mesopotamia, which was the sole commercial bank in the country, and of the industrial and agricultural credits that were extended by their respective banks. The same applied to the Real Estate Bank, which provided real estate credits very cheaply, on a large scale, and at low interest rates.

The Industrial Bank varied its interest rates according to region in a bid to encourage investment in areas that were less economically developed than the capital, Baghdad. Monetary authorities also tried to plan credits and establish an upper credit ceiling for borrowing sectors generally. Loans were highly concessional and soft. As a result, monetary expansion was large and domestic liquidity very high, including the liquid assets of the Bank of Mesopotamia.

Effectively, domestic and foreign public borrowing disappeared, thanks to abundant government funds from continued increases in oil revenues. For this reason as well, the Government enjoyed surpluses throughout the second half of the seventies. Its deposits in the Central Bank and the Bank of Mesopotamia increased, giving it a satisfactory financial standing. Because of its dominant position in the economy, the public sector received most of the commercial bank credits (about 75 percent) while it simultaneously increased its deposits in the Bank of Mesopotamia as a result of its substantial production and marketing activities.

What can be readily inferred from surveying the evolution of macroeconomic policy during the seventies is that it was generally aggressive, in both the oil and the non-oil sectors, and therefore high growth rates in GDP were realized. These rose from 7.7 percent during 1970–74 to 12.3 percent during 1976–80, and averaging 11.3 percent for the entire decade (1970–80) at 1975 prices. The manufacturing sector achieved a cumulative growth rate between 1970 and 1980 of just over 13 percent; agriculture grew extremely slowly during this period, at 1.4 percent, while growth in the oil sector reached 10 percent.

The per capita share of GDP, at 1975 prices, increased from ID 282.6 in 1970 to ID 356.2 in 1975, reaching ID 543.2 in 1980. As for fixed capital formation, its percentage share in GDP (again at 1975 prices) increased from 12.5 percent in 1970 to 25.9 percent in 1975, rising to 33 percent by 1980. The percentage share of the private sector in GDP, however, declined from 45.1 percent to 14 percent, then rose again to 21.7 percent, for the same three years.

All these figures reveal high growth rates, a substantial growth in capital formation, and an increasing dominance by the public sector over economic activity, in conjunction with the social imperatives of public authorities during the seventies. The same trends are evident in the contribution of the public sector to non-oil GDP, which rose from about 30.68 percent in 1968 to 43.7 percent in 1975 and reached 52.6 percent by 1980.[48] However, these figures also reflect the continued importance of the private sector in economic activity, which also increased (by about 47.4 percent), despite the expanded central role of the state in the economy.

During 1980–87, all macroeconomic policies were essentially aggressive, as the economy was transformed into a war economy. The aggressive nature of these policies was not surprising considering the extremely high costs of modern warfare. Invariably, these policies affected civilian investment, a substantial portion of which was redirected to supporting the military effort, which grew to an unprecedented level.

Among the first consequences of the war was a sharp drop in oil exports and revenues, impelling the Government to resort to domestic and foreign borrowing. At the same time, it tried to

[48]Ministry of Planning, Central Statistical Organization, *Annual Abstract of Statistics*, 1970–82.

revitalize oil production and exports by expanding production facilities and transferring oil by pipelines, which was accomplished. Oil exports increased in the later years, albeit at a much lower rate than at the start of the eighties. In another development, government spending was increased in all areas, especially the military, although social services also benefited and much was spent on construction of roads and buildings.

But the war also generated economic and financial problems. The oil sector retreated in both exports and prices, leading to the depletion of the country's foreign exchange and a reduced capacity to import or finance the growing public expenditures for both investment and consumption. The demand increased for domestic and foreign labor to operate productive projects and direct economic activity, which imposed greater financial burdens on the economy in general and on the balance of payments in particular.

The Government thus had to apply restrictive macroeconomic policy measures, whether in investment and consumption expenditures or in imports, while promoting increases in production and greater productivity in the public sector. At the same time, it sought to curb the relatively high rate of private consumption in a bid to mollify rising prices and limit the foreign debt burden.

Conclusions and Prospects

Perhaps the most important conclusion to be derived from this detailed study of the evolution of investment policy in Iraq over the past four decades is that oil was the cornerstone of this policy. It was and remains the principal source of investment financing and of the foreign exchange needed to finance the very large imports of capital goods that go into the country's development. It is clear from what has been discussed that economic development in Iraq was affected by developments on the oil scene—production, exports, and revenues. The rate of economic growth in the fifties increased when oil revenues increased, that is, following the fifty-fifty profit-sharing agreement negotiated with the foreign oil companies that operated in Iraq at that time. The same occurred in the mid-seventies, after the oil price adjustments and the nationalization of those foreign companies. Economic growth during the sixties declined, and this paralleled a recession in the oil sector that extended from the late fifties until the early seventies. The process is indicative of the close connection between oil revenues, investment, and noninvestment government expenditures, and the economic growth of Iraq.

GDP depended, and continues to depend, on oil production for the most part. The latter consistently made up a large percentage of the former, notwithstanding the decline of its contribution during the war years, which led to a proportionately higher share for non-oil economic sectors benefiting from the recycling of oil revenues in their direction by way of capital formation in these sectors. The relative decline in the contribution of oil was not so much due to significant growth in the other sectors as to the stagnation of exports and revenues because of the war and the recession that befell the advanced industrial countries at the turn of the eighties. Thus, growth in the non-oil sectors provides a more authentic picture of the condition of economic growth generally in Iraq than any debates over oil versus non-oil GDP growth.

The interplay of the oil factor, political change, and the social imperatives of the ruling party determined the size of investment, its form, and its direction in the various productive sectors. This study has described the evolution of investment policy side by side with the evolution of the forms of capital formation, sectoral and commodity. Perhaps the most important observation in this regard is that most of the accumulation was in the public sector, which suggests the importance of this sector for realizing investments based on oil revenues—which belong to the Government anyway. It is therefore not surprising to find public investment the principal source of capital formation specifically and of the country's economic development generally.

Large-scale and continuous development investment spending since the early fifties led to high growth rates for Iraq compared with other developing countries, whether in oil or non-oil. It also led to continuous improvements in per capita income and standard of living.

Having examined the changing imperatives of the Government in Iraq, we can attempt to forecast how trends will unfold in the nineties, other things being equal, including the social and political imperatives of this Government.

The public sector will continue to play a fundamental and leading role in the national economy by virtue of its size, while its relative importance will remain high even as its dominance over the economy is reduced. It is a necessity to a developing economy that continues to struggle for self-development under adverse external conditions and difficult internal economic conditions owing to the war, the country's foreign debt, and declining growth in oil exports.

Because of the continued relative importance of the public sector, government investment policies will still have a major impact on the country's development, in terms of volume of investment, sectoral assignments, and regional trends, and also because the oil sector remains central for financing development. Although domestic sources of financing will probably increase, they will remain limited in comparison with oil.

As the tacit assumption of unlimited financing for the country's development proved erroneous, and with the realization that unqualified dependence on oil export revenues is also a mistake, investment policies will tend to become more conservative in terms of investment volume, especially when the limits of absorptive capacity are taken into consideration.

The inclination will be toward horizontal expansion in the public sector, with greater attention being given to productive, financial, and administrative efficiency, to the rationalization of economic resources, and to reducing wastage of scarce resources through irrational or economically unjustified use. Also, public projects will most likely acquire greater freedom in the management of their resources, output direction, and product pricing.

An inclination now exists to deregulate prices, and this trend will probably continue into the next decade. However, the Government's role of monitoring from a distance will remain, to curb any economically unjustified price increases.

The private sector will be permitted a greater role in economic resource investment and will be given all forms of support and material and financial facilities. This will provide the banking sector with an opportunity to play a more active part in domestic investment financing, its management, and support.

Economic feasibility studies of projects will command greater attention and will preclude implementation; projects will also be examined for the efficiency of their performance.

We anticipate the devotion of greater attention to sectoral linkages and the forward and backward linkages of proposed projects in each sector.

We also anticipate revived interest in the agricultural sector because of its extreme importance as a food source, and in the prevention of bottlenecks in that sector. Its allocated investments will grow, and emphasis will be placed on efficient implementation and on preventing wastage in actual investment expenditures. However, we expect the development of the industrial sector and improvements in infrastructure to continue to command attention by virtue of their importance to development, and their sectoral investment allocations will therefore remain high.

Greater attention will be given to cultivating talents and scientific and managerial expertise and to developing middle management; emphasis on administrative efficiency will be placed above any other requirements unrelated to the effective and competent management of projects.

However, against these optimistic future projections, several qualifying conditions must be kept in mind:

First, Iraqi markets are characterized by either a general absence of competition in certain specific productive sectors or very limited competition. At best, the prevailing market situation is one of a few monopolies. Not even monopoly competition exists in the true sense of the word. What does exist is a sellers' market over which the sellers have clear control and with abundant liquidity among many social groups. This situation, along with large government spending, will inevitably lead to large increases in prices. Increases occur after the cancellation of price setting for many commodities, leading to high inflation in agricultural commodity prices in particular and in a very short time (no more than a few weeks), forcing the Government to return to pricing certain popular agricultural consumer goods.

Second, the primacy of the profit motive in the private sector contributes to this factor and is more important than the trend toward greater investment or consideration of the social or political consequences that may ensue. Thus, the private sector's preoccupation with limitless profit and short–term financial (rather than economic) returns will shape society's position (and that of the state in particular) toward that sector in future.

Third, a real risk of distortions exists in pricing and resource assignment if the two-tier system continues in the public and private sectors. This problem must be addressed, for it will definitely erode the effectiveness of the price system, whether in the un-regulated private sector or the regulated public sector.

Fourth, unqualified deregulation of prices leads to galloping inflation under conditions of postwar scarcity. It will be difficult to curb that inflation without government intervention, so that a certain measure of government monitoring of prices will be needed.

Fifth, continued adherence to an aggressive investment policy, without limit, can only aggravate these inflationary pressures and increase demand for both domestic and imported goods and services. This will increase the domestic and foreign deficits as well as the external debt, leading to a drawdown on foreign financial reserves, a deterioration of the actual and effective exchange rate of the dinar, reduced exports, stagnation of domestic liquidity and therefore domestic demand, and so on.

All of these require the adoption of a highly conservative investment policy for the coming decade.

Last, but certainly not least, is the danger of continued dependence on oil, its exports, and revenues. This danger and its negative consequences will remain with us as long as macroeconomic policies fail to emphasize the development of domestic economic resources as the basis for development, thereby minimizing the contribution of oil by developing other, non-oil sectors in the national economy.

Comment

Abdel Wahed Al-Makhzoumi

I would like at the outset to express my appreciation for this good study, which dealt with investment policy in Iraq over a period of close to four decades. Its treatment of the subject was organized and logically sequenced, which enabled the reader to get a clear idea of the message that the writer wanted to convey. I believe that a critique of this study will not be easy by any means, since I agree with most of the points raised in it. I agree in particular with the following points:

- That the revenues from oil exports were the mainstay during that period as a source of financing that investment policy, and they constituted a primary source of foreign exchange needed for the purchase of capital goods and for other development expenses that must be paid in foreign exchange to agencies implementing the investment projects.
- That the growth of the economic sectors, other than crude oil extraction and exports, reflected changes in those sectors during the period covered better than the overall growth rate of gross domestic product (GDP) (oil and nonoil). Isolating the impact of the crude oil sector, with its sharp fluctuations and high share in GDP, would give a clear picture of developments in other sectors of the economy.
- The author succeeded in highlighting the interaction and the interdependence during that period between oil and oil export revenues on the one hand, and political changes, social orientation, and ideologies of the ruling party on the other, and how they determined the size, pattern, and direction of investment. The investment policy of the Development Board in the fifties was conservative, implementation was low, and there was an ongoing emphasis on investments in the agricultural sector, mainly to satisfy the Development Board regarding its list of investment projects. There was a clear tendency toward involving the private sector in joint ventures with the Government in the industrial sector. This orientation

242

changed in the seventies to central planning; the diagnosis of obstacles to development; the specification of resources and potentialities and general development objectives; a shift of emphasis to the industrial sector; and high implementation rates. New sources of investment financing were sought, both domestic and foreign, including foreign borrowing that began with the Five-Year Plan 1961–65, and the pursuit of following what the author called a shock development strategy.

The author dealt with the investment policy in Iraq in that period in an objective manner. He is not an advocate of any policy followed during the period under consideration nor is he among those writers who sharply oppose any of these policies in such a way that their conclusions are clear from the outset. He presents faithfully what he knows, and in a manner that helps the reader understand the circumstances and the economic and noneconomic factors that had a clear impact on determining the form, content, size, and direction of investment policy in Iraq.

The evidence used in the intertemporal comparisons of annual growth rates and sectoral contributions to economic development is derived from the estimated figures of GDP growth rates and national income in Iraq, in real terms and in current prices during the period 1950–87. Because of the statistical situation in Iraq during that period, caution should be exercised in using these figures as regards the accuracy and comparability of some of them. They were prepared by various agencies and persons. Some were prepared based on different concepts and were modified to fit into a time series with earlier estimates; others were revised or reestimated by the same agency or by others.[1]

Regarding foreign investments in Iraq—excluding Arab investments—there were no direct investments following the Revolutionary Command Council's Decision No. 1646 of November 1, 1980, which decreed the liquidation of foreign participation in the capital of private companies in Iraq within a year. Arab nationals are not considered foreigners. But there are facilities for temporary investments accompanying the implementation of projects by foreign companies in Iraq.

---

[1]For more information, see "Development of National Income Statistics in Iraq," prepared by Abdel Hussein Zeini, published by the Baghdad Chamber of Commerce (1973).

The effects of macroeconomic policies in Iraq, as a developing country, were not different from those in most developing countries. However, financial policy, especially government spending, played a leading role, and the economy was open to the outside world to satisfy domestic demand depending on the availability of foreign exchange.

If I may add some remarks and ideas, the first thing that came to my mind was that the study needed a brief presentation of the methods followed by the planning bodies in investment planning in Iraq during the period under consideration, how the plans were prepared and finalized, the effects of changes in the plans (which were relatively many), and the extent to which planned objectives were achieved. Such a presentation would have added to the study's usefulness and would have been a summary of excerpts from various parts of it.

I expected also to find a comparison of forecasts or objectives of the various investment plans and the achievements realized. Such a comparison would usually take the form of comparative tables or charts showing GNP and the other major national account aggregates (normally agriculture, manufacturing industries, and other sectors). They would have shown the degree of realism in setting objectives and the benefits derived from the planning experience over the years.

With regard to the method of presenting the figures included in the text, and recognizing the difficulty of obtaining figures on the Iraqi economy in the form and detail necessary to present them suitably, I did not feel that my distinguished colleague established a base and then followed it.

The author leads us through an experiment in investment planning based on what was written about these plans and programs, or on laws and regulations that defined their powers and concepts, and on published results. We notice from this survey that an attempt was made to control government development spending through development programs during the period 1950–58. This attempt, which was disrupted by a political change, was characterized by centralized planning and implementation of government investment spending. After 1959, there was a period of centralized planning and decentralized implementation. After the enactment of the Planning Board Law of 1966, there was overall economic planning, which was not limited to economic aspects but extended

to coordinating economic, monetary, and trade policies, evaluating the draft of the annual state budget, and guiding private
sector activities to ensure that they conformed to development
plan objectives. This development took place after foreign borrowing emerged as a new source of investment finance in the 1961–
65 plan, and the attempt to link plan projects to the objectives
of Arab economic integration, and to coordinate (at the macroeconomic level) the investment policy with the financial, monetary,
credit, trade, and wage policies for the first time in the 1965–69
plan. The development plans covering the period 1965–80 were
established in the light of different political and economic developments, social orientations that differed from what went before,
and favoritism, which left a clear impact on the size of investments
and on the nature and direction of the investment policy. Reading
the study, however, it is not easy to find a clear itemization of the
outcome of all of these developments, whether they produced the
essential results and in which direction, and the extent to which
objectives were realized. I am confident that careful investigation
will yield positive results.

10

Investment Policies in Morocco

Bachir Hamdouch[1]

Morocco belongs to the group of the 17 heavily indebted middle-income countries. For a decade, it has been engaged in implementing a stabilization and structural adjustment program that has resulted in a reduction in macroeconomic disequilibria, but at the cost of a decline in investment rates and higher unemployment.[2] Moreover, the external debt burden, which was one of the main reasons for adopting the adjustment program, has not been lifted. Conversely, while overall debt more than doubled (from $9.7 billion in 1980 to $20.7 billion in 1987 and to $22 billion in 1988),[3] debt reschedulings have become the norm.

Morocco is a typical example of the paradoxical situation of many developing countries for which the decade of the 1980s has been a lost one as far as development is concerned. Morocco is also an illustration of the principle that growth is more rewarding than stagnation. However, since this principle was not accepted in time by the international community, many developing nations (including Morocco), which willingly or unwillingly committed themselves to rigorous adjustment, became locked into the vicious circle of debt.[4] The change in attitude in favor of growth (which has been in effect for the past few years with the Baker Plan and

---

[1]The views and opinions expressed in this paper are the author's and do not reflect the views of the Arab Monetary Fund.

[2]Bachir Hamdouch, "Adjustment and Development: The Case of Morocco," in *Adjustment Policies and Development Strategies in the Arab World,* ed. by Said El-Naggar (Washington: International Monetary Fund, 1987).

[3]World Bank, *World Debt Tables*, 1988–89 edition (Washington, 1988).

[4]From the limited resources available, funds were provided to ensure partial debt-service repayment at the expense of investment financing, which could have sustained growth and generated a surplus for debt repayment.

more recently with the debt-relief proposals that include particularly the Brady initiative) points clearly to a recognition both of the growth principle and of the concern for a reconciliation between the structural adjustment necessary and the equally necessary development-oriented growth in countries where basic needs are not always met, or where human living conditions are sometimes in jeopardy.[5]

These developments underline the importance of studying the issue of investment policies, an issue that lies at the heart of the problem. Indeed, it is a central theme in the crisis, in growth (and development), and in the debt issue. Moreover, while ill-considered or ill-adapted investment policies have contributed heavily to the crisis (particularly the debt crisis), and adequate investment policies are necessary, they alone may not be sufficient to resolve it.

This presentation makes a modest contribution to this debate by offering an analysis of the main features of investment policies in Morocco. The topic is vast and merits wider investigation, which was not possible given the time and scope of this seminar.

Impact of Macroeconomic Policies on Investment

Generally speaking, economic policy, in all its components, has a direct or indirect impact on investment. This point is certainly as true for general macroeconomic policy as for sectoral structural adjustment policies. Moroccan economic policies already in the 1960s and the 1970s had a strong impact on the volume and direction of investments. I shall briefly outline this impact to provide a perspective and to gain a better understanding of the policies pursued during the 1980s.

The Sixties and Seventies

The decade of the 1960s was marked by a moderate rate of growth and a modest rate of investment. This decade was specially distinguished by the stabilization plan of 1964, which produced a halt in growth and even led to a retreat in investment that extended

[5]See Statement by the Managing Director of the International Monetary Fund made before the Economic and Social Council of the United Nations (ECOSOC) on July 13, 1989, in *IMF Survey*, July 24, 1989 (Washington), pp. 26–28.

throughout the next two years (Table 1). Inflation seemed to have been successfully brought under control.

The sectors suffering most from the lack of capital accumulation included food crop production, industry, and social services (education, health, and housing). The distribution of gross fixed capital formation between the public and private sectors points to the predominance of the former, with 60–70 percent of the total (Table 2).

The pace of growth and investment during the 1970s was higher than in the preceding decade. Moreover, the mid-1970s were not marked by stabilization but by a strategy of accelerated economic growth. Table 3 shows the evolution in growth rates of gross domestic product (GDP), gross fixed capital formation (GFCF), and the cost of living index during this period.

The gross fixed capital formation growth rate was particularly high between 1974 and 1977 (34 percent in 1974 and 69 percent in 1975), raising the GFCF/GDP ratio from 13.9 percent in 1973 to 32.8 percent in 1977, with 6.4 percent and 19.6 percent, respectively, for the public sector alone.

Public investment became in effect the "engine of growth" during the period; its share in gross fixed capital formation was rising, particularly after 1973 (Table 4). Revision of the already ambitious objectives of the 1973–77 Plan as a result of the considerable increase in phosphate export receipts provided an opportunity for realizing finally the goal of rapid growth in which the state would assume a leadership role. Investments by the public sector and parastatal programs rose almost threefold, from DH 10.9 billion to DH 29.3 billion,[6] involving in particular the social services and the capital-intensive branches of the industrial sector. This policy, which was maintained even after the means of realizing the goal were no longer available, had considerable implications for the economy and made it necessary to adopt corrective policies in the next phase.

The Eighties: Impact of the General Adjustment Program

In July 1983, the Moroccan Government adopted a general adjustment program in agreement with the International Monetary

---

[6]World Bank, *Morocco: Economic and Social Development Report* (Washington: World Bank, 1981), p. 15.

Table 1.   Developments in Gross Domestic Product, Gross Domestic Investment, and Cost of Living, 1960–69

	1960	1961	1962	1963	1964	1965	1966	1967	1968	1969
GDP (at 1960 prices)[a]	909	838	993	1,048	1,061	1,081	1,066	1,136	1,276	1,287
Gross domestic investment (at 1960 prices)[a]	96	85	114	131	118	122	116	158	218	163
Cost of living index in Casablanca (1963 = 100)	88	90	95	100	104	108	107	106	106	109

Source: World Bank, *World Tables, 1976* (Baltimore: Johns Hopkins).
[a]In tens of millions of 1960 dirhams.

**Table 2.   Distribution of Gross Fixed Capital Formation
Between Public and Private Sectors, 1965–68**
(In tens of millions of dirhams)

	1965	1966	1967	1968
Public sector	—	92	115	140
State	*48*	*52*	*86*	*92*
Local communities	—	*12*	*13*	*14*
Public enterprises[a]	*31*	*26*	*16*	*34*
Private sector	—	61	74	57
Total	144	153	189	197

Source: World Bank mission report (August 1969), cited in A. Agourram and A. Belal, "Bilan de l'économie Marocaine depuis l'indépendance," in *Annuaire de l'Afrique du Nord*, 1969 (reproduced in A. Belal, "Impératifs du développement national" (Rabat: BESM, 1984), p. 79.
[a]Public enterprises not included elsewhere.

Fund to address general macroeconomic disequilibria. It was the first component in the structural adjustment program; the sectoral adjustment programs implemented with World Bank support were the second.

The two types of adjustment programs cut through the same areas of operation. Interest rate and exchange rate policies, which were the subject of both the general adjustment program and the sectoral adjustment programs in the financial, industrial, and foreign trade areas are an example. Such overlapping caused a coordination problem between various instruments of economic policy. The general adjustment program, as its title denotes, is general in scope; it outlines the measures to be taken and refers to the sectoral program for detailed information about the measures and their timing. This ensures a minimum degree of harmony, but has it been enough?[7]

What concerns us here is that the two types of adjustment program had an impact on investment. Let us start by discussing the impact of the general adjustment program.[8] Morocco has been implementing this program for more than six years and it still has a few years to completion. Adjustment had already been initiated, and the general adjustment program was in fact a "beefed-up"

[7]See discussion of this point in Hamdouch (cited in fn. 2).

[8]The impact of the sectoral adjustment program is discussed below.

Table 3. Evolution in Rates of Growth of Gross Domestic Product, Gross Fixed Capital Formation, and Cost of Living Index, 1970–78

(In percent)

	1970	1971	1972	1973	1974	1975	1976	1977	1978
GDP (at 1969 prices)	5.0	5.8	2.1	3.8	5.8	9.3	11.8	6.0	3.1
GFCF (at 1969 prices)	12.9	0.1	−11.0	−0.9	34.3	68.7	24.0	21.8	—
Cost of living index (1972/73 = 100)	—	—	—	105.0	122.0	132.0	143.0	161.0	176.0

Source: Secretary of State for Planning and Regional Development, reproduced in World Bank, *Morocco: Economic and Social Development Report* (Washington: World Bank, 1931).

Table 4. Distribution of Gross Fixed Capital Formation Between Public and Private Sectors, 1970–77

	1970	1971	1972	1973	1974	1975	1976	1977
Public sector	54.5	49.5	52.2	45.8	68.6	62.7	61.3	59.8
State	*19.4*	*17.4*	*22.3*	*18.4*	*24.0*	*24.3*	*26.1*	*30.3*
Other public sector	*35.1*	*32.1*	*29.9*	*27.4*	*44.6*	*38.4*	*35.2*	*29.5*
Private sector	45.5	50.5	47.8	54.2	31.4	37.3	38.7	40.2
Total	100.0	100.0	100.0	100.0	100.0	100.0	100.0	100.0
GFCF (*in tens of millions of 1969 dirhams*)	274.0	274.0	244.0	242.0	325.0	548.0	680.0	828.0

Source: Calculations based on World Bank, *Morocco: Economic and Social Development Report* (Washington: World Bank, 1981), Table 2.11.

extension of the stabilization program undertaken under the Three-Year Plan (1978–80) and was followed by the adjustment program of 1980–83.

In a nutshell, the general adjustment program considered that the major economic constraint in Morocco was the external disequilibrium with its corollary, indebtedness. Its main objective therefore was the restoration of "sustainable" equilibrium in the current account of the balance of payments by 1988. For this purpose, it was necessary to reduce the treasury deficit and to control the growth of private consumption so that domestic absorption could grow at a lower rate than GDP. However, the retained growth rate was only 3 percent on average. Thus, the adjustment effort was to be mostly undertaken by controlling the growth of overall demand and by reducing the investment ratio from 20 percent in 1983 to 16 percent in 1988.

The instruments used to achieve the objectives of the general adjustment program consisted of a number of economic policy measures covering the following areas:

- Public finance: fiscal restraint and reduction of investment in plant and equipment.
- Monetary field: reduction of liquidity in the economy and mobilization of savings.
- External economic relations: liberalization of trade, exchange rate depreciation, and debt stabilization.
- Structural reforms: to be generally implemented under sectoral adjustment programs in cooperation with the World Bank.

Adjustment may be carried out in many different and interrelated ways. Tables 5 and 6 summarize how it was implemented in Morocco. Table 5 shows the evolution in the components of overall expenditure expressed as a percentage of GDP, as well as the evolution in the resource gap. It demonstrates that

- GDP growth has been modest and uneven, mainly owing to varying crop results;
- gross public spending declined sharply owing to reduced consumption (especially public consumption) and reduced investment. At the same time, savings rose and the resource gap was sharply reduced,

Table 5. Evolution in Gross National Expenditures and in Resource Gap, 1982–87

	1982	1983	1984	1985	1986	1987
1. GDP[a]	100.0	100.0	100.0	100.0	100.0	100.0
2. Overall consumption	90.0	87.6	88.7	85.9	85.3	85.5
Private	*68.6*	*67.8*	*70.5*	*68.5*	*67.9*	*68.0*
Public	*21.4*	*19.8*	*18.2*	*17.4*	*17.4*	*17.5*
3. Investment	23.3	20.9	21.8	22.9	20.3	19.1
4. Gross national expenditures[b]	113.3	108.5	110.5	108.8	105.6	104.6
5. Resource gap[c]	13.3	8.5	10.5	8.8	5.6	4.6
6. Gross domestic savings	10.0	12.4	11.3	14.1	14.7	14.5
7. Exports of goods and services[d]	20.5	22.4	25.7	27.0	24.5	25.3
8. Imports of goods and services[d]	33.8	31.7	36.2	35.8	30.1	29.9
9. GDP/Real growth rate	6.8	2.3	2.1	4.4	5.8	1.0
10. Cost of living change	10.5	6.2	12.5	7.7	8.8	2.8

Source: Calculations based on Ministry of Planning, *National Accounts*, reproduced in reports of Bank of Morocco.
[a]Data from the previous national accounts series (base year 1969) are retained to ensure comparability with data of previous years and with earlier reports and studies, especially those prepared by the World Bank (the new series uses 1980 as a base year and goes back only to 1980).
[b]Item 4 = items 2 + 3.
[c]Item 5 = items 1 − 4 = 6 − 3 = 7 − 8.
[d]Nonfactor goods and services.

**Table 6. Evolution in Revenues and Expenditures of
Treasury and Financing of Deficit, 1982–87**
(as percentage of GDP)[a]

	1982	1983[b]	1984	1985	1986	1987
Current revenues	24.3	22.3	22.4	22.4	21.7	23.4
Expenditures	36.6	30.8	29.2	28.6	30.6	28.1
Current expenditures	22.7	22.8	22.3	22.5	22.1	21.3
Administrative expenses	*16.1*	*17.3*	*16.0*	*15.1*	*15.2*	*15.6*
Consumer price subsidies	*3.2*	*1.7*	*2.1*	*2.3*	*1.1*	*0.5*
Interest on public debt	*3.5*	*3.8*	*4.2*	*5.2*	*5.7*	*5.1*
Capital expenditures	13.9	8.0	6.9	6.1	8.5	6.9
Budget deficit	12.3	8.5	6.8	6.2	8.9	4.7
Change in arrears	2.3	—	−0.3	−2.7	3.4	−0.8
Financing requirement of						
Treasury	10.0	8.5	7.1	8.9	5.5	5.6
Net financing	10.0	8.5	7.1	8.9	5.5	5.6
External	10.4	4.5	6.4	4.6	−2.1	−0.4
Domestic	−0.4	4.0	0.7	4.3	7.6	6.0
Monetary financing	*−1.1*	*6.2*	*0.8*	*2.9*	*4.8*	*1.8*
Domestic borrowings	*0.7*	*0.2*	*−0.1*	*1.4*	*2.8*	*4.2*
Provision for authorized						
expenses		−2.4				

Source: Calculations based on annual reports of Bank of Morocco.
[a]See fn. a in Table 5.
[b]For 1983 onward, after debt rescheduling.

- in foreign trade, the reduced resource gap was due to increased exports rather than to lower imports; and
- inflation rates dropped.

Table 6 shows how adjustment was undertaken in public finance; it illustrates the evolution in the revenues and expenditures of the Treasury and the financing of the deficit, expressed as a percentage of GDP. It indicates that

- The financing requirement of the Treasury, expressed as a percentage of GDP, was reduced by almost half;
- the reduction in the financing requirement resulted not from any increase in the current revenues of the Government but rather from a sharp reduction in public expenditures, especially expenditures from the capital budget, which were cut by half; more than four fifths of this reduction was the result of reduced investment spending;

- current expenditures were not high, but their structure changed considerably, indicating a sharp reduction in consumer subsidies and a sizable increase in interest payments on public debt, especially on domestic debt;
- sources of financing the treasury deficit changed: until 1984, most of the financing was from external sources, while in 1986 and 1987 it came entirely from domestic sources;
- in domestic financing, borrowing grew in volume in 1987 and replaced financing from monetary sources; and
- by 1988, the sources of financing had changed, which was in effect a step backward: external financing again provided 31 percent of the financing requirement of the Government Treasury with monetary sources providing the rest.[9]

This partial adjustment of public finances was thus essentially undertaken at the expense of a sharp reduction in investment expenditures and was followed by a transformation in the structure of public expenditures in favor of current expenditures. Changes also occurred in the structure of current expenditures, and the financing of the treasury deficit gave rise to a problem of the effects of crowding out.

It is a valid question whether financing the needs of the Government Treasury on an increasing scale from domestic resources in past years had been done at the expense of private investment. In other words, had there been a crowding-out effect? This question becomes somewhat important when discussing the implications of macroeconomic policies for investment and investment policies. It serves no purpose to take back with one hand what was given with the other.

But the question is not easy to answer. It requires a more profound analysis and a special investigation that is not within the scope of this undertaking. However, some elements of the answer may be advanced, which could be developed in the course of the discussion or in other later investigations.

Financing the government treasury deficit can produce a crowding-out effect in three ways: first, by reserving to the Treasury the lion's share in money creation. Credit control mechanisms, especially credit containment policies (credit ceilings), tended to restrict credit distribution in favor of the Treasury. This fact was

---

[9]Bank of Morocco, *Annual Report, 1988*, Table A40.

evident in 1983 and 1986 and also in 1988. In 1983, claims on the Treasury grew by 28.1 percent, compared with 11.5 percent for credit to the rest of the economy, with the Treasury capturing 72.5 percent of domestic credit, leaving only 27.5 percent to the rest of the economy. In 1986, the corresponding rates were 22.2 percent against 8.6 percent and 73 percent against 27 percent. In 1988, they were 17.2 percent against 9.2 percent and 68.6 percent against 31.4 percent. During these three years, claims on the Treasury represented more than half of the money supply counterparts, with a record of 53.2 percent in 1983.[10] The credits above the ceiling (uncontained credits), such as investor credits and export credits, have developed in recent years and reached 18 percent of total credit in the economy in 1988.[11] Without these, credit distribution between the Treasury and the rest of the economy would have been more unbalanced. They served to mitigate the crowding-out effect, and they constituted some type of safety valve.[12]

Second, the Treasury can exert a crowding-out effect by capturing private savings; savings here could be either voluntary or compulsory. In the area of voluntary savings, the Government in recent years has launched a program of borrowing on attractive terms (higher interest rates and tax breaks), where participation was limited to the nonbank private sector. Considerable funds were raised through this channel in 1986 and 1987, representing 2.8 percent and 4.2 percent of GDP, respectively (Table 6). As for compulsory savings, these related to treasury arrears in payments to its suppliers, whether public or private enterprises. In 1986, government arrears grew by a figure equivalent to 3.4 percent of GDP (Table 6).

Third, the crowding-out effect can be exercised through the interest rate—a higher interest rate can be a disincentive to investment. The increase in real interest rates that occurred in Morocco in recent years was due to three main factors The first was the desire, within the framework of the adjustment program, to encourage savings by offering positive real interest rates through

[10]Ibid.

[11]Ibid.

[12]Consideration is now being given to eliminating credit containment and to introducing other control techniques such as statutory reserves. See statements by the Minister of the Economy, *La Vie Economique* (Casablanca), September 1989.

raising nominal rates. The second was the rewarding rates offered on public borrowings, while the third related to the reduction of inflation rates.

A situation emerged where real interest rates on medium-term credits, which were zero or even slightly negative in 1981–82, exceeded 11 percent in 1987.[13] Such rates have the effect of increasing the cost of capital and may discourage investment, especially in capital-intensive branches of the industrial sector, which is what actually happened in 1987, particularly following the removal early in that year of the 2 percent discount on interest rates offered on credit to the industrial sector.[14]

The risk of a crowding-out effect is usually higher in the presence of multiple exclusion factors, as was the case in both 1986 and 1987. In 1986, a combination of crowding-out effects resulted from the capture by the Treasury of credits and savings, and in 1987 from public borrowings and higher real interest rates. Therefore, the monetary authorities had to reduce interest rates in 1987. This move was firmly established and widened in scope in 1988. It touched particularly on medium- and long-term credits, where interest rates fell by 1.5–2 points.[15]

Assessment of the results of the crowding-out effects and countereffects is not easy, especially when account is taken of other factors that influence investment, including economic conditions at home and abroad, expectations of economic transactors, the sectoral adjustment programs, and the financial and fiscal incentives to investors (investment codes). Account must also be taken of the use by the Government of captured credit or savings, which gives an idea of the total effect on the economy: consumption versus savings and in which sectors. We have clearly seen that the Government's propensity to invest declined during the 1980s. Finally, the element of timing should be taken into account, as the

---

[13]See nominal interest rates and inflation rates in the reports of Bank of Morocco.

[14]Public investments declined in 1987 by 20.6 percent in the chemical and parachemical sector, 15.8 percent in mechanical and metallurgical industries, and 13.8 percent in the agro-foodstuff industries, which led to a 9.5 percent decline in investments in the manufacturing sector as a whole. See Ministry of Trade and Industry, "Situation des industries de transformation," Fiscal Year 1987 (Rabat, December 1988), p. 11.

[15]Report of Bank of Morocco, 1987 and 1988, Table A57.

direction and magnitude of the implications of these effects and countereffects may vary in the short, medium, and long term.

The Eighties: Impact of the Sectoral Adjustment Programs

The intention here is not to present an analysis of the different sectoral adjustment programs undertaken by Morocco but rather to see to what degree they have had an impact on investment.

The results of the sectoral adjustment programs have been mixed in terms of their respective impact on investment. The impact of the adjustment program in the area of pricing has been diffused and unclear.

As for the adjustment program in the financial sector, the increase in real interest rates stimulated savings, which rose from a ratio of 11.3 percent of GDP in 1984 to 14.1 percent in 1985. But this movement soon lost momentum, and the ratio of savings stagnated at about 14.5 percent in both 1986 and 1987.[16] Furthermore, the Treasury, as mentioned above, dug deeply into savings in recent years (producing a crowding-out effect). Adding to this the rapid increase in real interest rates, which led to the higher cost of capital, it seems improbable that the interest rate policy could have had a net positive impact on investment.[17]

It is too early to judge the impact of the adjustment program on private investment in agriculture. Its impact on public investment was, however, more direct and clear cut, as we shall see in the following section.

Owing to the magnitude of private capital in industry and the renewed importance of industrial exports in the structural adjustment policy as a whole, the impact of the industrial adjustment program on investment and the direction of investment assumes particular significance. The annual survey of the Ministry of Trade and Industry enables us to trace developments in the manufacturing sector. Table 7, reproduced from the survey, shows the average annual growth rates for exports, investment, and manufacturing by sector for 1984–87. It shows that only the textile and leather sector achieved the highest rates of growth in respect of both

[16]Calculations based on reports of Bank of Morocco.

[17]On the relationship between interest rates and investment, see Jacques J. Polak, *IMF Survey*, July 24, 1989, p. 237.

Table 7. Growth Rates in Exports, Investment, and Industrial Production by Sector, 1984–87

Sector	Exports	Rank	Investment	Rank	Production	Rank
Agro-foodstuffs	25.0	2	12.5	5	14.5	3
Textiles and leather	30.5	1	28.1	1	13.4	4
Chemicals and parachemicals	1.1	5	23.5	2	9.0	5
Mechanical and metallurgical industries	14.8	4	23.2	3	19.7	1
Electrical and electronic industries	19.6	3	16.1	4	16.4	2
Total	14.6		20.4		13.1	

Source: Ministry of Trade and Industry, "Situation des industries de transformation," Fiscal Year 1987 (Rabat, December 1988).

exports and investment. The agro-foodstuffs sector occupies second place in terms of export growth, but comes only in fifth place in terms of investment growth, while the situation is just the opposite in the chemical and parachemical industries. The two remaining sectors are in an intermediate situation, which would seem to indicate that, except for the textile and leather industries, the most dynamic sectors in terms of exports are not so dynamic in terms of investment (and production) and vice versa.

The textile industry is fairly significant; alone it represented 35 percent of industrial exports and 19 percent of total investments during 1984–87, and more than 64 percent of the exports of finished goods in 1987.[18] Industrial exports have thus strengthened in recent years, but this situation gave rise to a problem of export concentration by product and also by destination.[19]

The adjustment program in the industrial sector—which envisaged the promotion of export-led industrial growth—is yet to

[18]*La Vie Economique* (Casablanca), March 18, 1988; Office des changes, Division des études et de la balance des paiements, *Statistiques des échanges extérieurs du Maroc.*

[19]In 1987, 75 percent of textile exports consisted of ready-made clothing; 85 percent of these were imported by countries of the European Economic Community (75 percent by France). Having exceeded its quota under the Multifiber Agreement, Morocco had to suspend "voluntarily" its exports of trousers to France in the summer of 1988. See *La Vie Economique* (Casablanca), July 29, September 16, October 16, and December 2, 1988.

have a significant and widespread impact on investment in industry. (However, a deeper investigation of the branches and subbranches might reveal some activity that could augur well for the future.)

Public Investment Policy

Public investments have played—and are still required to play—an important role in Morocco's economic development. They represented over 60 percent of total investment during the 1960s and 1970s. Public investment policies underwent changes in the past three decades and were also influenced by the structural adjustment program.

Evolutions in Policy

The direction of government choices in the areas of public investment can be discerned from an analysis of the successive Moroccan development plans. Table 8 shows the distribution by sector of capital expenditures effected by the Treasury. The figures indicate that certain elements of policy have remained constant and others have undergone change.

The policy constants consisted of the priority or preferential treatment accorded to two sectors: agriculture and infrastructure. By virtue of its priority status, agriculture received the lion's share of public investments during the 1960s and 1970s. Midway through the period, the share of capital expenditures in agriculture from the state budget reached 43 percent (see Table 8). In real terms, investment was even higher, since two thirds of government capital expenditures in the agricultural sector went into construction of barrages ("barrages policy") and irrigation works, including in particular construction of large hydraulic systems. This concentration of capital expenditure was made at the expense of rainfed farming—which produces the essential food crops—and of small and medium-sized hydraulic systems.

The favorable treatment accorded to infrastructure is illustrated by the fact that it has regularly received about one fifth of government investment expenditures. It indicates a preference for the strategy of growth by "an excess in infrastructure" (A.O. Hirschman).

Table 8. Evolution in Sectoral Distribution of Public Capital Expenditures, 1965–80

(In percent)

	1965–67	1968–72	1973–77	1978–80
Agriculture and barrages	27.4	42.9	24.3	26.7
of which: Barrages	(4.4)	(16.1)	(6.5)	(9.3)
Irrigation	(14.7)	(13.2)	(8.9)	(10.4)
Other productive sectors	28.2	18.6	15.7	11.8
Infrastructure	21.8	21.5	19.6	19.6
Education and training			11.6	17.6
Social services and housing			8.1	5.9
Regional development	22.5	17.0	9.9	11.5
Administrative and unclassified expenditures			10.8	6.8
Total	100.0	100.0	100.0	100.0
Total investment[a] (millions of current dirhams)	2,132	5,478	17,923	15,960
Average annual capital expenditures (millions of 1981 dirhams)[b]	2,146	3,320	6,489	6,467

Sources: Economic and Social Development Plans and World Bank estimates.
[a]Includes capital transfers but excludes defense expenditure and debt service.
[b]Constant dirhams are derived by deflating current dirhams by the implicit deflator of the gross fixed capital formation in the national accounts (growth of the deflator in 1981 is estimated at 10 percent).

The policy changes covered two main areas: the productive sectors other than agriculture, and the socioadministrative sectors. The other productive sectors (manufacturing, mining, and energy) saw their share in capital expenditures falling sharply and continually during the period: from over 28 percent in 1965–67 to less than 12 percent in 1978–80 (Table 8). It should be observed, however, that investment in these sectors grew through public enterprises that have their own budgets and that grew in size and importance, particularly during the 1973–77 period.[20] Several projects were undertaken, generally in capital-intensive activities such as phosphate and cement production, sugar plants, and oil refineries.

[20]Public enterprises received capital transfers amounting to 40 percent of government capital expenditures in 1973–77. These transfers financed about one third of capital investments by these enterprises.

Conversely, the socioadministrative sectors (education and training, housing, health, regional development, and administrative services) saw their share in government capital expenditures rise sharply in the 1970s. Their share jumped from 17 percent in 1968–72 to 40 percent in 1973–77 and to 42 percent in 1978–80 (Table 8). It has thus grown 2.5 times during the period. But this sharp increase was at the expense of the productive sectors (including agriculture), whose share in capital expenditures from the government budget was cut by more than half: over 60 percent in the early 1970s and 40 percent or less during the rest of the decade.

The trends during that period included an acceleration in public investment, illustrated by a tripling in less than ten years of the annual average investments expressed in constant dirhams (DH 2.1 billion in 1965–67 and DH 6.5 billion in 1973–77). A massive concentration of investment in capital-intensive projects with questionable profitability also occurred. Some of these projects were long term and others were of undetermined duration. Moreover, the sectoral distribution of investments tended to assume a less productive character. The contribution of investments to growth was poor; faster growth rates could have been expected, considering the increased level of investment, particularly in the mid-1970s.

As a result, the incremental capital-output ratio in the economy increased rapidly from 2.6 in 1965–72 to 6.7 in 1979–82.[21] Private capital also turned to import-substitution, capital-intensive industries, in the presence of often excessive protection and sharp distortions in the regime of incentives.

There was massive recourse to external borrowings to finance both government and public enterprise investments after a fall in phosphate receipts. Accordingly, public investment was responsible for the debt crisis in that the projects implemented were not generally export oriented, which would have ensured the availability of the foreign exchange necessary for debt-service payments—except for phosphate and its by-products.[22]

[21]World Bank, *World Development Report, 1985* (Washington: World Bank, 1985), p. 52.

[22]World price fluctuations, however, contribute to the uncertainty of this commodity.

Adjustment

The policy of public investment has been undergoing adjustment since 1978, but the adjustment effort became more rigorous in 1983. To mitigate the deficit in public finances and its implications for current payments, public investments were reduced as of 1978. Projects already started were stopped, and others considered to be priority projects were continued. Despite the cuts, annual capital expenditures from the Treasury during 1978–80 were kept at the same level as those for 1973–77. Moreover, the 1981–85 Plan had practically doubled the volume of investment in constant dirhams (DH 12.3 billion, against DH 6.5 billion annually during the 1978–80 period).

Although an improvement did take place in the basic equilibria, the imbalances remained serious, and external debt indicators became even more alarming. There was accordingly no justification for this new surge toward expansion, which may be explained by the oscillation between adjustment and growth that marked Moroccan economic policies at the turn of the 1980s.

The debt crisis had set in. Adjustment became imperative, and the bulk of the fiscal adjustment effort was to focus on the capital budget, particularly as large appropriations totaling DH 75 billion had remained unexpended in the first four years of the Plan. The general adjustment program limited the volume of appropriations committable in the last year of the Plan to 20 percent of the total, and it was decided that the investments should be programmed on the basis of compatibility with the foreseeable resources and on the principle that their financing should not aggravate the debt profile.

Sectoral investment programs were reviewed with World Bank assistance. The key words in the process were efficiency and resource economy. The principles were to improve stock capital efficiency by ensuring maintenance and institutional restructuring or reform; to establish priorities in project implementation, since all projects cannot be implemented simultaneously, given the scarcity of financing and limited absorption capacity; and to improve the Government's "capacity to invest" using the basic techniques of planning, budgeting, and project monitoring.

The criteria were adequate economic and financial profitability, shorter gestation periods, and lower recurrent expenses; an emphasis on labor-intensive projects (less capital-intensive projects);

a net positive effect on the balance of payments; and the availability of financing.

The 1988–92 Plan is guided by this spirit. It assigns the private sector "a crucial role in realizing the objectives of the 'Orientation Plan'. This sector is to be encouraged, especially in the areas where it is called upon to intensify its investment."[23]

Private Investment Policy

The special place reserved to the private sector in the 1988–92 Plan—this sector is called upon to make up 60 percent of industrial investments—reflects a continuation of the attitude toward private capital in Moroccan economic policies since the early 1960s. Such policies have evolved over time but always in a direction favorable to private investment, until 1988, which saw an end to the escalation of incentives to private initiative.

This preferential treatment is targeted both to the Moroccan private sector and to foreign capital, with some minor variations. The foreign investor is entitled to repatriate income from investment and the invested capital itself. This advantage was recently extended to Moroccans residing abroad as an incentive to them to invest in Morocco. The clause in the investment codes of 1973 limiting incentives to Moroccan enterprises no longer appears in the investment codes of the 1980s.

The Investment Codes

Incentives to private investors are numerous and are generally listed in the investment codes, which are sets of fiscal and financial measures designed to encourage private investment. Individual sectors of economic activity are covered by a set of related measures, or codes of investment.

The earliest code, dating back to 1958, provided for various measures to stimulate investment in the industrial sector, including partial or total exemption from payment of customs duties on imports of new materials and equipment, tax breaks, and guarantees for the repatriation of profits and of foreign capital under certain conditions. The results, however, were disappointing.

[23]"Plan d'orientation pour le développement économique et social, 1988–92."

A second code on industrial investment was therefore adopted in 1960 that maintained the incentives of the former code and added new ones, which included the possibility of constituting funds exempted from taxes on profits to acquire new equipment, the allocation of an equipment allowance (equivalent to 15 or 20 percent of the total amount of the investment), and relaxation of conditions attached to the repatriation guarantee, which became virtually automatic. The average value of the advantages accorded under this code represented approximately 14 percent of the realized investment. The 1960 code was generally well received. Private investors, however, did not respond either in terms of volume or behavior to the expectations of the Moroccan authorities.

The third code on industrial investment (1973) accorded more advantages than its predecessor, making the granting of advantages virtually automatic. The advantages were modeled according to the levels of regional development, with the aim of decentralizing industrial growth. The code provided for the possibility of combining its advantages with those granted under the industrial export promotion code.

In reality, the 1973 code comprised six such codes for investments in industry, handicraft industries, mining, maritime transport, tourism, and promotion of industrial and handicraft exports. For the establishment of large-scale enterprises (investments of more than DH 30 million) or investment in specific sectors (automobile assembly lines, tire-making, edible oil production, sugar or oil refining, flour-milling, etc.), the Government, under contractual agreements with prospective investors, may grant even more advantageous conditions than those prescribed in the code. The 1973 code was favorably received in foreign business circles.

This code did not prevent the promulgation in 1983 of a fourth industrial investment code that contained more liberal provisions, including wider tax benefits, more business opportunities, interest rebates, substantial incentives for job creation activities, and, most important, the removal of the stipulation that only Moroccan companies could benefit from these advantages. This provision allowed fully owned foreign companies to enjoy the advantages provided for in the code, particularly the guarantee of unlimited automatic transfer of dividends, capital, and capital gains in the event of liquidation.

Does this not mean that private investment, and more particularly foreign investment, was becoming less sensitive to the financial stimulants? In any case, investment codes were promulgated, at times with excessive incentives, for the other sectors: agriculture in 1969 (the agricultural tax was removed in 1984 until the year 2000); export firms in 1977; real estate in 1980 (a 15-year tax holiday);[24] tourism investments in 1983; maritime transport investments in 1984; real estate promoters in 1985; and mining investments in 1986.

The trend in granting investors further advantages was reversed in 1988. Under pressure of budgetary imbalances that were becoming more difficult to reduce further, the Government revised the investment codes (with the exception of the code on agricultural investment), reducing the advantages and limiting in particular the exemption from the tax on business profits and on corporations (where the tax exemption period was cut from 10 or 15 years to 5 years with the level of exemption reduced to 50 percent).[25]

Other Incentives

Several other incentives were granted to encourage private investors. Of the six types of incentives, two were sharply reduced because of the structural adjustment program, though they were the most important. The first related to the various subsidies in the agricultural sector, which were gradually eliminated under the sectoral adjustment program for agriculture. The second related to the tariff and quantitative protection of the industrial sector. Although this protection may have been justified for "infant industries," it was often granted on a case-by-case basis and sometimes depending on the identity of the investor. Such protection was often excessive and was maintained even after the enterprise had grown out of "infancy." Under the sectoral adjustment program for industry and foreign trade, this protection was reduced and became more orderly.

The third related to the sets of measures ("regimes") applied at customs, including exemptions (or suspensions) of customs duties,

[24]A. Akesbi, "Paradis fiscal pour les promoteurs" (Tax holiday for promoters), *Liberation*, No. 302, March 6, 1981.

[25]For further details, see *La Vie Economique* (Casablanca), February 12, 1988.

in addition to those advantages extended under the investment codes to encourage export industries in particular. This classical list of incentives consisted of bonded warehouse storage, temporary entry, temporary importation, temporary export for foreign processing, temporary exportation, transit, drawback, and customs clearance at domicile.[26]

The fourth advantage consisted of the establishment by the state of "industrial parks" to be made available to investors at moderate cost, while the fifth related to the incentives accorded under the selective credit policy, including lower interest rates and/or the provision of credit.

The sixth consisted of incentives to remittances of Moroccans working abroad, including exchange premiums and interest on checking accounts held in Moroccan banks. These incentives were later canceled. However, because of a drop of almost 20 percent in 1988 in this primary source of foreign exchange in Morocco,[27] various measures were adopted, including relaxing foreign exchange controls and extending the same repatriation guarantees that were formerly granted to foreign capital invested in Morocco to housing loans and credits for small and medium-scale industries.[28] A bank (Bank Al-Amal) was established to finance investment projects in Morocco of nationals working abroad, especially in industry. The acquisition of housing has always been the principal investment of Moroccan expatriate workers.[29] With the onset of reverse migration—particularly from Europe— investment in small and medium-scale industries was an attractive proposition, considering that the funds in question were considerable and presented a twofold advantage as sources of foreign exchange and of investment financing. Assistance in this area was to be provided by the government agencies responsible for the encouragement of investments.

[26]For more details, see ODI (Industrial Development Office), *Guide de l'investisseur* (Investor's Guide), August 1989.

[27]DH 10.7 billion in 1988 compared with DH 13.3 billion in 1987 ($1.3 billion and $1.7 billion, respectively).

[28]*La Vie Economique* (Casablanca), June 24, 1988.

[29]Bachir Hamdouch, "Réflexions sur les effets de l'émigration des travailleurs marocains à l'étranger," *Revue de l'INSEA*, No. 7, January 1984; Bachir Hamdouch and others, "Migration Internationale au Maroc," INSEA-UQAM, Rabat, 1981.

Role of Investment Promotion Agencies

Encouragement of private investment by the Government and public agencies is carried out through the management of incentives granted under the investment codes and the provision of services to facilitate project implementation, including capital participations or setting up entire projects.

Administration of Incentives

The administration of incentives passed through three main phases. The Investment Commission was set up in 1958 to select projects eligible for benefits under the investment code. This interministerial body was coordinated by the Ministry of Economy until its dissolution. It met whenever it received a project application from the technical ministry concerned.[30]

As the granting of advantages under the 1973 investment code became automatic, the *raison d'être* of the Investment Commission no longer existed. Consequently, each technical ministry dealt with project applications under its respective jurisdiction merely to ensure that they met the requirements of the applicable regulations. If so, the ministry would issue an "in order visa" and notify the Ministry of Economy accordingly. Once an application was so approved, the investor had to apply to a financing agency: the National Economic Development Bank (BNDE) or a commercial bank.

Thus viewed, the procedure seemed simple and swift. In reality, it was long and cumbersome owing to the numerous departments through which the project had to pass at both the local and central levels (to illustrate the lengthy character of the procedure, an investment project application had to be submitted in 17 copies).

Thus the idea of a single focal point was born. It had been envisaged in the 1973–77 Development Plan, but had not been accepted for several reasons, the most important of which was that it would have cast doubts on the way in which the administration conducted its business. It may also have meant adding an extra agency instead of replacing the existing ones. Questions were also raised about the power that such an authority would

[30]A similar formula was applicable for a Contracts Commission.

have vis-à-vis the other departments and about its eventual effectiveness. It was suggested that the investors themselves, or their accredited representatives, could best deal with their own affairs and would be quicker to get through. In fact, the single authority system did operate in Morocco for some time in the form of a "Welcome Center" for investors, but it had no power whatsoever.

A major development in the field of private investment was a Royal Letter addressed to the Prime Minister, in June 1989, denouncing the "slowness" and "multiplicity of administrative procedures." It concluded

> Consequently we have to put an end to this situation. Henceforth, every properly-constituted application of an investment project shall be deemed as having obtained the approval of the Administration if the latter fails to take any action thereon *within two months* from the date of its submission. In case of rejection, the decision of the Administration must be duly explained. This decision shall take effect immediately and shall appear forthwith in the provisions of all our investment codes, where it must be inserted.[31]

Steps for the enforcement of this decision are under way. Attempts are being made to establish an administrative structure to handle private investment matters, which would be characterized by a simplified procedure, transparency, and speed. It is also intended to establish "an investment follow-up committee" at the provincial level.[32] The 1988–92 Plan envisages measures aimed at streamlining administrative procedures and incorporates the notion of "a sole interlocutor at the local level."

Investment Services Agencies

Two bodies play an important part in private investment promotion,[33] namely, the Industrial Development Office, a public agency, and the National Economic Development Bank, a semipublic body. Their actions are on the whole complementary.

---

[31]*Le Matin du Sahara* (Casablanca), August 25, 1989 (author's italics).

[32]Circular letter from the Prime Minister in *Le Matin du Sahara* (Casablanca), August 25, 1989. See also the letter from the Minister of the Interior to the governors on the same issue.

[33]A third body, the National Investment Company (SNI), could also have played an important role. This semipublic holding company should have activated the financial market in Casablanca. However, its activities were generally limited to the management of equity portfolios received at the time of its establishment.

The Industrial Development Office (ODI) is an industrial promotion agency that acts on its own behalf or in association with private national and/or foreign investors. Four types of interventions may be identified in the ODI effort:[34] (a) reception, information, and assistance in project implementation; (b) sectoral studies and assistance in project identification, pre-feasibility, and feasibility studies, upon the request of private industrial promoters; (c) technical assistance to small and medium-scale industries, ranging from project identification to enterprise management; and (d) equity participation in, or support for, the implementation of projects of national or regional interest, and pilot projects or projects with a high technological content. In companies other than its affiliates, the ODI maintains minority equity as a general rule, although its participation is usually higher than 20 percent to enable it to play an active part in the project. Once the project is launched, ODI may relinquish its equity to the private sector, thus freeing it to engage in other projects. The ODI group currently comprises some 30 industrial companies, 10 of which are affiliates.

The National Economic Development Bank acts mainly as an agency for financing private industrial projects. It has a secondary function as an organ of promotion and assistance. In nearly thirty years of activity, Bank interventions consisted of direct loans (62 percent), rediscounted medium-term credits (37 percent), and equity participation (1 percent).[35] Investments or financing operations with BNDE participation represented close to 30 percent of gross fixed capital formation in terms of plant and equipment in Morocco during that period.

Effectiveness of Private Investment Promotion Policies

The enactment of several investment codes in succession, with progressively more liberal provisions, calls into question the effectiveness of these codes and raises the issue of whether the results were adequate in relation to the advantages that were granted.[36]

[34]ODI, *Statement of General Policy, Review of Activities in the Last Ten Years,* and *Report on Activities,* 1987.

[35]BNDE, "Au service de l'entreprise" and *Annual Report, 1987.*

[36]A general feeling exists in Morocco that there was a degree of "inadequacy" between the advantages offered in the investment codes and the results. This was

Accordingly, I shall attempt an analysis of the results and the factors that have influenced investment decisions.

Results

First, little information is available on the investments approved within the framework of the investment codes. The only updated data available in sufficient detail concern the industrial sector. These investments, however, were those that the Ministry of Industry judged eligible for the advantages offered under the investment codes, but that were not necessarily implemented. No information is available to permit comparison between the investments approved and those that were actually implemented.[37]

In the 1970s, private investment followed the growth of public investment, though at a slower pace. Expressed as a percentage of GDP, it rose between 1970 and 1979 from 7 percent to approximately 13 percent (5 percent and 8 percent excluding investments in housing), while the ratio of overall investment rose from 15 percent to 33 percent during the same period.[38]

During this time, corporate investment in Morocco by the foreign private sector, which represented 5–6 percent of the gross fixed capital formation at the beginning of the decade, dropped sharply by almost one half since 1973 and was no more than 2–3 percent of gross fixed capital formation through the rest of the decade.[39] The effect of "Moroccanization" and the introduction, in the 1973 codes, of the clause that a company had to "Moroccan" to enjoy the advantages had become evident.

An analysis of the developments with regard to approved investments in the activities covered by the investment codes of 1973 (manufacturing, handicrafts, mining, fishing, and tourism) shows

---

referred to in the above-mentioned royal letter to the Prime Minister which reads in part: "As regards the advantages that have been thus approved, Morocco still remains far from obtaining all that it could legitimately and reasonably have expected" (*Le Matin du Sahara* (Casablanca), August 25, 1989).

[37]The rate of implementation would be about 80–85 percent according to sources at the Ministry of Trade and Industry.

[38]See World Bank, *Morocco: Economic and Social Development Report* (Washington: World Bank, 1981), p. 25.

[39]ODI, *Review of foreign private investments from 1968 to 1976*; BMCE, Bulletin No. 136, December 1978.

the same rapid growth. The total volume of approved investments multiplied 6.7 times (in current dirhams) between 1973 and 1977. Manufacturing alone represented 60 percent of the total. It should be pointed out that the volume of approved industrial investments stagnated in the early years of the decade.[40]

We have already seen that public investments were declining in the 1980s. Can the same be said of private investments? The volume of approved investments in the industrial sector (the only investments for which data are available) grew from 20 percent to 30 percent annually between 1984 and 1987,[41] with the exception of 1985, in which investments of public enterprises fell by 60 percent under the impact of the adjustment program. The strong growth in private investment was attributable to the new industrial investment code of 1983.

Table 9 shows the distribution of approved industrial investments by type of investor from 1984 to 1988. It shows a sharp drop in public enterprise investments, which represented a mere 2 percent of approved investments in 1988; the share of Moroccan private investments remained strong and stable, representing close to four fifths of total investments; and the share of foreign private investments was not negligible, representing close to one fifth of the total. The foreign element in equity of the manufacturing sector reached 14 percent in 1987.[42]

In brief, private investment grew rapidly following the enactment of the investment code of 1973 (except for foreign private investment). There was also an accelerated growth in private industrial investments approved after the adoption of the 1983 code.

Two indicators may be used to evaluate the effectiveness of the private investment promotion policy, namely, the degree of capital intensity in industrial projects and the geographic distribution of the investments. The results in the 1970s failed to achieve the objectives of the development policy as enunciated in the development plans, and were particularly negative when compared with

[40]World Bank, *Morocco: Economic and Social Development Report* (Washington: World Bank, 1981), Statistical Annex, p. 22.

[41]Realized industrial investments grew at an average rate of 20 percent between 1984 and 1987; see Table 9.

[42]Ministry of Trade and Industry, "Situation des industries de transformation," Fiscal Year 1987 (Rabat, December 1988), p. 15.

**Table 9. Sources of Approved Investments in Industrial Sector,
1984–88**

(In percent)

	1984	1985	1986	1987	1988
Public enterprises	10	4	3	8	2
Domestic private sector	73	80	72	76	78
Foreign private sector	17	16	25	16	20
Total	100	100	100	100	100
(In millions of dirhams)	2,780	2,830	3,550	4,690	5,780
Percentage change	22	1	25	32	23

Source: Ministry of Trade and Industry.

the objectives of the investment code of 1973 with respect to job
creation and decentralization of productive activities. This outcome was partly due to the distortions in the regime of incentives.
Investment for each job created in approved projects rose sharply:
DH 54,000 in 1970, DH 77,000 in 1973–74, DH 89,000 in 1975,
DH 144,000 in 1976, and DH 87,000 in 1977. Geographic concentration of industrial investment remained strong in the projects
that were again approved in the late 1970s, as the region of Casablanca (Zones I and II) and the other major urban centers (Zone
III) absorbed 94 percent of the investments in 1979 (see Table 10).

Has the situation improved following the revision of the industrial investment code in 1983 and the adoption of the sectoral
adjustment program for industry and foreign trade? After a few
years during which adverse influences (or habits) led to the concentration of industrial investment in the region of Casablanca,
decentralization of investment progressed as of 1986 (Table 10).
Meanwhile, the amount of investment for each job created tended
to stabilize between DH 90,000 and DH 100,000: DH 99,000 in
1984, DH 92,000 in 1985, DH 101,000 in 1986, DH 86,000 in
1987, and DH 97,000 in 1988. Accounting for inflation, this result
was an improvement in relation to the situation in the mid-1970s.

Factors Influencing Investment Decisions

Numerous factors influence investment decisions; some are economic in nature while others are not. They vary, and their relative
weight also varies, according to the type of investment (national
or foreign), the socioeconomic environment, and the regulatory

Table 10. Geographic Distribution of Industrial Investments Approved in 1979–88

	1979	1980–82	1983	1985	1986–88
Zones I and II[a]	55	37	52	50	43
Zone III[b]	39	45	39	36	35
Zone IV[c]	6	18	9	14	22
Total	100	100	100	100	100

Source: Ministry of Trade and Industry.
[a]Region of Casablanca.
[b]Other major urban centers.
[c]Rest of Morocco.

and administrative regimes under which the investment is to be made.

A number of these factors have already been described and their impact on investment identified, including the investment codes and other incentives, the general adjustment program with its impact on investment through credit and interest rate policies, the policy on financing of the treasury deficit, and the sectoral adjustment programs, with their impact on the correction of price distortions and on resource allocation.

These are the factors that eventually influence the competitiveness of the economy, and they assume particular importance when the investments focus on export-oriented activities and/or when the investor is foreign. The foreign investor will consider the comparative costs (or comparative profitability) that determine his decision to take his project to Morocco (and where to locate his project inside Morocco) or elsewhere. Also to be considered are the high costs of certain production factors in Morocco,[43] such as industrial fuel (owing to the "oil premium" imposed by the state), electric power (the rates of which are paradoxically higher for industry than for households), and the cost of transport services, banking, and insurance. Other factors relate to the general economic conditions and the long waiting period to acquire foreign exchange, which undermine the creditworthiness of Moroccan enterprises abroad, aggravate their financial burdens, and damage Morocco's image; finally there are the awkward administrative

[43]See cost of production factors in Morocco in ODI, Industrial Investors Guide.

delays that discourage foreign investors more than national investors.

Certain measures have been taken or are under way to remedy this situation, including measures to shorten the waiting period for the purchase of foreign exchange, as permitted by an improvement in the external account, to reduce the Government's domestic arrears, and to streamline administrative procedures in the investment field.

That the investment decision is influenced by many factors makes it difficult to attribute any variation in investment to a particular factor. It also raises the problem of the relative weights of individual factors in the investment decision. An attempt at such an analysis was made on the basis of a survey of industrial enterprises in Morocco.[44] The objective was to identify investment factors in the light of the incentives granted under the industrial investment code of 1973. The main conclusions of the analysis were

- The determining factors include the presence of a growing demand for familiar products on the market and a sufficient level of profitability.
- While appreciable incentives are offered under the investment codes (they represent 40–50 percent of gross operating revenues depending on geographical location), their absence would have completely jeopardized only one tenth of the total number of projects: 40 percent of the projects would have been completed on schedule and the remaining 50 percent would have required rescheduling either in start-up operations or in implementation phases.
- Customs protection constitutes a fundamental incentive (not included in the code).
- Those incentives provided in the code that intervene at the establishment phase (financing, interest rates, exemption from import tax on materials and equipment) influence the investment decision more significantly than those granted at the

[44]The sample comprised 74 enterprises and was considered by the authors to be sufficiently representative of the manufacturing industries. See B.H. Boulghasoul, "L'incitation à l'investissement industriel au Maroc," in *Politiques de sortie de crise et relations Nord-Sud*, text compiled and presented by Bachir Hamdouch (Rabat: SMER, 1989); B.H. Boulghasoul and A. Boujenoui, "Evaluation de l'impact de la politique d'incitation des investissements industriels au Maroc" (Rabat: INSEA, 1984).

operational stage (exemption from corporate income taxes and the accelerated depreciation).

- Exemption from the business tax is not a sufficient incentive for decentralization of investment.

Revision of the code thus became imperative, as did the restructuring of the entire regime of incentives, together with the system of administrative procedures just put in place. However, is this a sufficient incentive for private capital (domestic or foreign) to take the place of public investment in the promotion of growth?

Conclusion

For Morocco, the 1960s represented a decade marked by lack of investment. The transient increase in phosphate export earnings in the mid-1970s provided the opportunity to redress the investment shortage by a surge in public investments. The country therefore moved from a situation of too little investment to one of too much investment; the latter in respect of "the capacity to invest" in a rational manner. This resulted in serious waste and macroeconomic disequilibria. The 1980s has been a decade of economic policy adjustment and restructuring of the productive system.

Much has been done, but more remains to be done, including continued adjustment of the economic structures and steering investment back in the right direction. There has been a movement from one extreme to the other. The country has again moved from a situation of too much public investment to insufficient public investment. Public investment is irreplaceable, at least in some sectors, in a Third World country like Morocco. Moreover, if the complementarity that exists between public investment and private investment is not safeguarded, the risk of blocking private investment may arise. Finally, the stock of public capital is no longer maintained, or is insufficiently maintained, which again leads to loss of efficiency and to waste.

It is necessary therefore to revive investment and growth.[45] Structural adjustment is easier and faster under conditions of growth.

[45]The World Bank seems to share this viewpoint and is of the opinion that more importance should be attached to infrastructure. See Press Release and Statement by the President of the Bank during his visit to Morocco in July 1989 in *La Vie Economique* (Casablanca), July 23, 1989.

It rhymes better with growth than with stagnation, and so does social peace. Such a revival is also essential if another serious issue is to be addressed, namely, the distressing problem of external debt, which exercises a crowding-out effect not only on public investment but also on the country's overall investment, and which eats up most of its economic surplus. But this is another issue.

Comment

Abdelrazaq El Mossadeq

The paper on investment policies in Morocco presented by Mr. Hamdouch seems to me to be comprehensive. It contains a series of detailed information and reviews the progress of Moroccan economic policy in general and investment in particular.

Therefore, my comments will be restricted to pointing out certain facts, proposing a re-reading of the policies followed by the state, and analyzing the figures in a different way. I will limit myself to the industrial sector.

These comments will be centered on two main points of the paper: the adjustment program and investment policy.

Adjustment Program

Morocco, like most countries, has for several years been following adjustment programs. I could even say that adjustment is a matter of necessity or, if you wish, the continuous adaptation of the management of a country or a firm.

To me, a healthy economy is an economy in perpetual adjustment, continuously questioning its structure, adapting to market needs, taking into consideration new economic conditions, and above all, innovating. No market can be taken for granted, and no situation is immobile. The world changes and the power of the economy is to reach out and control these changes.

What is an adjustment program? It is nothing more than obvious reorientation of policies. In my understanding, an adjustment program should have as its major objective to equalize or at least to bring the economic profitability of any project closer to its financial profitability. In other words, the incentives policy, legal or illegal, should be neutral from one sector to another and from one activity to another. The administration should not intervene to guide an economic activity or to slant an investment choice. The rationalization of expenditures is the final objective and with it the elimination of waste and the optimal use of resources by directing them

279

to profitable activities at the national level. An adjustment program should concern not only the productive sectors but also and above all the "administrative" sector.

I make these comments because, to my knowledge, only the industrial sector has started an adjustment program, which is still under way. All the adjustment measures that were taken have been in the industrial sector. Of course, certain sectors benefited from these measures (tourism, for example, with the currency devaluation), but these were not the decision makers' main concerns; they were induced benefits or, to use an economic term, external economies.

We cannot talk about the success or failure of an adjustment program that has not been implemented. We *can* say that the small achievements of the other sectors in comparison with the industrial sector show that an adjustment program with the same conditions has more chance for success than failure.

At this level, the statistics used in Mr. Hamdouch's paper show that the manufacturing industries sector achieved positive results. The annual rate of newly established enterprises has increased by 8 percent annually since 1985, industrial employment by 6 percent, turnover by 20 percent, and exports by 25 percent. Investments increased also by 20 percent, with a higher contribution by foreign investment (20–25 percent of the total) and a net decrease in public investment (less than 2 percent in 1988). The volume of production exported doubled between 1983 and 1988 to reach 25 percent. Moreover, about 213 investments approved in 1988 have part or all of their production targeted to foreign markets.

We note that the textile sector was the most dynamic in recent years, and on this subject two remarks can be made: the textile sector covers a wide area, including the clothing industry, spinning, weaving, finishing, dying, and hosiery. It is true that about one third of the investment in 1987–88 was allocated to the clothing industry, but even in this activity, which seems to be unappreciated by many because of its "banality," large investment opportunities remain open to investors.

The goal of an adjustment program, as stated earlier, is to direct the investments only to activities where conditions for success exist: infrastructure, markets, factor costs, qualified manpower, etc. Industry cannot be learned or enacted, it is the result of favorable conditions and of qualified and experienced people in management and in technical fields but also of people willing to take risks. We should avoid merging industries on a whim; those who did it are paying the price.

Investment Policy

The investment decision is the result of a long process of research and study and of a sequence of events that is just as long. If the implementation of an investment within a specific framework depends only on the decision maker, its success of course depends on the decision maker's choice and on his competence but also on the framework and on the external conditions in which the investment develops. Since the investment is the only means of consolidating, making profitable, and reinforcing the production capacity of a country, public authorities in different countries have always tried, each in their own way, to direct their policy toward realizing the maximum possible investment compatible with their information and resources, and to create a framework with the best conditions for the success of this investment.

Much progress has been achieved in the science of economics. It now allows better control of data and a reduction in the margin of error. The investment codes adopted by many countries, and sometimes by many regions, have tried to improve the return on capital invested in industry by correcting the distortions caused by external conditions. These codes have also been used to improve the relative position of a country in international competition as it seeks to attract the maximum foreign capital.

However, the profitability of a project does not depend only on quantifiable factors. Nonquantifiable factors are often more critical when it comes to the choice of the investor. Among these factors are stability, continuity in economic policy, basic infrastructure, the existence of an industrial base, and administrative procedures.

Public authorities in Morocco have acted on two levels. I will try to explain this later by highlighting the role of the Government in overall industrial investment, and in the regionalization of industry in particular.

Since independence, Moroccan investment policy has been characterized by reliance on private initiative and by the ability of the private sector to contribute significantly to the economic growth of the country. This choice is not synonymous with a *laissez-aller* or *laissez-faire* approach. In fact, the state has always stepped in when necessary to control the growth appropriate for the development of the economy. Since the 1956–60 period, which was characterized by control of the economic decision centers and the establishment of investment, promotion, and financing institutions (Bank of Morocco, State Industrial Participation Institution (BEPI), the National Bank for Economic Development (BNDE), and the Caisse de Dépôt et de Gestion (CDG)), the state has been working hard to attract private investment, whether national or foreign, and to invest itself, if necessary.

The 1960 investment code sought to reassure private investors and to define the rights and obligations of these investors as well as those of the public sector. It is perhaps worthwhile mentioning that the public sector has no monopoly on investment. Almost all economic sectors are open to private promoters, except in those sectors where state intervention is necessary because of the nature of the sector or because it is under monopoly. Far from the privatization movement that is now in fashion, let us remember that sectors such as education and urban transportation have for a long time been "open" to private investors.

However, during 1956–60 the records show that foreign investment was zero, or even negative, and the national private sector was not yet prepared to assume its obligations because of lack of experience, maturity, and technical or financial means. In this situation the state has to show the way and to demonstrate in fact that it believes in industrial investment and in the positive contribution that foreign capital and technical know-how can make. This is the explanation behind the large state participation in industrial investment, either alone or in association with the private investor.

Let me mention the launching of the sugar plan (the first sugar plant was completed in 1963) and the phosphate plan envisaged as processing about a third of the country's phosphate production (with the completion of Maroc-Chimie in 1967). As for public investments in association with foreign investments, we can mention SAMIR (with the IRI), Berliet-Maroc (with Berliet), SOMACA (with Fiat and Simca), and General-Tire Maroc. The strong presence of the public sector in industrial investment in the 1960s led some people to call this period the decade of public investment.

The end of the 1960s and the beginning of the 1970s saw the emergence of private investment, and this situation pushed the public authorities to change the 1960 code that refers any project to an investment committee, and to replace it in 1973 with a more flexible code that refers to the committee only certain investments in sectors considered strategic or investments over a certain amount (30 million dirhams). At the same time, the BEPI was changed to the Industrial Development Office (ODI), which was given the responsibility of promoting industry in association with the private sector. Of course, the state continued to invest directly in the sugar plan, the phosphate plan, and even to implement new plans such as those for cement, the iron and steel industry, and dairy products.

ODI has been the determining element in public industrial investment but almost always in association with private investors in various sectors such as diesel engines, cement, spinning, machine tools, agro-industry, electrolysis, and the clothing industry. It can even be asserted that the two clothing units launched by ODI in 1976–77, because of their success after a difficult start, were a good model for many promoters looking for profitable investment opportunities. The 1970s can be considered without doubt the decade of private investment, as it represented more than half the value of the investments made during the period.

The end of the 1970s and the beginning of the 1980s were marked by the difficult financial situation at the international level. Industrial investment declined. The public sector limited its role to projects already under way (Loukkos sugar plant, Nador steel project, Maroc phosphate project) or, through ODI, to investments requiring low capital. The import-substitution policy reached its limits. All potential sectors were virtually covered and some industries even started to branch out into some smaller subsectors. Moreover, the financing capacity of the country was limited and it was necessary to encourage foreign capital. But the 1973 code may have been an obstacle to foreign investment in Morocco because, out of its concern to create a spirit of cooperation between the national and the foreign private sectors, it stipulated that for the investment to obtain benefits, more than half of the capital should be nationally owned.

The new 1983 code eliminated this condition. Henceforth, industrial investment was to enjoy the same benefits regardless of the origin of the capital. Since 1983, foreign capital has represented

20–25 percent of industrial investment, compared with less than 10 percent in previous years. The code also provided certain additional benefits for export activities. It should be recalled that the first export law and customs legislation were promulgated in 1973. But we think that the change in the structure of protection of national industry—with the goal of making export activities as profitable as activities directed toward the local market—has given a new dimension to the industrial sector and has stimulated exports. The results were shown above.

Before ending this section, it is useful to make two points that I believe are essential for Morocco's investment policy. First, industrial investment has never been subject to the approval of the authorities. Except for activities such as the refining of edible oils and automobile assembly plants, which are regulated by specific legislation, the authorities' prior approval is not required. The decision to invest is the responsibility only of the project promoter, who should take into account the general economic environment. Second, public investment in industry does not enjoy special status or special benefits. The role of the state investor in industry is limited to its part as shareholder. It is put under the same conditions as the private investor. Moreover, as stated above, the public sector does not have any monopoly in this matter.

The regionalization policy is another aspect of the investment policy in Morocco. We can say that the state has acted directly by establishing or encouraging the development of certain economic development zones. In this regard, we can name the Gharb zone for the processing of sugar cane and sugarbeet, the Mohammedia zone for the petrochemical industry (SAMIR, SNEP, and lubricant oils), the Safi zone for phosphate processing, the Agadir zone for the fishing industry, the Tadla zone for the processing of industrial production of cotton and beet, and the Nador zone for the steel industry.

ODI has been assigned the main task of contributing to the regionalization of industrial investment. Besides SNEP in Mohammedia, no other ODI investment has been carried out in the Casablanca region. ODI has also participated in decentralizing away from Casablanca certain industrial activities, such as the dairy industry, the mechanical industry, cement plants, yeast, ethyl alcohol, and textile industries. The various investment codes have provided for benefits first in the form of equipment bonuses and then in the form of tax exemptions enacted in inverse ratio to the economic development of the regions.

From the end of the 1970s, the state, moving away from direct investment in industry, changed its role by acting on three levels: technical assistance, the infrastructure necessary for industrial units, and financing. Small and medium-sized industry was put at center stage. It is considered to be the driving force of this policy or of any self-sustaining development policy, more equitable, better distributed, and seeking to ensure a large diffusion of the investment spirit and a taste for enterprise.

A technical assistance department to assist promoters of small and medium-sized industry was established at ODI in 1979. A department for small and medium-sized industry was also established at the Ministry of Industry. This body conceived and proposed various special benefits for this type of industry, and these proposals were taken into account in drafting the 1983 investment code. At the same time, the medium- and long-term financing of industrial investment, which had until then been a BNDE monopoly, was extended to various commercial banks, which were better located in the regions with their many branches. Better conditions were introduced, particularly in the amount of financing. Recently, new arrangements have been added to this favorable environment: credit facilities, venture capital, and the establishment of Bank Al-Amal. Moreover, the feasibility study for the establishment of industrial zones in Morocco was launched and began to be implemented in 1982. Several industrial zones are now established. The preparation of industrial zones has been decentralized and entrusted to a central body (the CDG) but also to regional establishments or to any other body selected by the local authorities interested in the establishment of a zone. This program has contributed largely to solving one of the major bottlenecks of industrial regionalization.

It is true that up to now the Casabanca region continues to attract a relatively significant part of investments. However, this part is declining considerably. The results of such a process, which is by nature long and complex, can only be perceived over a long period of time. Casabanca has over the last three years attracted only 43 percent of industrial investments, compared with 55 percent at the beginning of the 1980s and 75 percent in the mid-1970s. It is difficult to say that these results are only the consequence of the decisions listed above. They are also certainly due to natural evolution resulting from the significant increase in the price of industrial land in Casabanca, for example. But we can say, without doubt, that these decisions played a determining role in moving investment in the right direction.

List of Participants*

Moderator
   Said El-Naggar
   Former Professor of Economics
   Cairo University, Cairo
   Egypt

Authors
   Bachir Hamdouch
   Arab Monetary Fund
   Abu Dhabi
   United Arab Emirates

   Heba Handoussa
   Department of Economics
   American University, Cairo
   Egypt

   Abdullah Al-Kuwaiz
   Assistant Secretary-General for Economic Affairs
   Gulf Cooperation Council
   Riyadh, Saudi Arabia

   Abdel-Monem Seyed Ali
   Professor of Economics
   Baghdad, Iraq

   A. Shakour Shaalan
   Director, Middle Eastern Department
   International Monetary Fund
   Washington, D.C.

   Ibrahim F.I. Shihata
   Vice President and General Counsel
   World Bank
   Washington, D.C.

   Abdel Rahman Taha
   Director of Operations
   Inter-Arab Investment Guarantee Corporation
   Safat, Kuwait

*The titles and affiliations listed for participants are those they had
at the time of the seminar (December 1989).

John W. Wall
Europe, Middle East and North Africa Regional Office
World Bank
Washington, D.C.

Dale Weigel
International Finance Corporation
Washington, D.C.

Commentators
Fareed Atabani
Economic Consultant
Khartoum, Sudan

Mohamed A. Diab
Economic Consultant
Kuwait

Mohamed El-Diri
Ministry of Finance
Rabat, Morocco

Abdulaziz M. Al-Dukheil
President, Consultative Center for Investment and Financing
Riyadh, Saudi Arabia

Nour El-Din Farrag
General Manager and Chief Executive Officer
Arab Petroleum Investment Corporation
Zahran, Saudi Arabia

Ahmed El-Ghandour
Faculty of Economics
Cairo University, Giza
Egypt

Abdelrazaq El Mossadeq
General Manager
Department of Industry
Ministry of Industry and Trade
Rabat, Morocco

Mahsoun Galal
Managing Director and Chairman
National Manufacturing Company
Riyadh, Saudi Arabia

Abdel Wahed Al-Makhzoumi
Central Bank
Baghdad, Iraq

Ezzedin M. Shamsedin
Advisor to Executive Director
World Bank
Washington, D.C.

Participants
Ahmed Abushadi
External Relations Department
International Monetary Fund
Washington, D.C.

Hussein Youssef Alani
Head, Arab Authority for Investment and Agricultural
    Development
Khartoum, Sudan

Mirvet Badawi
Arab Fund for Economic and Social Development
Kuwait

Mourad Benachenhou
Executive Director
World Bank
Washington, D.C.

Osama J. Faquih
Director General and Chairman of the Board
Arab Monetary Fund
Abu Dhabi, United Arab Emirates

Farag Bin Ghanem
Mission of the People's Democratic Republic of Yemen
Geneva, Switzerland

Mohieldin Al-Ghareeb
Chief Executive Officer
Public Authority for Investment and Free Zone
Cairo, Egypt

Saleh Al-Gibali
President and General Manager
Industrial Phosphoric Acid and Fertilizers Co.
Tunisia, Tunis

Abdlatif Y. Al-Hamad
Director General and Chairman of the Board of Directors
Arab Fund for Economic and Social Development
Kuwait

Tayseer Abdel Jaber
Executive Secretary
Economic and Social Commission for Western Asia
Baghdad, Iraq

Abdelrazaq Khaled Al-Zaid Al-Khaled
President, Kuwaiti Economic Association
Safat, Kuwait
Kuwait

Rasheed O. Khalid
Arab Monetary Fund
Abu Dhabi, United Arab Emirates

Azizali Mohammed
Director, External Relations Department
International Monetary Fund
Washington, D.C.

Abdalla Al-Mulla
Economic Advisor
Gulf Cooperation Council
Riyadh, Saudi Arabia

Yusuf A. Nimatallah
Executive Director
International Monetary Fund
Washington, D.C.

Nasser Al-Nuweis
General Director
Abu Dhabi Fund for Economic and Social Development
Abu Dhabi, United Arab Emirates

Hanna Ouda
Former Minister of Finance
Amman
Jordan

Jassem Khaled Al-Saadoun
General Director
Al-Shal for Economic Advisory Service
Safat, Kuwait

Sabry Zaer Al-Saady
Economic and Social Commission for Western Asia
Baghdad, Iraq

Abdel Karim Sadek
Kuwait Fund for Arab Economic Development
Kuwait

Fawzi Hamad Al-Sultan
Executive Director
World Bank
Washington, D.C.

Samir Tobar
Dean, Faculty of Commerce
University of Zakazik
Egypt

Ismail El-Zabri
Director, Technical Department
Arab Fund for Economic and Social Development
Kuwait

Abdel Hassan Zalzala
Former Assistant Secretary General
Arab League
Ottawa, Canada

Tawfik El-Zir
Economic Researcher
National Center for Financial and Economic Data
Riyadh, Saudi Arabia